Business Review

Business Review: Advanced Applications

Edited by

Anton Ravindran and Farid Shirazi

CAMBRIDGE
SCHOLARS
PUBLISHING

Business Review: Advanced Applications,
Edited by Anton Ravindran and Farid Shirazi

This book first published 2013

Cambridge Scholars Publishing

12 Back Chapman Street, Newcastle upon Tyne, NE6 2XX, UK

British Library Cataloguing in Publication Data
A catalogue record for this book is available from the British Library

Published by Cambridge Scholars Publishing in collaboration
with the Global Science and Technology Forum

ISBN (10): 1-4438-5029-2, ISBN (13): 978-1-4438-5029-2

TABLE OF CONTENTS

Introduction 1
Anton Ravindran and Farid Shirazi

Chapter One 4
Emerging Cloud Computing Paradigm and its Impact on Enterprises
Anton Ravindran

Chapter Two 21
Controller's Perspective on Implementing Rolling Instruments
Robert C. Rickards

Chapter Three 48
Valuing Risk Exposure and the Expected Cost of Margin Calls:
The Case for a Secondary Market in Redistributing Liquidity Liability
(Margin Credit Swaps)
Timothy E. Zimmer, Valerien O. Pede and Andrew M. McKenzie

Chapter Four 61
Standard of Living in the European Union
Jana Stávková, Pavel Žufan and Naďa Birčiaková

Chapter Five 87
The Quality of Disclosure in the Annual Report: Analysis of Different
Approaches
Alain Devalle and Fabio Rizzato

Chapter Six 106
Diversity in the Board Room: A Business Case or Rhetoric?
Daniel Kipkirong Tarus

Chapter Seven 136
Human Resource Intangible Assets Connected to the Organizational
Performance and Productivity
Marko Kesti and Antti Syväjärvi

Chapter Eight 174
Promoting Knowledge Based Economy and Minimizing Digital Gap in Arab Countries with special reference to Saudi Arabia: A Qualitative Study
Khalil Elian Abdelrahim

Chapter Nine.. 196
Information Systems and Internal Control Systems
Fabrizio Bava and Alain Devalle

Chapter Ten 216
The Impacts of ICT Expansion, Legal and Institutional Framework on FDI Flows: A Comparative Study between Asia-Pacific and the Middle Eastern Economies
Farid Shirazi

INTRODUCTION

In today's networked society, Information and Communication Technology (ICT) plays an important role in economic growth. It is assumed that ICT expansion improves the efficiency of the industrial infrastructure by enhancing business activities, strengthening the competitive capacities of firms and improving the efficiency of governments, as well as enhancing the provision of education and health.

ICT has also had an enormously positive impact on organizational structures in areas such as education, R&D, health, and business. For example, ICT enables firms to redistribute their organizational structures in terms of flattening hierarchies, delegating responsibilities and reengineering business processes. As such, the "New Economy" is also referred to as the "post-industrial society," the "information society," the "innovation economy," the "knowledge economy," the "network economy," the "digital economy," the "weightless economy" and the "e-conomy" (Cohen et al., 2000). Each of these terms emphasizes different aspects of structural change, but each of them is vulnerable to misinterpretation (Pohjola, 2002). However, the core argument of the New Economy focuses upon the intensive use, production, and adoption of ICTs, both as outputs from ICT-producing industries and as inputs into ICT-using industries (Pohjola, 2002). In this context, organizations normally choose ICT tools and applications to promote their business, taking up opportunities offered by the adoption of new technology. This selection is also made as a response to dissatisfaction with old procedures and practices. Dissatisfaction can arise as a result of the perceived deficiencies of existing systems or as a result of a comparative evaluation with better systems. Thus, deficiency is the inability of a system to respond to the challenges introduced by technological change. The new technology also presents challenges to firms and organizations with respect to global market competition. Sciadas (2006) argues that the empirical evidence strongly supports the claim that the diffusion and appropriate utilization of ICT not only presents enormous opportunities for economic and social development, but also that its absence seriously threatens the sizable gaps that exist between the 'haves' and 'have-nots' in the so-called 'digital divide'.

This book discusses some of the new empirical evidence regarding the opportunities and challenges offered by the new technology.

In Chapter 1, Ravindran discusses how emerging Cloud technology is reshaping the existing computing landscape and the impact this is having upon enterprises. He argues that Cloud Computing is neither a new nor a revolutionary technology, but rather that it is a new paradigm with the capacity to enable new business models, new opportunities and new revenue streams. The chapter discusses the main characteristics and implications of Cloud Computing for businesses today. Chapter 1 also highlights the challenges and risks associated with Cloud Computing, including issues related to security, privacy and compliance. In Chapter 2, Rickards and Ritsert compare and contrast traditional static controlling tools with newer and more dynamic tools, by analyzing the results presented in several surveys. Their study focuses mainly on the implementation of rolling planning instruments. The authors propose a twelve-point strategy for controllers, which could facilitate the adoption of rolling planning instruments, particularly in small and medium-sized enterprises (SMEs). In Chapter 3, Zimmer, Pede and McKenzie analyze the major issues surrounding price volatility in grain markets. They provide a benchmark pricing structure according to which these products could be evaluated and initially priced, prior to auction and exchange. In Chapter 4, Stávková, Žufan and Birčiaková analyze the standard of living in five selected EU countries (the Czech Republic, Finland, France, Spain and the United Kingdom) by measuring income disparity and poverty issues, as well as government spending on social protection. In Chapter 5, Devalle and Rizzato discuss a range of different research approaches used in evaluating the quality and reliability of firms' disclosures of annual reports and financial statements.

In Chapter 6, Tarus discusses the demographic characteristics and firm outcomes for predicting the Top Management Team (TMT) characteristics in firm performance. Drawing upon various theoretical perspectives, the chapter discusses whether there is a business case for diversity or merely rhetoric. In Chapter 7, Kesti and Syväjärvi discuss the important role of Human Resources Management in increasing performance and productivity. Using the action research approach, they argue that improved human competences, in the form of better and more effective information management, may lead to growth in organization revenue. In Chapter 8, Abdelrahim discusses the importance of knowledge management in minimizing the digital gap among Arab countries. In Chapter 9, Bava and Devalle discuss the role of Information Systems in protecting data and in ensuring the reliability of financial information, from a managerial and internal control perspective. Finally, in Chapter 10, Shirazi discusses the bi-directional relationship between ICT development and the growth of Foreign Direct Investment (FDI), through a comparative study of emerging regions, namely Asia-Pacific and the Middle East.

Editors: Dr. Anton Ravindran and Dr. Farid Shirazi

CHAPTER ONE

EMERGING CLOUD COMPUTING PARADIGM AND ITS IMPACT ON ENTERPRISES

ANTON RAVINDRAN

PRESIDENT, GLOBAL SCIENCE & TECHNOLOGY FORUM (GSTF)
CEO & FOUNDER, RAPIDSTART
VISITING PROFESSOR/RESEARCHER, INSTITUTE FOR RESEARCH IN APPLICABLE COMPUTING (IRAC),
UNIVERSITY OF BEDFORDSHIRE
ADJUNCT PROFESSOR, BINUS UNIVERSITY

Abstract

The increasing rate of growth, change and significance of information technology shows no sign of slowing. Cloud Computing has emerged as a new approach in computing, and its data centres are growing at an unprecedented rate. This has attracted a lot of attention from the scientific, research and business communities. Cloud technology represents an evolution and a shift away from the traditional IT paradigm. Many scholars have argued that the Cloud Model is evolutionary, while a few others have suggested that it is revolutionary and that computing will become the fifth utility. This chapter investigates how this emerging Cloud technology is reshaping the existing computing landscape, and the impact this is having on enterprises.

Keywords: *Cloud Computing, Business Strategy, IT Strategy, Strategic Alignment, Transformation, Innovation, Elasticity, Scalability, Disruptive Technology, Utility Computing.*

Introduction

The new normal is rapid change. In a relatively short time span, computers and communications technology have helped to create modern global markets and the digital economy. This process, driven by IT leaders, has resulted in an explosion of communication and collaboration, and to a level of access to information which is unprecedented in the history of mankind. There is no doubt that the emerging technological development of Cloud Computing, which some argue is revolutionary and others claim is evolutionary, can only bring new dimensions, unique experiences and value propositions for enterprises.

'It is not the strongest species that survive, nor the most intelligent, but the ones most responsive to change' (attributed to Darwin). In the 'New Economy' (a term which refers to the impact of IT on the economy, introduced on the basis that conventional measures of value are no longer valid due to rapid changes in the market driven by the internet and advances in technology), everything changes faster. McCallum (2001) said 'enterprises that do not adapt are in for a lot of trouble. The problem is change: The more rapid the pace of change, the direr the consequences of stubbornly sticking to old ways'. According to Vega-Gonzalez (2005), technological developments have divided human history into six different time periods. The era of technological revolution began with the advent of printing, and the second resulted in the advent of the steam engine, electricity and industrial technology. This was followed by the first phase of the third era, driven by electronics, software and communications technologies (Vega-Gonzalez, 2005). We are now living in a period of transition between the Information Age and the Cyberspace Age, which Vega-Gonzalez considers to be the second phase of the third technological revolution, in which information is the driver of change. This new technological development will perhaps be more significant than any of those which preceded it.

Throughout the annals of history, there have been various forms of disruptive technology. Any new technology which has a serious impact on the status quo, and which revolutionizes the way we live and work, is disruptive (Christensen, 1997). From the electric light to the automobile, history is filled with examples of new technologies which have changed the way in which people live, conduct commerce and run their governments. Peha and Strauss (1997) state that 'Computing technology, which stores and processes information, has been growing at a phenomenal rate'. Driven by information technology, the rate of change continues to accelerate. Peha and Strauss (1997) go on to state that 'every few years, ICT innovates beyond recognition'. Every three to five years, our understanding of ICT tends to change dramatically, as new assumptions and ideas are accepted, and what was previously considered esoteric becomes accepted as common knowledge. We are living through a transitional period between the Information Age and the Cyberspace Age, and Vega Gonzalez (2005) claims that 'this new technological revolution will perhaps be bigger than all previous ones'. IT, which is the most important commercial and technological development of the last four to five decades, is undergoing a significant transformation, from being an asset procured by companies to being a service procured from vendors. According to Carr (2005), the shift from a 'fragmented capital asset to a centralized utility service will be momentous'. The Cloud Model is likely to alter the existing computing paradigm and to affect users, vendors, enterprises and markets (Carr 2005).

Trends in IT Spending and Growing Importance of IT

The increasing rate of growth, change and significance of information technology shows no sign of slowing. According to Gartner Dataquest's (2012) statistics, in April 2002 one billion computers were shipped, and by April 2012 this figure had risen to two billion. Therefore, while it took nearly twenty-seven years to reach the one billion mark, there has since been a rapid acceleration, and the figure has doubled in only ten years. At the same time, the cost of memory has dropped from US$ 10,000 in 1956 to US$ 1.26 in 1996 and to US$ 0.08 in 2010 (Wikipedia). On January 12, IBM (Computer World, 2012) announced that after five years of work, its researchers had been able to reduce the number of atoms required to create a bit of data from one million to twelve. In the meantime, wireless and mobile applications are setting the stage for a further upsurge in penetration and in the importance of ICT, and this will change the way we compute and how businesses compete.

According to the latest study by Gartner (2012), spending on Information Technology by organizations reached $ 3.68 trillion in 2012. Gartner's (2012) study, of 175 board members of companies with more than $ 250 million in annual sales, found that 64% of the respondents said they planned to increase their investments in IT, despite the gloomy market outlook. 50% of the directors interviewed agreed that IT was the way to change the competition.

The growing complexity of Information and Communication Technology (ICT), and its inherent strategic importance in the success or failure of any business, poses new challenges for managing the delivery of

IT solutions. It is the goal of every purchasing decision made in IT today to be faster, cheaper and better. There is no doubt that IT has become the engine of growth for business: it underpins business operations, ties together far flung supply chains and, increasingly, links businesses to the customers they serve (Carr, 2003). Hence, IT departments, headed by the Chief Information Officer (CIO), are faced with a growing responsibility to manage these rapid changes and to leverage from technological advances.

ICT has shifted from being an asset owned by companies, in the form of hardware and software, to being a service purchased from service providers (Carr, 2005). Studies show that this shift has been making gradual progress over the past two decades. According to IBM, ‘the trend toward Cloud Computing started in the late 1980s with the concept of grid computing when, for the first time, a large number of systems were applied to a single problem, usually scientific in nature and requiring exponentially high levels of parallel computation’ (cited in Sharma, 2009). Many analysts forecast growth rates for Cloud Computing in excess of 20% to 30% year on year, and Gartner has predicted that the market for Cloud Computing services will grow to over $ 150 billion by 2013. However, according to Kesner (2003), ‘The vendor community and at times IT leadership tend to oversell the value and understate the required investment and difficulties in enabling IT to bear’.

Twitter is a good example of a start-up that has fully leveraged from Cloud Computing in reaching out to its global audience. Carr (2005) and others have envisaged that Web and Cloud will lead to a ‘World Wide Computer—Compute from anywhere’ paradigm. The Cloud Model is expected to make computing a lot less expensive (Braiker, 2008; Wyld, 2009; Armbust et. al., 2009) and to provide access to computing resources, for individuals and enterprises, without having to make capital investments in infrastructure, resources and maintenance.

The term ‘Cloud Computing’ originates with the cloud symbol which is often used to represent the Internet in diagrams. The underlying concept of utility computing dates back to the 1960s, when the American computer scientist Herb Grosch envisioned that ‘computation may someday be organized as a public utility’. The first academic definition was provided by Chellappa (1997), who said that Cloud Computing ‘is a paradigm where the boundaries of computing will be determined for economic rationale rather than technical limits’.

Figure 1: Growth & Evolution of Computing

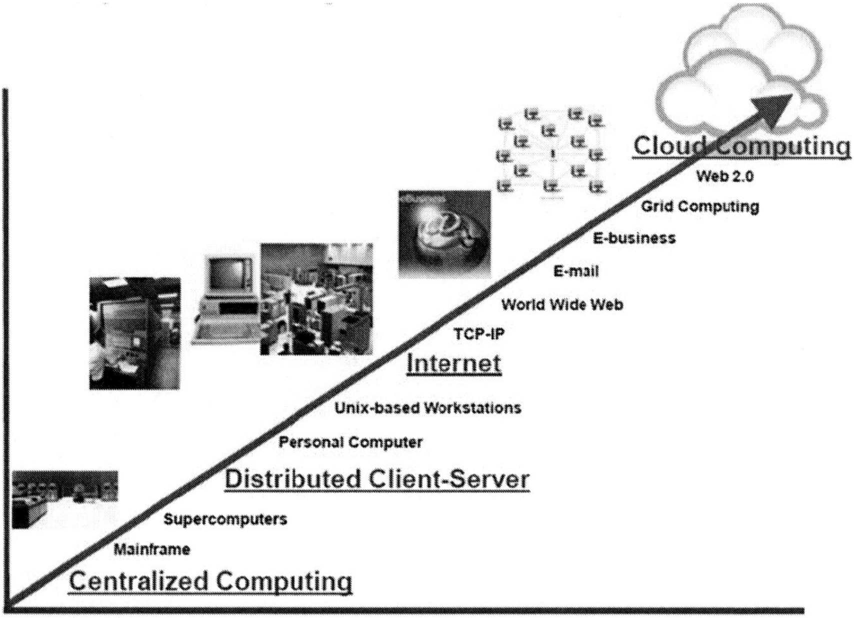

Adapted from IBM, 2010

What is Cloud Computing?

The following sections will examine several developments in cloud technology, including deployment models, drivers, challenges, and impact. Firstly, is it Outsourcing 2.0—a new technology, or a new business paradigm? Cloud computing is a new way of delivering computing resources and applications on demand via the internet, with the ability to scale dynamically across shared resources. It is therefore different from outsourcing. Bohm et al., (2009) state that 'Cloud Computing is sometimes used to refer to a new paradigm—some authors even speak of a new technology—which offers IT resources and services over the internet'. IDC defines Cloud Computing as 'an emerging IT development, deployment and delivery model, enabling real-time delivery of products, services and solutions over the Internet' (cited in Hugos & Hulitzky, 2011). The analogy often used to describe the Cloud Model is that it is like buying electricity instead of self-performing, self-developing or self-generating. According to Kern and Willcocks (2002), outsourcing is a relationship between a client and a supplier, where the former contracts or purchases IT services from the latter (cited in Bergkvist & Fredriksson, 2008). However, whilst the Cloud Model and outsourcing both involve the procurement of IT services from a supplier, there are significant differences.

The difference between Cloud Computing and outsourcing can be best illustrated by examining the challenges which outsourcing faces (Bohm et al., 2009). On the one hand, customers expect cost-effective, efficient and flexible delivery of IT services from their service providers. Alongside advances in technology, customers are now also demanding innovation, personalization and customer-specific innovation from service providers. Advances in technology have been the driver for the shift from the traditional manufacturing 'one-size-fits-all' mass production model to 'today's consumer–mandated, consumer-producer value co-creation model towards a mass customization model' (Shih, 2006). Unlike outsourcing, Cloud Computing aims to provide a technical basis which meets the consumer demand for flexibility. It achieves this by providing services on a needs basis, for which customers pay based on their usage. This emerging model of computing and service procurement is having a significant impact on how IT services are procured and consumed by enterprises.

In addition, unlike the outsourcing model, according to which physical infrastructure and resources are kept by the customer or service provider, Cloud Computing is a model for the flexible and virtual asset-free provision of IT resources and services. To that end, Bohm et al. (2009) opine that Cloud Computing can be considered as the 'consequent evolution of the traditional on-premise computing spanning outsourcing stages from total to the selective, and from multi-vendor outsourcing to asset-free delivery'. In fact, Cloud service providers provide essential data centres for outsourcing vendors as well. Lastly, in contrast with outsourcing, the Cloud Model is an on-demand and highly scalable pay-per-use model.

Definitions and Key Features of Cloud Computing

Although various definitions of Cloud Computing have been proposed, most researchers agree that the Cloud Computing model encompasses a general shift in computer processing, storage and software delivery, and moves away from the desktop, local servers and leverages from the internet. Instead, Cloud Computing delivers services by leveraging from next generation data centres hosted by large infrastructure companies such as Amazon, Yahoo, Google, Microsoft or Sun (Abadi, 2009).

Cloud Computing represents a new paradigm shift from computing-as-a-product to computing-as-a-service. This is a transition from buying hardware and software as products which are installed, configured, used and maintained to treating computing infrastructure and applications as services to be paid for only when used. Rehman and Sakr (2010) state that Cloud Computing 'is a disruptive technology, in that it embodies a major conceptual shift and is rapidly changing the way developers, users, and organizations work with computing infrastructure'. They claim that this will have a significant impact on how IT is procured and consumed.

According to Armbust et al. (2009), Cloud Computing refers to computing services delivered over the internet to the computing infrastructure in the data centres which provide these services. These services are known as Software as a Service (SaaS). The data centre hardware and software is called a 'Cloud'. When Cloud services are made available to the general public via the internet on a pay-as-you-go basis, this is known as a Public Cloud, and the services sold are known as utility computing. A Private Cloud refers to a business or an organization's internal dedicated data centre. Hence, Cloud Computing is the sum of SaaS and Utility Computing, though this does not include Private Clouds. In contrast, Vaqueo et al. (cf. Bohm et al., 2009), claim that Clouds are a large pool of easily accessible and virtualized resources, such as hardware, development platforms and/or services. These resources can be dynamically reconfigured, in order to adjust to a variable load and to meet the specific requirements of customers. This pool of resources is typically offered on a pay-per-use model, in which guarantees are offered by infrastructure providers by means of customized SLAs. On the other hand, the National Institute of Standards and Technology (NIST, 2011) defines Cloud Computing as a model for enabling convenient, on-demand network access to a shared pool of configurable computing resources (e.g., networks, servers, storage, applications and services), which can be rapidly provisioned and released with minimal management effort or service provider interaction.

Although there are a range of existing definitions, the majority of authors agree that the key features of Cloud Computing are the following: service, hardware, software, scalability, pay-per-use and internet. This is shown in Table 1, which summarizes the key features of Cloud Computing as these are defined by a range of authors.

Table 1: A comparison of various Cloud Computing definitions

Author	*Service*	*Hardware*	*Software*	*Data*	*Development*	*Pay Per Use*	*Off Premise (Public)*	*Scalability*	*No Upfront*	*Virtualization*	*SLA*	*Deterministic*	*Internet /Network*	*Automation*
Armbust et al	X	X	X			X	X	X	X				X	
Breiter/ Behrendt	X	X				X		X		X				X
Briscoe/ Marinos	X	X	X					X		X			X	
Buyya		X						X		X	X			
Foster et al	X	X		X				X		X			X	
Gartner	X	X	X		X			X					X	
Gorssman /Gu	X	X		X									X	
Gruman/ Knorr	X	X	X		X								X	
IDC	X	X				X		X					X	
Kim	X	X	X	X		X		X					X	
McFred-ries	X	X	X	X						X				
Nurmi et al	X	X	X					X				X		
Vaquero et al	X	X			X	X		X		X	X			
Vykoukal	X	X				X		X					X	
Wang et al	X	X	X	X										
Weiss	X	X	X					X						
Youseff et al	X	X			X	X		X		X	X			

Source: Bohm et al., 2009

Characteristics and Implications of Cloud Computing

Hardware, software and applications have previously been run on an 'ownership' model, and have been treated as capital expenditure requiring investment in infrastructure, implementation, training, ongoing maintenance and, every few years, additional investments in upgrades and platform migration. This has been considered to be the responsibility of IT departments. This traditional model of development and deployment of IT applications has been facing problems related to cost and time overruns. A recent study by Flyvberg and Budzier (2011) reported that a US $ 5 million project to implement SAP led to a $ 192.5 million loss at Levi Strauss, which resulted in the termination of its Chief Information Officer (CIO)'s contract. Flyvberg and Budzier (2011) go on to state that the average cost overrun stands at 27%, with the average schedule overrun standing at approximately 70%. One of the key benefits of Cloud Computing is that it spares companies from having to pay for underutilized resources (Hofmann and Woods, 2010).

The Cloud Computing model can help enterprises and their IT departments to address these challenges. As the Cloud is based on a pay-per-use model, it not only shifts the risk to the service provider, but also allows the customer to purchase computing resources based on need, thus providing elasticity of resources. In the Cloud Model, computing resources are not capital expenditure but operating costs. Thus, Cloud Computing has eliminated huge upfront investments in computing infrastructure, and has allowed business to scale up quickly. This emerging paradigm has the potential to transform a large part of the IT industry. It is likely to make software which can be purchased as a service based on demand more attractive, while reshaping the way IT hardware is designed and purchased (Armbrust et al., 2009).

Deployment Models of Cloud

The Cloud Model presents enterprises with various deployment options. This section will briefly outline the widely accepted Cloud deployment models.

Private Cloud: These are Clouds provided, operated, managed and maintained exclusively for a specific organization. The term 'Private Cloud' refers to an internal data centre which is not publicly accessible (Armbust et al., 2009). Large organizations are likely to see the Private Cloud model as the most logical one for the purposes of mission critical applications and sensitive data. According to a recent study in the UK, reported in CIO magazine (2012), CIOs are in agreement that enterprises are now beginning to leverage from the Private Cloud model, which has now reached maturity.

Public Cloud: This is the most common and widely known form of Cloud. A Public Cloud is accessible to anyone, and its infrastructure and applications are owned by the service provider. The key challenges for a Public Cloud are security and control (Shekhawat and Sharma, 2012). As such, SMEs and start-ups have been the first to adopt this model, while large enterprises have leveraged the Public Cloud for 'non-core' business functions.

Community Cloud: These Clouds are optimized for use by particular industry sectors, such as financial or health care services, or by groups of users seeking to meet specific objectives such as mission, policy, compliance or security requirements.

Hybrid Cloud: These Clouds combine of two or more of the above Cloud Models (Private, Public and Community). This model allows for selective implementation, and may be used to address issues relating to security, compliance and loss of control, whilst at the same time enabling the adoption of Public Clouds which offer cost benefits and further application options. According to Kundra (2010), a U.S CIO, this model provides the best of both worlds—the security of the Private Cloud and the cost benefits of the Public Cloud.

Distinct Levels of Cloud Values

Dean and Saleh (2009, of the Boston Consulting Group (BCG) have identified three distinct levels of value in Cloud Computing. According to their observations of customers, each level builds upon the previous one, and requires a shift away from current business processes. Each level also leads to value creation which is much greater than at the prior level.

Utility Level: This is the basic level of Cloud, where enterprises benefit from the pay-per-use model and from lower costs and higher levels of service, which may not be otherwise available. Although small and medium enterprises (SME) and start-ups have been the early beneficiaries of Cloud Computing, large companies and even public sector organizations are beginning to leverage from applications such as email and calendar services (Hofmann and Woods, 2010). Dean and Saleh opine that CIOs and their IT departments are now able to spend less time worrying about 'keeping the business running' and to allow IT staff to focus more upon improving the features and the functionality of applications. This allows the CIO to focus on strategic initiatives and to work on transforming the organization.

Process Transformation Level: Dean and Saleh (2009) say that CIOs and IT departments can play a role in introducing new and improved business processes by leveraging from the elasticity and collaborative nature of the Cloud Model. Legacy systems often lack standardization of applications and data formats, and this has resulted in inherent inefficiency. The Cloud Model, which embraces standards, will lead to process transformation and efficiency across the organization (Dean and Saleh, 2009).

Business-Model-Innovation Level: By leveraging from access to resources, the Cloud Model could lead to the next generation of innovative business models and reshape existing ones, resulting in extensive collaborative efforts with partners, suppliers, distribution channels and customers (Dean and Saleh, 2009).

Benefits and Challenges of Cloud Computing

Cloud computing offers a slew of benefits to users, both individuals and enterprises. However, it also presents challenges and poses risks. By embracing and deploying Cloud Computing, enterprises can leverage from its benefits while ensuring that these risks and limitations are addressed. The diagram (Figure 2) below identifies three key areas in which enterprises could leverage by embracing the emerging Cloud Model. These are (a) Operational Excellence (b) Strategic Value and (c) IT Value.

Figure 2: Key sets of Values to Enterprises

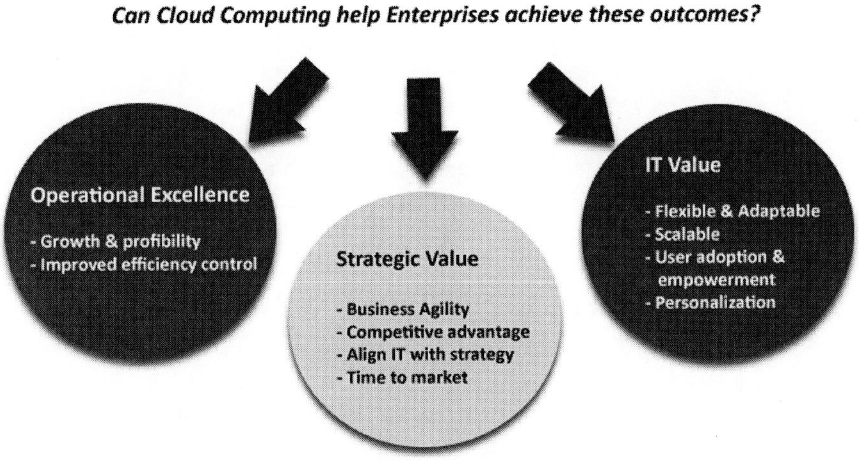

Benefits of Cloud Computing

A Public Cloud eliminates significant capital expenses on computing infrastructure, upfront license costs, maintenance costs, migration costs and upgrade costs (Brynjolfsson, Hofmann and Jordan, 2010; Hofmann & Woods, 2010; Wyld, 2009). Cloud applications can be deployed instantly and simultaneously to thousands of geographically dispersed users. Developers can experiment and test new and innovative ideas without having to invest in infrastructure. Cloud Computing offers scalability and elasticity which meets on-demand peak and seasonal computing resources (Hofmann & Woods, 2010). The Cloud has opened up a world of opportunities for big and small enterprises alike (including individuals) by providing access to computing resources without the need to implement, administer, maintain or buy those resources, and this has increased business agility. The key features and drivers of the Cloud Model are depicted in Table 2 below.

Table 2: Features & Drivers of the Cloud Model

Features	Flexibility On-demand elasticity Scalability Compute from anywhere, location independence Self-service IT Elimination of maintenance, upgrades and migration of applications No update disruptions Enhanced security for SMEs
Business Benefits	On-demand provisioning /buy or release on demand Virtual/mobile Access—'compute anywhere' Business Agility Reliability through redundant sites Ability to easily meet evolving IT requirements Immediacy—quick to deploy applications Effective utilization of resources
Economic Benefits	No or low capital investment No or low running cost Utility-based, pay-as-you go model No need pay for underutilized resources No long term contract/commitments

Challenges and Limitations of Cloud Computing

Is the utility analogy accurate for Cloud Computing? There are concerns about the Cloud Model, and general challenges associated with data security and the risk of unauthorized access to customer data, proprietary information, trade secrets and classified information, as well as concerns about system availability and business continuity. It is a fact that running Cloud applications results in ceding control to the service provider as regards the protection and location of the data. Although some researchers (Carr, 2005) have argued for the vision of computing becoming the fifth utility, the fact that Cloud Computing simply cannot achieve the same plug-and-play simplicity as electricity and security is one of the greatest challenges to the model. Hofmann and Woods (2010) argue that the utility analogy doesn't hold true, as most enterprises don't spend any time worrying about whether electrical wires are being compromised. In contrast, a violation of data security is a serious concern for an organization. However, for small and medium enterprises, with limited resources and skills sets, data may be more secure with a cloud service provider than if it is held at the organization's premises.

The other major concern affecting the deployment of a Cloud is that it should meet the compliance standards of legislative requirements, such as Sarbanes-Oxley (SOX) in the US, and the Data Protection directives of the European Union (EU) (Hofmann and Woods, 2010). While data protection requirements in the EU are consistently applied across its member countries, in the US data protection requirements can vary from state to state. In fact, these issues are slowing down the deployment of Cloud services, though many organizations have adopted the hybrid model in order to address these concerns (Wyld, 2009).

Hoffman and Woods (2010) argue that 'as long as we rely on fiber-optic cables, we're limited by network speed' and that the transfer of large volumes of data using Cloud technology has resulted in a bottleneck. Cloud technology has therefore been found unsuitable for business applications such as stock trading, where a large amount of data needs to be transferred with great speed and with split-second precision. Bryanjolfsson, Hofmann and Jordan (2010) opine that infinite elasticity and scalability remains an unattainable goal in the foreseeable future, as Cloud Computing isn't simply a matter of adding an infinite number of servers. Some problems and processes cannot be solved by adding more servers, as these require different architectures for processing, memory and storage. RDBMS applications are widely used for major business applications. These database systems face limitations, as they are unable to write concurrently on two different nodes. As such, Hoffman and Woods (2010) highlight the fact that it is difficult for high volume mission critical applications to run using Cloud technology. However, they suggest that Cloud technology could be revolutionary for start-ups and for small and medium enterprises.

In addition, there is a lack of standards, as well as other technical limitations. For example, Hofmann and Woods (2010) state that Cloud providers speak different languages, and that all the major vendors of storage, such as Amazon's Dynamo, Google's Big Table and Facebook's Cassandra, are proprietary applications,

Given that there is no scientific solution for scalable relational database management systems (RDBMS) as yet, this leaves no option but to choose between proprietary storage and the huge challenges faced by interoperability (Hofmann and Woods, 2010). In contrast with the case of electricity, the different Cloud platforms and applications are not necessarily interchangeable and interoperable. In the case of an electricity grid, a customer can plug in without having to be concerned about the power supply. Furthermore, Cloud penetration is also hampered by a lack of uniform standards, although efforts have been undertaken by The Open Grid Forum to develop an Open Interface, and there are ongoing efforts by the Open Cloud Consortium to develop Cloud Computing standards and practices.

Cloud Computing technology is a means to an end, not the end itself (Muller, 2011; Wyld, 2009). Today's CIOs and their IT departments are expected to deliver more than the development and implementation of the latest technologies: they are expected to deliver measurable business value. Increasingly, technology is becoming a commodity. Goldstein (2008) offers a very thought-provoking and somewhat pragmatic assessment of the Cloud Model, and he highlights the fact that the model is able to free CIOs from constant worries about IT investments, thereby presenting an opportunity for CIOs to focus on more strategic issues and to play a different role, devising novel ways to take advantage of Cloud technology. The benefits of the Cloud Model to enterprises are significant. However, as Muller (2011) highlights, it is unlike other utilities because it is not a one-size-fits-all solution. Hence, companies and CIOs will need to develop unique strategies, in line with their business objectives, in order to fully leverage from the cloud model.

Conclusion

The Cloud Model has been widely accepted as a paradigm of new technology in the literature, and it is fast gaining prominence in the industry. It has been suggested by some that the Cloud Computing model shows the potential for disruptive evolution, in terms of how enterprises have leveraged from technologies such the internet over the past two decades. It is evident that the rate of change and ubiquity of computing is showing no sign of slowing. The exponential growth of mobile applications and social media are generating new data and information at an astonishing speed and an unimaginable magnitude. According to Gartner, the Cloud Computing services market will reach over $ 150 billion in 2013. Cloud Computing is a paradigm shift in ICT which has begun to alter the computing model, to increase business agility and scalability and to increase access to computing resources (storage, communication and processing) for both enterprises and individuals. The unique aspects of Cloud Computing, such as its provision of access to unlimited computing resources, pose new challenges and security risks. By implementing appropriate controls and by applying due diligence, Cloud Computing has the potential to offer significant benefits to enterprises and to transform businesses in ways which are as yet unheard of and still to be conceived.

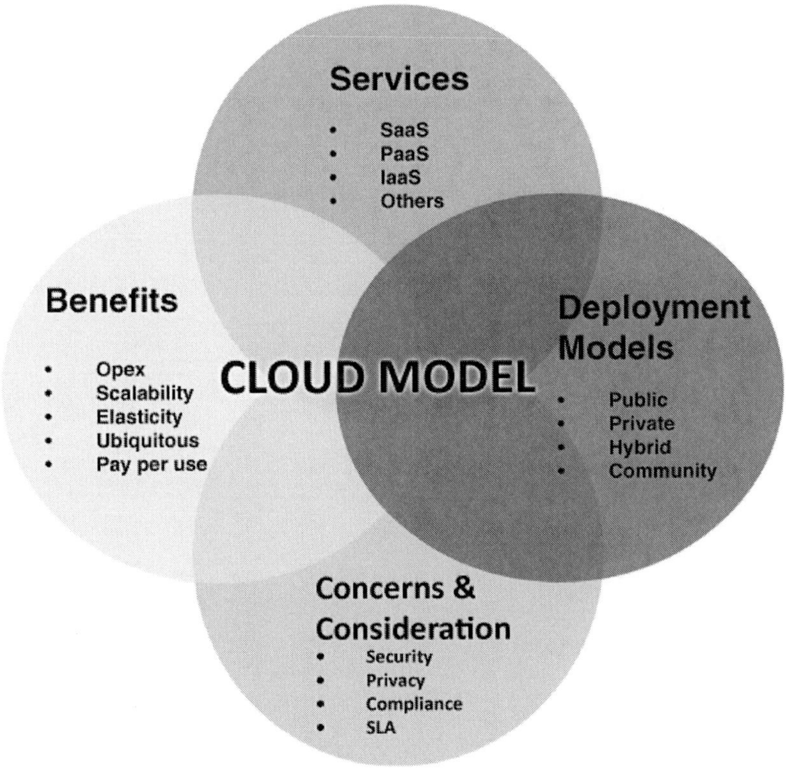

Figure 3: An Overview of Cloud Model

In summary, it is evident that the Cloud Model offers significant benefits. It is indisputable that it has proven to be a major commercial success and that it will continue to evolve. It also poses challenges and has limitations. There is universal agreement about the power of Cloud Computing and its potential impact on enterprises, in spite of concerns about privacy, security, control and lack of standards. Cloud Computing will uncover and unleash new growth and revenue opportunities for businesses. Cloud Computing is neither a new nor a revolutionary technology, but a new paradigm which will generate new business models, new opportunities and new revenue streams. It presents new challenges relating to security, privacy and compliance. In order to operate securely in the Cloud, enterprises must ensure that service providers deploy aggressive security and risk management solutions. There is a need for heightened due diligence in identifying and selecting service providers, with regular reviews of privacy and IP policies, security measures and disaster recovery plans. There is also a need to carefully evaluate and manage contractual transfers of risk through indemnities and warranties.

CHAPTER TWO

CONTROLLER'S PERSPECTIVE ON IMPLEMENTING ROLLING INSTRUMENTS

ROBERT C. RICKARDS
MUNICH BUSINESS SCHOOL
GERMAN POLICE UNIVERSITY
AND ROLF RITSERT
GERMAN POLICE UNIVERSITY

Abstract

The business environment's increased volatility following the 2007-2009 financial crisis has forced many enterprises to rethink their approach to planning. Advocates of rolling planning instruments believe they are superior to traditional, static tools, especially given their ability both to signal and to respond rapidly to environmental change. Yet only a minority of enterprises employs them. By analyzing results from several surveys, this study briefly compares and contrasts traditional, static controlling tools with their newer, more dynamic counterparts. It then considers why many enterprises so far have failed to implement rolling planning instruments. The study concludes with presentation of a 12-point-strategy controllers and management accountants could use to facilitate their adoption, particularly in small- and medium-sized enterprises (SMEs).

Keywords: *business drivers, controlling, forward visibility, rolling budgets, rolling forecasts, scenario analysis*

Introduction

Traditionally, classic business administration has had a clear orientation on the fiscal year. Both the statement of comprehensive income and the closing statement of financial position are annually-based. The high general acceptance of an annual orientation creates a framework, which facilitates time-series comparisons of a single enterprise's performance and comparisons at a given point in time between enterprises. However, the environmental conditions of many enterprises often are so unstable that annually-oriented plans require updating several times in the course of a business year. Accordingly, a survey of over 200 organizations found that 80 percent of them expected to have quarterly rolling forecasts and budgets in place by 2005 (Parmenter 2007). Despite the touted advantages of rolling instruments, though, seven years later still only a minority of enterprises employs them.

On the other hand, the marked increase in various forms of economic volatility (demand, overall business conditions, input and output prices, exchange rates and costs of workforce talent) in the aftermath of the 2007-2009 financial crisis appears to be forcing companies to rethink their approaches to planning (The Hackett Group 2011). For example, a survey of budgeting practice in UK corporations found that 40 % of the responding finance managers already had implemented a rolling forecast or were giving it careful thought (Clarke 2007). In 2010, Unilever scrapped its annual budget and now relies on an eight-quarter rolling forecast. Norton Lilly International, Statoil, and American Century Investments also eliminated their static, 12-month budgets with no tears. Observers expect larger, well-known enterprises to follow suit (Banham 2011).

At least for some enterprises, the world thus seems to be moving too fast to plan even one year ahead. Furthermore, by focusing solely on annual goals, management risks steering the enterprise in the wrong direction due to its failure to take important information beyond the fiscal year's end adequately into consideration.

Hence, as shown below, recent survey results indicate that, while still far from ubiquitous, the usage of rolling planning instruments indeed seems to be increasing – albeit often in tandem with traditional annual budgets (Sivabalana et al. 2009). This study explains why more enterprises generally, and SMEs in particular, don't have them in their controlling toolkits yet. To do so, it begins by describing the classic, static planning instruments most enterprises employ, together with these tools' shortcomings. It then turns to the more advanced, rolling forecasting and budgeting instruments found at leading firms. In comparing and contrasting static with continuous planning instruments, it reports results from various surveys, conducted mostly in German-speaking countries, about their use. After discussing reasons why the employment of dynamic devices is less widespread than it might be, it develops a strategy to facilitate their adoption and implementation.

Traditional, Static Instruments

With the traditional, static approach, planning takes place in keeping with rules contained in a handbook (Rickards 2008). These rules serve the purpose of fundamental coordination, quality assurance, and communication. Reporting focuses largely on comparison of actual results with plan data. Strategic planning encompasses goals, scenarios, and initiatives. The overall planning process tends to seek qualitative results rather than produce quantitative guidelines. Furthermore, strategic and operational planning are separate processes with limited linkages and different responsibilities.

In classic planning, setting ambitious budget goals generally is more important than predicting actual results precisely. Financial and historically oriented key performance indicators (KPIs) dominate operational planning. For example, the main basis for the financial portion of the annual master budget is the operational sales revenue targeted in the planned statement of comprehensive income. In contrast, planning for the statement of financial position relies heavily on historical values.

There are many direct data inputs from a variety of sources (Heer and Lamorte 2010). Typically, the controlling service is responsible for sales revenue and direct costs in planning the statement of comprehensive income, while bookkeeping supplies the data for operating profit on that statement and the numbers for the statement of financial position. Cash-flow planning occurs largely independent of that for the statement of financial position.

Resource allocation takes place via annually negotiated budgets based on bottom-up-planning with numerous coordination rounds (Leyk et al. 2006). Strategic goals are not disaggregated for individual functions. Sales planning, therefore, is a decentralized process characterized by high input levels of manpower and time. Short-term changes are difficult to integrate into the budget. Planning for production, procurement, and various support areas relies on historical data. Moreover, this planning comes about in separate functional silos, each often with its own assumptions, so production bottlenecks tend to persist.

With regard to forward visibility, the traditional, static approach bases its prognoses on the planned statement of comprehensive income, whose close linkage to the budget hinders meaningful gap-analyses. To the extent scenario planning occurs, one prepares the scenarios manually and uses them mostly to support investment decisions. The financial prognosis, annual budget, and reporting of actual results display a high level of detail.

Finally, IT-support for classic planning involves a variety of different tools, often Excel-based. Indeed, 82 % of surveyed enterprises report using such Excel-based tools (Business Applications Research Center 2008). Whether developed in-house or purchased off-the-shelf, though, these applications typically are process- or business-unit-specific. Enterprises usually introduce new instruments only on a reactive basis.

Shortcomings of Static Instruments

Many managers still view traditional budgeting as an organizational imperative to control costs and financial performance (Frow et al. 2010). Although classic planning and budgeting enjoy widespread use, they are subject to serious criticism for impeding efficient resource allocation, encouraging myopic decision-making, and facilitating budgetary gamesmanship. The following are some of the many other shortcomings of traditional planning and budgeting:

- Time-consuming to prepare, but already out of date when finally authorized (Schmidt 1992)
- Too costly for the few benefits they produce
- Promoting rigid planning and incremental thinking (Hope and Fraser 1999)
- Ignoring key drivers of shareholder value by focusing too much attention on short-term financial indicators
- Tying the organization to an often risky, twelve-month commitment, based on forecasts of uncertain reliability
- Imposing a vertical command-and-control structure and centralized decision-making,
- Being unable to reflect changes in the company's organization and processes (Schmidt 1992)

In sum, the core of adverse criticism seems to be that classic planning and budgeting do not meet the demands of competitive environments in the information age (Hope and Fraser 1999). Particularly in the aftermath of the 2007-2009 financial crisis, the traditional approach's inability to signal and respond to rapid environmental change has become obvious (Hackett Group 2011; Banham 2011).

Results from a survey among controllers in Austrian, German, and Swiss small- and medium-sized enterprises (SMEs) with regard to the quality and costs of their planning illustrate nicely the Janus-like view managers have of traditional, static planning. On the one hand, they complain about the large amounts of time and money consumed relative to the modest utility gained from preparing annual forecasts and budgets. In this regard, strategic plans take just 5 % of planning resources, while forecasting consumes 10 % and annual budgeting 85 % (Kopp and Leyk 2004). On the other hand, most managers don't believe they can make do without these static instruments (Kuhn and Pick 2006)! In fact, over 80 % of surveyed enterprises still employ them, either alone or in combination with some more modern tools (Seufert et al. 2008).

In answering a question about the resources budgeting alone consumes, 10 % of the surveyed firms reported needing more than 20 man-months to complete this task. Only 39 % of the businesses said they needed fewer than 3 man-months. Results from a survey of larger enterprises are broadly similar. In over 68 % of the companies, the controlling staff reported annual budget preparation requiring between eleven and twenty weeks. More than half the enterprises took between 4 and 6 months for their operational planning and budgeting. Indeed, several firms said they spent more than 31 calendar weeks on these processes (Leyk et al. 2006)!

Results from a third survey are particularly interesting because the researchers repeated their 2006 study with the same panel in 2010. The number of full-time equivalent (FTE) positions devoted to budgeting per 1 billion € in sales revenue grew from 5.56 to 7.49. Meanwhile the number of drafts necessary before authorization of the budget rose from three to four, and the number of workdays required for planning and budgeting increased from 60 to 80. On average, budget preparation alone consumed twenty-eight days, with a quarter of the firms reporting they needed more than forty-five days to complete the task (Barkalov et al. 2010). Results from a second research team that conducted its surveys in 2008 and 2010 also found a clear shift toward longer durations of the budgeting process (Weber et al. 2010). Supporting the findings about these trends, another survey discovered 64 % of controllers saying their planning took too much time and 47 % of them expecting planning costs and efforts would be higher in 2011 than in 2010 (ICV 2011).

Furthermore, the amount of detail involved in annual budget planning is very high. Over 50 % of the surveyed SMEs budget at least 50 cost centers, while 25 % base their budgets on more than 100 cost centers. The same is true for the number of general ledger accounts taken into consideration (Kuhn and Pick 2006). It is noteworthy that the degree of detail increases with the number of positions planned. Yet details about the incorporation of strategic measures into annual budget planning often are inadequate – or altogether absent (Leyk et al. 2006; Barkalov et al. 2010).

In larger enterprises, the high degree of detail in budget planning is an important influence on the amounts of manpower and time consumed too. Decomposing the overall budget problem down to the lowest hierarchical level requisite for detailed analysis consumes large quantities of such resources. Moreover, wasteful resource consumption occurs every time negotiating partners loop through the planning cycle to revise their draft until they finally approve the annual operating budget. Large firms usually commit 75 % to 95 % of their total controlling capacity to operational planning during the time they are engaged in budget preparation (Kopp and Leyk 2004).

Also worthy of mention is the fact that only 36 % of the respondents really believe in their budget. 57 % of them assess the crunched numbers generated from all that work as moderately realistic at best. Comparison of actual results with forecasts shows further that this self-assessment markedly overestimates budget quality. After only three months, events have overtaken more than half of all traditional, static budgets. Relative to the planning period, only about 6 % of the budgets examined proved to be reasonably accurate. In addition, linking the budget numbers to benchmarks in the form of personal performance contracts hardly improves budget accuracy (Kuhn and Pick 2006). Comparable figures from another survey show 12 % of controllers don't think their own plans are worth the paper on which they are printed, while another 53 % view them as a point of orientation at best. Moreover, 54 % of controllers believe their budgets always are overtaken by events within six months of authorization and the other 46 % think that often to be the case (ICV 2011)!

Among the reasons given (multiple responses possible) why actual results vary from forecasts and budget plans, the most frequently mentioned are: changes in the business and economic environment (67 %), imprecise or too aggressive forecasts (54 %), and poor data quality or missing data (41 %). Participants also cited the overly long duration of the budgeting process itself (23 %) (Leahy 2005).

In fact, the relationship between accuracy and the length of time required for forecasting and budgeting apparently is an inverse one. While 50 % of the enterprises needing less than a week produced actual results within ± 5 % of their predictions, only 11 % of the companies taking a month or more were equally precise (Wolleswinkel 2008). A similar study of the relationship between the efficiency of forecasting and budgeting processes and their effectiveness arrives at the same conclusion (Barkalov et al. 2010).

Researchers therefore rightly wonder whether highly detailed forecasts and budgets really are necessary and efficient. Unfortunately, top management seldom considers the high cost involved relative to the meager benefit derived from such detailed instruments. It then is no wonder that cost, product, and strategic controlling considerations often receive little attention in the planning process. Whatever their utility in the past, traditional, static budgets apparently no longer constitute an adequate basis for modern operational controlling. It therefore is all the more surprising that five of six surveyed controllers can't imagine working without them (Obermüller 2006)! Likewise controllers either don't view reduction of planning cost and effort as an important topic (41 %) or, while recognizing it as an important problem, have not done anything about it yet (24 %) (ICV 2011)!

More-effective forecasting-and-budgeting capabilities were top-of-the-mind for CFOs in 2011, with 84 % making them a priority, followed closely by improving the accuracy, shortening the cycle time, and increasing the efficiency of forecasting performance at 81 % (multiple mentions possible) (Hackett Group 2011). Greater accuracy (42 %) and closer linkage between strategy and execution (31 %) long have been high priorities, whereas CFOs generally have held shorter cycle time (9 %) and switching to rolling instruments (7 %) to be less urgent (PwC 2007).

Although not viewed as their top priority, CFOs nevertheless have clear ideas about what would boost confidence in their forecasts the most. Those measures (multiple responses possible) would be: further automation of IT-systems and -tools (42 %); more scenario planning and sensitivity analyses (42 %); switching to a rolling format (40 %); reduction in detail as well as a stronger focus on business drivers (35 %); and better input data quality (34 %) (KPMG 2007).

What are Rolling Forecasts and Budgets?

To deal with the drawbacks of traditional instruments, firms face a choice among three alternatives: accept their shortcomings and maintain them; improve them; or abandon them and possibly replace them with something better. Studies of enterprise planning reveal interesting, practice-led developments. As noted earlier, some companies employ rolling forecasts, produced on a monthly or quarterly basis, to supplement their annual static budgets (Montgomery 2002). Other organizations see them as the main alternative to annual operational planning (Hope and Fraser 1999; Ekholm 2000; Weber et al. 2010). Yet use of both rolling forecasts and rolling budgets appear to be the most frequently chosen alternative (Neely et al. 2002; Hansen et al. 2003; Durfee 2006; De Waal et al. 2010).

Rolling forecasts and budgets are key elements of a planning system distinguished by regular adjustments and increasing detail as the information situation improves (Horváth and Reichmann 2003). In principle, the "rolling concept" is not new because enterprises have been preparing certain sub-budgets on a continuous basis for a long time (Hahn 2003). Cash planning, undertaken every month or quarter, probably is the most familiar of these sub-budgets. Both midterm and long-term plans are rolling instruments too. In actual practice, though, a rolling approach to operational budgeting remains unusual.

The most important characteristics of rolling plans in contrast to traditional forecasts and budgets are:

- Constant time horizon independent of the fiscal year
- Periodicity (as a rule, quarterly preparation)
- Combination of more detailed planning in early periods and less detailed planning in later periods
- Planning focuses mainly on monetary and nonmonetary business drivers that influence monetary results (revenues and costs)

Underlying all rolling forecasts and budgets is a constant time horizon. In a given individual case, the dynamism and complexity of the environment determine the number of the quarters or months for prognostication (Büchner et al. 2000). Normally the time interval covered lies between five quarters (or thirteen months) and eight quarters (or twenty-four months), because beyond two years' time the reliability of the prognosis declines markedly. Survey results show about two-thirds (67 %) of enterprises still rely exclusively on traditional, static budgets. Of the 33 % of enterprises, whose planning system contains at least some rolling elements, 7 % have a time horizon of four quarters, 6 % five quarters, 4 % six quarters, 9 % a flexible number of quarters, and 7 % some other time span such as two quarters or three years (Wolleswinkel 2008).

Many enterprises, which have introduced both rolling forecasts and budgets, use them in combination with a traditional annual budget plan. This approach determines the lower boundary of five quarters (or thirteen months), because at the latest with the beginning of the fourth quarter (or twelfth month) forecast, budget values must completely cover the next fiscal year. In addition, the inclusion of at least five quarters (or thirteen months) facilitates comparison of the same quarter (or month) of different years (e.g., the first quarter of 20XX with the first quarter of 20XX+1). Especially in the construction industry and the merchandising sector, with their strong seasonal variations in revenues, such comparisons are helpful for controlling an enterprise's operations.

Rolling revisions ensure that, despite the passage of time, the length of the period covered remains constant, while currently available, improved information is integrated into them. In doing so, one distinguishes between the quarters with regard to the degree of detail. As shown in Fig. 1, one generally prepares more detailed forecasts and budgets for the next quarter (Q1 in January 20XX) than for the later quarters (Q2 20XX, Q3 20XX, Q4 20XX, Q1 20XX+1)

Figure 1: Rolling Forecasts and Budgets

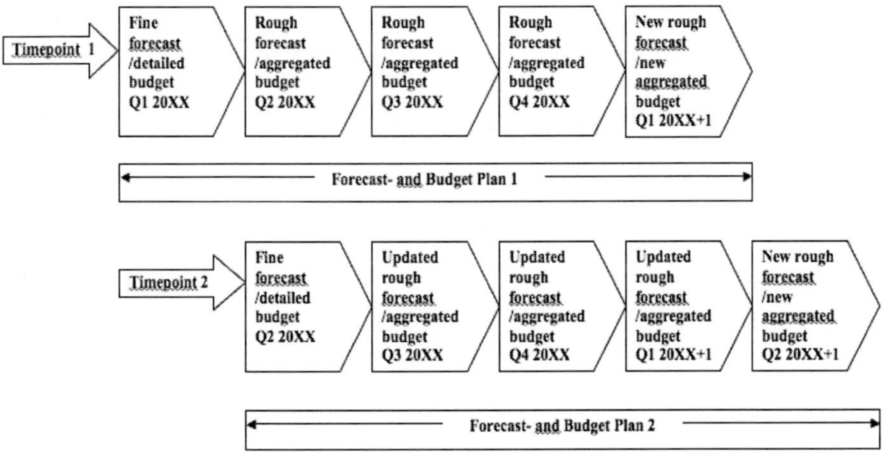

Relative to traditional, static planning as an annual one-time event, rolling forecasts and budgets offer an enterprise's management clear gains in near-time controlling information. These gains pertain not only to the revenue budget, but also to the production budget, and to the budgeting of inputs as well as to work-in-process and finished goods inventories. Because they always are based on the most recent information available, a high degree of actuality is an important characteristic of rolling instruments. Near-time information is important above all for exchange-listed companies because the share price is sensitive to forecasts of the business's future development. With rolling instruments, one already can make a statement at the beginning of the second quarter 20XX, based on the latest information available, about how an enterprise's business likely will develop during the first two quarters of 20XX+1. In this fashion, continuous planning provides much earlier guidance for stakeholders' expectations than traditional, static methods afford. If one chooses the appropriate degree of detail and the enterprise does entirely without a classic annual budget, then planning with a rolling detailed forecast and a rolling detailed budget for a quarter also avoid duplicative work and thus save time.

In conceiving and constructing enterprise-specific rolling instruments, one needs to be mindful of the following considerations:

- **Frequency and time horizon** – the more dynamic and complex the environment, the shorter the time horizon should be and/or the more frequently preparation should take place.
- **Depth of detail** – in order to minimize effort and expense, reports for top management based on rolling instruments need only include critical, profit-related information.
- **Linkage to longer-term goal-setting** – the strategic planning framework with its distant time horizon represents the action and orientation corridor for rolling, operational planning, which includes the measures necessary to attain the enterprise's midterm goals.

Unfortunately, the terms "rolling forecast" and "rolling budget" often are used as synonyms for a dynamic, continuous planning process. This imprecision leads to confusion because the two terms actually apply to related, but different instruments. The important difference concerns their goal orientation. A rolling budget usually has linkage to a binding service contract between the management levels with relative goals (ideally defined through benchmarking) to be attained within certain guidelines and on the basis of specific, concrete measures. Management periodically re-evaluates and adjusts these goals accordingly. The adjusted rolling budget thus represents an authorized plan of action to attain a certain goal condition.

In contrast, in the case of rolling forecasts, there generally is no monthly or quarterly goal adjustment process. Instead, the purpose is to predict the future state of the enterprise's business development as accurately as possible. The goals remain constant for a fiscal year, so that one can calculate an updated "standard cost-forecast variance." The rolling forecast then just provides a framework, in which individual business units plan their operational activities. Accordingly, it somewhat resembles the flexible budget, also frequently used in cost accounting, where the degree of capacity utilization serves to correct the standard costs involved.

Practical Example

A mid-size enterprise with two divisions produces PC-peripherals and the machines for manufacturing them. With about 1,100 employees it operates in both Germany and China. Before reform of the enterprise's planning process, its staff devoted over four months each year to preparation of the annual budget. The company then set itself the goal of reducing the time spent on operational planning to less than two months within a time period of three years. The reformed, best-in-class planning process embodies many advanced budgeting principles (Kopp and Leyk 2004). In particular, it includes the following features:

- Linkage of strategic and operational planning
- Top-down-determined goals, derived from the enterprise's strategy
- Detailing of budgets only where necessary and reasonable
- Rolling perspective for both forecasts and budgets

In order to reduce the degree of detail and to determine the variables on which to focus the rolling instruments, the firm first analyzed its cost accounts. Together, just eight of 56 cost accounts, on the basis of which the enterprise formerly prepared its operational plans, constituted 87 % of its entire cost volume. Today, over half of this company's cost categories no longer appear individually in its forecasts and budgets. Instead, planners treat them as an aggregated value (sum of the prior year's actual results times current year's *kaizen*-factor) in the operating budget. Doing so greatly simplifies the planning process, while freeing up manpower and time to concentrate on the major elements in the firm's forecasts and budgets. At the same time, these rolling instruments nevertheless continue to reflect planned total costs.

This approach means that the enterprise now controls its aggregated costs differently than formerly. Previously, the company controlled them individually both on the level of the entire firm and also on the product manager level. Although many cost accounts today are less important from the perspective of the overall enterprise, they remain relatively important for product managers. In order to attain goals set for their products by top management, they continue to need more highly disaggregated data in their cost calculations, in order to discover where they can save material as well as labor or machine time. Accordingly, planners prepare more narrowly focused, but more detailed tools for the product managers' use.

Because operating income (EBIT) is the company's most important planning variable, it appears in both rolling forecasts and budgets. In addition to the abovementioned eight key cost accounts, both instruments break out each division's respective unit sales, revenues, and deductions from sales revenue. Table 1 reproduces these instruments' framework. Omitted here due to space limitations and privacy considerations are the detailed forecast and the detailed budget supplementing columns 1 and 2 as well as all line-item financial information.

Planners prepare the firm's rolling instruments quarterly – both on the level of the two divisions as well as at the overall enterprise level -- for five quarters. In practice, here, at the latest, it becomes evident that these tools are not meant for detailed controlling in every cost center, but rather to support decision-making at higher management levels.

Information inputs from various managers are necessary for preparing rolling instruments. This information comes chiefly from the responsible cost centers, not the controlling service. For example, the sales manager and the respective managers of the business divisions are responsible for the revenue data. After all, they stand closest to customers and competitors and therefore can foresee many future business developments best. Similarly, the production manager is best-positioned to estimate labor costs, and so forth. Besides responsibility for identifying and forecasting certain business drivers' values, the controlling service nowadays has mostly a cross-functional, coordinating function. It must ensure that managers participating in the planning process start from the same assumptions in estimating forecast values. Only in this way do rolling prognoses and budgets yield reliable predictions about future developments.

Table 1: Contents and Suppliers of Information for Rolling Instruments (Monetary Variables in Mio. €)

		Column 1	**Column 2**	**Column 3**	**Column 4**	**Column 5**	**Column 6**	**Column 7**
		Σ BY	**Q3 20XX**	**Q4 20XX**	**Q1 20X1**	**Q2 20X1**	**Q3 20X1**	**Σ Q3-Q3**
Supplier	**Planning Variable**	**T A+F V**	**T F V**	**T F V**	**T F V**	**T F V**	**T F V**	**T F V**
BA I	Units sold (PU)							
BA II	Units sold (PU)							
BA I	Sales revenue							
BA II	Sales revenue							
BA I	Sales deductions							
BA II	Sales deductions							
	Net sales revenue							
MM	Vendor materials I							
MM	Vendor materials II							
MM	Other Materials I							
MM	Other Materials II							
	Cost of materials consumed							
Production	Personnel Costs I							
Production	Personnel Costs II							
	Personnel Costs							
M&R	Maint. & Rprs. I							
M&R	Maint. & Rprs. II							
SCM	Freight and Storage Costs I							
SCM	Freight and Storage Costs II							

Controlling	Incidental costs I							
Controlling	Incidental costs II							
Controlling	Administrative costs							
	General and administrative costs							
	EBITDA							
BK	Depreciation							
	EBIT	41 38 3	8 7 1	9 9 0	10 9 1	10 5 5	8 6 2	45 36 9

Business-Year Perspective:
Sum of Quarters Q1 and Q2 20XX (Actual-Results) plus Q3 and Q4 20XX (Forecasted/Plan-Results)

Rolling Perspective:
Sum of Quarters Q3 20XX through Q3 20XX+1 (all quarters in the Forecast/Budget)

Σ BY = Sum of Values for the Business Year, T = Target Value, A = Actual-Result, F = Forecast-Value, V = Variance, BA = Business Area, PU = Product Units, MM = Materials Management, M&R = Maintenance and Repairs, SCM = Supply Chain Management, BK = Bookkeeping

One reads the rolling forecast and the rolling budget in Table 1 as follows: At the time-point of preparation, the second quarter already has closed. The values for the third quarter 20XX and fourth quarter 20XX relate to the current business year. The first quarter of 20XX+1, the second quarter of 20XX+1 and the third quarter of 20XX+1 pertain to the next business year. In the columns there always are three numbers:

- The target value (T) of the respective line, which is derived from "top-down" midterm planning,
- A projected value, which is the sum of the actual value for the completed quarters of the business year and the forecast values for the remaining quarters until yearend (A+F), or the forecast values (F) for the remaining quarters of the current and the next business years,
- The variance (V) between the actual and target, or between the forecast and target values.

In column 1, the forecast-values of the third and fourth quarters of 20XX are summed with the actual values of the first and second quarters of that year. The results are compared with the plan values of the current year, in order to make a prediction about goal attainment or staying within the budget. This procedure is similar to the approach taken in traditional, static forecasts and budgets, except that the latter contain planning data, which already are between twelve and fifteen months old! From the business-year viewpoint, there already is a variance of 3 mio. € below the EBIT-target. Hence, the forecast shows the enterprise likely will not attain the current year's plan result with the existing measures. Countermeasures therefore are necessary!

Columns 2 to 6 reveal the quarters, in which one must reckon with the largest business shortfalls. Column 7 sums all target and forecast values of columns 2 through 6 (i.e., the respective quarters), for which the enterprise has projected forecast values. The variance of 9 mio. € indicates that, if management fails to implement additional measures, the company also likely will miss its midterm planning goal by a considerable margin. One simply cannot gain such valuable insights through analyses of traditional, static forecasts and budgets. With their fixation on the end of the current business year, they here would predict a yearend variance from the targeted EBIT of only 1 mio. €. As a result, any countermeasures introduced by management probably would be too little and too late to attain the midterm EBIT goal.

The projected small variance from plan values in the current year, however, is only a weak, early warning signal of the serious need for decisive action in the quarters following it! Considering that measures need time from their introduction until they become fully effective, a delayed intervention probably could not offset the threatening unfavorable development. Although the high detail of classic instruments facilitates very good control of ex post results, it clearly can prove much less useful for attaining a firm's future goals.

The rolling, cumulating forecast and the rolling, cumulating budget, in combination with the midterm planning goals, here yield additional value with regard to goal attainment. Simultaneously, they constitute a practical example of how a controller can present information about complex structures in simplified form that nevertheless is highly useful for managerial decision-making.

Rolling Instruments

To overcome the shortcomings of traditional, static tools, enterprises with better or advanced methods use at least some rolling instruments in their planning. The following description, though, applies just to those few enterprises, whose planning practices are best in their class. Environmental changes, not the fiscal year, trigger their planning. Accordingly, they continuously adjust their planning framework to internal and external events. While they also have clear rules to coordinate planning and to resolve disputes, coordination and quality assurance are independent of the planning process. Their reporting is flexible and scenario-based.

They understand the most important variables driving their business and use them as an integral element of their departments' controlling and reporting. The inclusion of key business drivers in all planning models provides linkage between strategy and operations. It also facilitates a reduction in planning detail, thus promoting greater efficiency and effectiveness. Because 20 % of the ledger accounts comprise 80 % of an enterprise's total expenses, one can focus attention largely on them. For purposes of controlling the remaining 80 % of the ledger accounts, comparisons of actual results from the prior and current periods often are adequate, thus reducing planning effort markedly and minimizing the number of coordination rounds required (Leyk et al. 2006). Responsibility for the planning model and the associated drivers lies with the operational business units.

Best-in-class enterprises quantify the effects of strategic initiatives and link them with both operational planning and business drivers. They establish fixed feedback loops in their strategic planning in order to make the adjustments necessary to obtain the "buy-in" of subordinated operational units. In setting operational goals for these units, best-in-class enterprises rely on performance comparisons relative to internal and external benchmarks ("beat the competition and beat the budget"). For performance evaluations, they eliminate factors over which managers have no influence ("split luck from effort"). For resource allocation purposes, on the other hand, best-in-class enterprises use an internal marketplace, where a project's contribution to value serves as the basis for investment decisions.

Best-in-class enterprises understand planning as a continuous process, linked to rolling prognoses. Built on key business drivers, the prognoses undergo regular, periodic updating as well as revision in response to environmental changes. Because prognoses can lead to coordinated, cross-functional operational countermeasures, their accuracy is a crucial item in the responsible managers' personal performance contract.

In their financial and sales planning, these businesses use scenario modeling with both internal and external parameters. Largely automated, this modeling is grounded on enterprise-wide assumptions as the core elements of all planning and decision processes. The planning staff generates detailed supplements and emergency schemes for certain scenarios and risks as required.

The prognoses and plans also include future-oriented elements like sales-funnels as well as measures of market potential and sales effectiveness. Planning for production, procurement, and support functions also concentrates on key business drivers in a uniform model. Production and supply chain planning simulates different levels of capacity usage and product priorities, while paying close attention to the efficiency of various manufacturing sites. A "make or buy"-decision framework is in place for introducing products, managing risk, and compensating for demand peaks.

Best-in-class solution support provides for acquisition of new hard- and software based on a long-term strategy, which in turn is coordinated with the enterprise's strategy. It covers the complete planning cycle, linking horizontal functional areas with vertical hierarchical levels. It thus facilitates enterprise-wide, efficient cooperation, coordination, and communication. The solution support promotes complex scenario modeling at all echelons, while systematically including available actual-data as the foundation for planning and prognoses.

Why Aren't All Firms Striving to Become Best-in-Class?

In view of the advantages described above, the question naturally arises as to why many firms still engage in traditional, static planning. Indeed, top management's behavior in this regard seems contradictory. On one hand, the senior management team sees the desirability of reducing the amount of detailed planning content (33 %), in part by making more realistic assumptions and adopting top-down guidelines for budgeting. On the other hand, in practice, only 28 % say they use a top-down planning approach (Leyk et al. 2006).

Further instances of such schizophrenic behavior abound. For example, CFOs view linkage between strategic with operational planning as a key success factor (98 %), but more than a quarter of them (26 %) admit they do not have it in place in their own enterprise. 45 % of CFOs agree that scenario planning is important or very important, yet just 15 % of them engage in it. 53 % of CFOs believe first-class IT support is essential for successful planning efforts, but only 22 % of them report having automated planning support in their organization (Leyk et al. 2006).

For practical reasons, both executives and operational managers may prefer more detailed budgets. They offer executives a vehicle for maintaining greater control over subordinates. They also afford managers with operating responsibilities greater security that they are making "correct" decisions. Among other reasons researchers give for companies nevertheless retaining traditional planning instruments are the following (Lynn and Madison 2004; Oehler 2008):

- The annual goal-setting process in the sense of management by objectives by itself is rather costly in terms of manpower, money, and time. To repeat this process every quarter or month simply could prove to be prohibitively expensive.
- Furthermore, organizations may budget for reasons not considered by critics of traditional planning instruments. Most budget research and practitioner criticism focus on the use of budgets for evaluation reasons (Hansen et al. 2003). However, annual budgets also serve the important, practical purpose of formal financial control (De Waal et al. 2010).
- In this connection, one can't ignore the annual basis of various planning objects such as the planned balance sheet. Many firms have tied management incentive schemes to the attainment of annual goals, necessitating generation of corresponding numbers. Moreover, an annual orientation is inherent in many standard business practices and external stakeholders expect a similar orientation in enterprise planning. For example, the payment of bonuses, which underpins managers' behavior, results from their attainment of annual, not monthly or quarterly, goals. Liquidity planning, including the taking up

of loans and use of operating loans, typically is also on an annual basis. Most managers and employees therefore have little experience orienting themselves temporarily in a different fashion.

- An annual orientation promotes stability. Too frequent adjustments can cause managers to doubt the binding nature of the budget plan. It is seldom the case that all the decisions involved have been reached by consensus. Calling the planned goals and measures to attain them into question every month or quarter could touch off unproductive squabbling, potentially paralyzing management when it needs to take action.
- Simple ignorance of the possibilities of combining periodic and continuous planning inhibits adoption of rolling instruments too.
- Instead of taking the necessary time to alter their enterprise's culture and adjust its internal processes, some users of rolling instruments tend to search for quick solutions. Proceeding in this manner invariably leads to further problems due to contradictions inherent in continuous planning. For example, top-down guidelines may decrease the time consumed by forecast and budget preparation markedly. Nevertheless, they are more suggestive of a "command and control" mentality than of advanced-budgeting leadership principles. Successful introduction of new controlling instruments presupposes decentralized, participative decision structures. If a firm continues to rely largely on top-down guidance and a traditional incentive system, it should not be surprising that subordinated instances carry on padding their budgets in order to attain the given goals more readily. Furthermore, to ensure future budgets contain substantial hidden reserves to meet unforeseen eventualities, they always consume their annual budgets completely, thereby wasting scarce resources.
- If, however, decentralization and participation of department heads and employees is successful, one consequently no longer can make the controller and CFO solely responsible for planning failures. Managerial unwillingness to accept responsibility also sometimes inhibits the introduction of rolling instruments.
- Because advanced-budgeting advocates champion the employment of BSCs and KPIs in connection with rolling instruments, the task of integration involves not only IT-technical aspects, like merging standard software from different makers with internally-developed software. It also has aspects that pertain to the company's controlling concept itself. The differing importance of monetary and non-monetary indicators is a case in point. If input prices increase, say, 3 percent in a month, that could lead to initiation of countermeasures in the

procurement or production departments as well as in product price formation. If, in contrast, surveys reveal customer satisfaction in a particular month lays 3 % below its benchmark, immediate initiation of countermeasures may not necessarily be appropriate. That is because such non-monetary results normally vary from month to month and are subject to a certain margin of error. They thus are less reliable as indicators of a real need to act.

The above reasons are somewhat surprising because the specific combination of periodic and rolling instruments necessary for implementation of best-in-class planning, of course, varies across organizations and stages of business development. Thus, for example, an immediate switchover to continuous forecasts and/or rolling budgets may prove useful in one company, but not in the next. In addition, the possibility of gradual implementation within an organization is an important characteristic and a great advantage of best-in-class planning. Managers and employees thus can learn how to use the new instruments step-by-step and consequently fewer problems are likely to occur during the introductory phase. Over time, users become increasingly adept in applying the instruments and can plan operational measures without difficulty. Accompanying this development is a gradual, forced reduction in the importance of traditional, static planning instruments.

CFOs themselves give more reasons for their reluctance to introduce rolling planning: the time taken from other controlling tasks for the necessary administration and merging of the data involved (53 %); the time responsible personnel from the respective cost centers and functional areas must spend making revisions (47 %); resistance of the responsible managers to investing the time necessary to revise forecasts and budgets more frequently (42 %); and the financial costs of additional forecasting and budgeting rounds (25 %) (Leahy 2005).

It is noteworthy that CFOs especially "fear" the mechanical activities of administration and data merging. These areas are precisely the ones in which IT-tools can be most helpful. Automation thus appears to be a critical factor for the success of rolling planning.

Strategy for Introducing and Implementing Rolling Planning

Given the circumstances, how should one now proceed to introduce rolling planning instruments? Adopting a pro-active stance is important. In light of the ambivalence and reluctance associated with top management's behavior described in the previous section, an element of stealth may be necessary too. The project itself then could consist of the following twelve points:

- Obtain commitment of top management and the finance team. Both need to comprehend and commit themselves to the rolling instrument methodology. They must understand that the business drivers will tie back to strategic decisions that senior managers may need to make in the future and the financial consequences associated with those decisions. It also is important that top management and the finance team agree that rolling forecasts and budgets will make the planning process easier, quicker, and more realistic. Here, workshops with presentations by experts, organizations with rolling forecasts, and an in-house team, whose members are likely candidates to lead such a project, should prove helpful. Assuming top management commits to the project, it then will need to set aside time to give more feedback on business drivers, visit sites already employing rolling instruments, and approve the investment in the chosen planning software, all on a "tight" time schedule. It also is important to have agreement from all the accountants to abandon any ingrained fixation on looking at details. Top management must be mindful that forecasting and budgeting are core activities and require adequate financing.
- Start fresh. It is important to avoid constructing the new planning instruments around the (often Excel-based) tools existing in the organization. A recent benchmarking survey notes that companies relying heavily on spreadsheets, for example, typically take 30 days longer to complete their budgets than those enterprises using integrated systems (Player 2009). The new planning structure and instruments therefore should suit the model, not the previous planning tools' capabilities. To begin moving top management's thinking in this direction, one might begin by interviewing senior managers to identify key business drivers and questions they likely will want answered in the future. One way to do so is to brainstorm with them about plausible future scenarios and then build the key business drivers into the planning model's design (Parmenter 2007).
- Progress by stealth. Unless top management decides to take the lead in introducing rolling instruments, the best way to implement the required changes may be by stealth. This approach may involve first justifying investment in the planning system to improve forecasting and end-of-month reporting. Then, when the system is in place and the forecasting and budgeting instruments are running smoothly, top

management well may be willing to switch from a fiscal-year to a rolling focus.

- Choose a small team. Depending on the enterprise's size, the project team in principle should have between three and seven members with in-depth organizational knowledge and an appropriate mix of skills including: self-starters, innovators, good presenters and communicators as well as closers; ability to bring others onboard; and general ledger experience. Its members should be committed at least half-time to the project to avoid meeting cancellations due to other responsibilities. Project coordinators at the different business units will support the team with information about their business unit's operations and feedback about their area. Top management's involvement should be left to an advisory capacity. In the future, the individuals principally maintaining the forecast should be its primary users.
- Find external expertise for independent advice and internal promotion, but design the model in-house. The project team will need an on-call external adviser to provide intelligent counsel without becoming a team member. This mentor should ensure that the team keeps the project's "big picture" in view and thus avoids losing itself in details, while also safeguarding against the software provider's consultants taking the team in a direction it should not go. At the same time, the project team must focus as much on marketing the new concept to budget holders as it does on the need to train them. Budget holders must grasp how the new planning process is going to facilitate management of their business. They will need to hear success stories throughout the implementation phase. Accordingly, the project needs PR-expertise behind it. The project team should issue no presentation, email, memo, or paper unless the PR-expert has vetted it first. In contrast to seeking advice and PR-assistance from outside the organization, project team members always must design the model themselves. That means the proper roles for planning tool consultants are advisers and trainers, but definitely not designers. Circumscribing consultants' role in this fashion saves substantial amounts of money, while ensuring that the model's designers are people who thoroughly understand the enterprise's business.
- Avoid overly complex models. Some accountants and planners design extremely complex Excel-based models, which are both difficult and time-consuming to use, lack version control, produce consolidation headaches and low levels of confidence in the resulting numbers. One should remember that the purpose of forecasting is to

inform decision makers and thereby to help shape planning and budgeting outcomes, not to predict the future exactly. What these managers really need is an unbiased forecast with a narrowing degree of uncertainty, which implies that any occurrences over-forecast would offset the ones under-forecast. The focus has to be on understanding causes and effects in order to react more quickly. For this reason, model planning tools ought to be relatively simple to employ. Nevertheless, in-house staff members will need to attend in-depth training, so they can be fully aware of the planning system's capabilities and have had the opportunity to use it themselves.

- Apply Pareto's 80:20 rule. The team needs to spend its time forecasting and budgeting the major categories requiring substantial creative thinking and short-circuiting categories subject to automation. Examples of the former are: revenues; salary and wages; benefits; training, travel, and conferences; operational equipment; property costs; and promotional activities. Some examples of readily automated categories are: repairs and maintenance of operational equipment; office equipment, computers, and consumables; telecommunication costs; motor pool costs; building maintenance; depreciation; miscellaneous costs. Several useful rules-of-thumb are: limit the categories forecast by budget holders to no more than twelve; identify categories subject to automation and provide those numbers; display individual lines only if they represent 20 % of the total (e.g. show an individual revenue line only if it constitutes more than 20 % of total revenue). This latter rule applies at both budget holder and consolidated levels. However, forecasts should be detailed enough for any news, good or bad, to be translatable into action. It also is important to allow budget holders some flexibility in choosing the categories so as to reflect their operation best.
- Information from outside the organization should drive the rolling planning process, which also should reflect all the information available inside the organization. External information is essential. Without it the forecast simply is a recast of what already is known and therefore provides little benefit for users. Furthermore it is difficult to forecast out to a meaningful time horizon without using indicators of demand from outside the organization.
- Don't link the planning system to fixed targets for incentive schemes. Simply stated, targets are where a company wants to go (Player 2009). Thus, they typically represent medium-term aspirations or goals that often get converted into quantified annual targets. In contrast, forecasts highlight a company's strategic direction. When the

two differ, many organizations use forecasts to "close the gap." That means managers, who are motivated by prospective bonuses, but find themselves behind on an actual basis, show their organizations catching up to target values in forecasts. The problem with this approach is that it blends both current trends with expected results of future action plans. As a result, it obscures details of the action plans needed to attain the targets and limits discussion of risks associated with them. So, to the extent possible, keep the planning system free from the influence of personal contracts and incentives. Where necessary, use relative targets (say, growth in market share > market growth by 1 %). Of course, there may be sales targets or goals for cost reduction, but avoid assuming one will achieve them. However, if there are planned events, which will help achieve those goals, rolling forecasts and budgets should include them.

- Have trend graphs for every category forecasted. One can achieve better quality through trend analyses. There is no place for hidden reserves when a budget holder is accountable for past and future trends. In addition, if available for all categories budget holders must forecast, trend graphs may increase forecasting accuracy.
- Ensure there always are sufficient in-house experts on the new system, one of whom should "own" it. Again depending on firm size, select from two to five in-house staff members to become experts on the planning system, one of whom should be the CFO, and ensure they are in the focus group. Until rolling planning becomes more widespread, these individuals very well may be recruited by other enterprises to head their projects for switching over to rolling planning. So, one should maintain this level of in-house competence continuously.
- Always test the planning system to see whether it is influencing forecasting and budgeting behavior as intended and whether managers consequently are making better decisions.

Conclusion and Suggestions for Future Research

When planning with rolling instruments, it is worth reflecting upon a prognosis, with which everyone is familiar – the weather forecast. It presents us with two interesting characteristics that we accept without question. The first characteristic is integrity. We assume that one has updated it recently, and that it embodies all there is to know about the influences upon our weather. If it turns out to be wrong, we accept that it was due to something unknown or unpredictable (Plowman, n.d.).

The second characteristic is trust. If the forecast suggests bad weather ahead we don't normally ignore it, or seek a second opinion. We get out the umbrellas.

Where successfully implemented, rolling instruments should lead to major changes in managers' behavior. These tools now should drive the search for new business. For example, they should form the basis for capacity planning in plants and in overhead areas. They should support managers in negotiations with customers. They should prompt critical reviews of overheads required for the future. They should be the cornerstone of midterm and longer-term plans. Whether such normative changes in actual behavior indeed occur, forecasts become more precise, budget variances smaller, profits larger, and share price growth higher are important, proper questions for future research.

References

Banham R. (2011). Let it roll: Why more companies are abandoning budgets in favor of rolling forecasts, *CFO* (May), 42-47.

Barkalov I., Martin J., & Wagner P. (2010). *Forward Visibility*, Capgemini Consulting, Frankfurt.

Büchner H., Krause S., & Weigand A. (2000). Anforderungen an die Planung in Turbulenten Zeiten. In: Horváth & Partners (ed.) *Früherkennung in der Unternehmenssteuerung*. Schaeffer-Poeschel, Stuttgart, 127-142.

Business Application Research Center (2008). (ed.) *Planung und Budgetierung in europäischen Unternehmen*. Würzburg, 2008

Clarke P. (2007). The rolling forecast as a catalyst for change, *Accountancy Ireland*, 39, 22-24.

De Waal A., Hermkens-Janssen M., & van de Ven, A. (2010). The evolutionary adoption framework: explaining the budgeting paradox. *Journal of Accounting & Organizational Change*, 7, 316-336.

Durfee D. (2006). Alternative budgeting: Companies are still looking for better ways to set performance targets, *CFO* (June), 28.

Ekholm BG, & Wallin, J. (2000). Is the annual budget really dead? *The European Accounting Review*, 9:519-39.

Frow N., Marginson D., & Ogden S. (2010). Continuous budgeting: reconciling budget flexibility with budgetary control. *Accounting, Organizations and Society*, 35, 444-461.

Hahn D. (2003). Grenzen der Unternehmensplanung. In: Horváth P, Gleich R (ed.) *Neugestaltung der Unternehmensplanung. Innovative*

Konzepte und erfolgreiche Praxislösungen. Schaeffer-Poeschel, Stuttgart, 89-101.

Hansen S. C., Otley D. T., & Van der Stede W. A. (2003). Practice developments in budgeting: an overview and research perspective. *Journal of Management Accounting Research*, 15, 95-116.

Heer R., & Lamorte B. (2010). Application requirements for rolling forecasts. Retrieved 26 December 2011, from http://www.alightplanning.com/sites/default/files/Rolling_Forecasts.pdf.

Hope J., & Fraser R. (1999). Beyond budgeting. Building a new management model for the information age, *Management Accounting*, 16–21.

Hope J., & Fraser R. (2003). *How Managers Can Break Free from the Annual Performance Trap.* Boston, MA: Harvard Business School Press.

Horváth P., & Reichmann T. (ed.) (2003). *Vahlens großes Controllinglexikon*, 2nd edn. Vahlen, München.

Internationaler Controller Verein (ICV) (2011). Umfragen. Retrieved December 11, 2011, from http://www.controllerverein.com/Umfragen.158871.html.

Kopp J., & Leyk J. (2004). Effizient und effektiv planen. In: Gaiser B, Kopp J, Leyk J (ed.) *Beyond Budgeting umsetzen – Erfolgreich planen mit Advanced Budgeting*. Schaeffer-Poeschel., Stuttgart, 1-13.

KPMG (2007). *Forecasting with Confidence – Insights from Leading Finance Functions*, n.p.

Kuhn B., & Pick H. (2006). Sinn und Unsinn der Budgetierung. The 6th Controlling Innovation Conference Berlin 2006, Controlling – Wandel aktiv gestalten, Berlin.

Leahy T. (2005). Stuck in neutral: 2005 Budgeting and reforecasting survey. Retrieved December 3, 2005, from http://www.businessfinancemag.com/magazine/archives/article.html?articleID=14466.

Leyk J., Müller M., & Grünebaum D. (2006). Der Ansatz des Advanced Budgeting in der Unternehmenspraxis: Empirische Ergebnisse des Horváth & Partners CFO-Panel zum aktuellen Anwendungsstand. *Der Controlling-Berater*, No. 4, 469-479.

Lynn M., & Madison R. (2004). A closer look at rolling budgets, *Management Accounting Quarterly*, 6, 60-64.

Montgomery P. (2002). Effective rolling forecasts, *Strategic Finance*, February 2002, 41-44.

Neely A., Sutcliff M., & Heyns H. (2002). *Driving Value through Strategic Planning and Budgeting*, Research Report, Cranfield School of Management and Accenture, Cranfield.

Obermüller J. (2006). Controlling – Wandel aktiv gestalten, *Der Controlling-Berater*, No. 7, 841-847.

Oehler K. (2008). Rolling Planung: IT-gestützte Umsetzung, *Der Controlling-Berater*, No. 7, 921-956.

Østergren K., & Stensaker I. (2011). Management control without budgets: a field study of 'beyond budgeting' in practice. *The European Accounting Review*, 20, 149-181.

Parmenter D. (2007). *Pareto's 80/20 Rule for the Corporate Accountant.* Wiley, New York.

Player S. (2009). *Managing through Change: The Power of Rolling Forecasts*, Ottawa.

Plowman, B. (n.d.) (2011). Rolling forecast. Retrieved December 18, 2011, from http://www.managers-net.org/plowman/forecasting.html.

Price Waterhouse Coopers (2007). *Budgeting and Forecast Study*, n.p.

Rickards R. C. (2008). *Kostensteuerung kompakt.* Oldenbourg Verlag, München.

Seufert A., Sexl S., & Oehler K. (2008). Unternehmensplanung und Wertbeitrag von IT – eine zentrale Gestaltungsaufgabe für das Controlling. In: *Controller-Leitfaden, Zürich*, 1-17.

Sivabalana P., Bootha P., Malmib T., & Brown D. A. (2009). An exploratory study of operational reasons to budget. *Accounting and Finance*, 49, 849–871.

The Hackett Group (2011). *Key Issues Study.* Cited in CPA Trendlines, *Good-Bye Annual Budget. Hello Rolling Forecast.*

Weber J., Voußem L., & Rehring, J. (2010). Aktuelle Ergebnisse aus dem WHU-Controllerpanel: Benchmarks und Trends in der Budgetierung. *Zeitschrift für Controlling und Management*, 54, 323-327.

Wolleswinkel M. (The Hackett Group) (2008). *World-Class Enterprise Performance Management*, Cognos Finance Forum, Wiesbaden.

CHAPTER THREE

VALUING RISK EXPOSURE AND THE EXPECTED COST OF MARGIN CALLS: THE CASE FOR A SECONDARY MARKET IN REDISTRIBUTING LIQUIDITY LIABILITY (MARGIN CREDIT SWAPS)

TIMOTHY E. ZIMMER
INDIANA DEPARTMENT OF WORKFORCE DEVELOPMENT
VALERIEN O. PEDE
INTERNATIONAL RICE RESEARCH INSTITUTE, PHILIPPINES
AND ANDREW M. MCKENZIE
UNIVERSITY OF ARKANSAS

Abstract

Noticeably starting in 2008 and beyond, volatility in grain markets has exposed vulnerability in the current hedging practices with regard to margin call risk and liquidity requirements. We explore the issue and support with others the creation of a secondary market, such as margin credit swaps. We argue that a margin credit swap market would efficiently redistribute the liquidity requirements imposed by grain futures exchanges from small hedging firms to larger financial institutions. We further investigate this research by providing a benchmark pricing structure by which these products can be evaluated and initially priced prior to auction and exchange.

Keywords: *Margin Call, Margin Credit Swaps, Futures Market, Commodity Exchange, Commodity Hedging.*

Introduction

The liquidity crisis experienced by grain elevators in 2008 brought into focus the vulnerabilities of current hedging practices employed at future exchanges. Traditionally, the role of a grain elevator is to function as a servicer in the processing of grain. The grain elevator provides a farmer with a contract to purchase their grain at the completion of harvest at a future point. Grain elevators often hedge some portion of this risk on the futures market to minimize their exposure to price variation. The current hedging system has traditionally worked reasonably well in providing grain elevators with a low cost method of dealing with their risk exposure. The degree to which an elevator moves from pure hedging towards speculation is an area of significant and acknowledged research (Working, 1960; Hieronymus, 1977; Peck, 1979; Peck and Budge, 1987, Stulz, 1996), but does not influence these results and is beyond the scope of this study.

In recent years, the commodity markets have continued to witness extreme price volatility (see figure 1). Thus the liquidity problems first observed in 2008 are now the market norm. The factors contributing to increased price volatility are numerous. However, some of the increased volatility is inevitably blamed on commodity speculation (Masters, 2008; Masters and White, 2008). Defense for the role of speculation in the commodity markets has been robust (Irwin et al., 2009), and has tried to explain the benefits of speculation in commodity markets. Though the merits of blaming speculators for volatility are highly disputed, the negative impact that volatility has had on market participants needing to manage price risk is indisputable.

Indeed, the increased price volatility in commodity markets has had the unintended consequence of revealing inadequacies of current hedging techniques practiced by grain elevator operators. As an example, suppose a grain elevator on Apri1 01, 2008, forward contracts with a farmer to handle (buy) the farmer's upcoming harvest, and under the terms of the contract it is agreed that the crop will be delivered to the elevator in November 2008. The forward price offered to the farmer will be based upon the current corn futures contract price for December 2008 delivery adjusted for the elevator's expected harvest time basis. The basis is the difference in the local cash price of grain and the futures price of grain. The grain elevator will subsequently hedge this commitment on the futures exchange. In the futures market, the grain elevator contracts to sell a bushel of corn at the current corn futures contract price for December 2008 delivery. The initial sale of December 2008 futures contracts will require the elevator to post money in a hedging margin account administered by a futures broker, who is in turn a member of the futures exchange. Current hedging margin requirements, as of September 18th 2012, for trading corn futures on the Chicago Board of Trade (CBOT) are set at $2,000 per contract. Based on the settlement price, as of September 18th 2012, for December corn futures, ($7.40 per bushel) this represents 5.4% of the face value of the futures contract. From the grain elevators perspective, by selling December futures contracts, price risk has been eliminated and the elevator can concentrate resources on attracting additional farmer production and thereby increasing grain throughput.

Figure 1. CBOT Hedging Margin requirements and Annualized Corn futures price volatility.

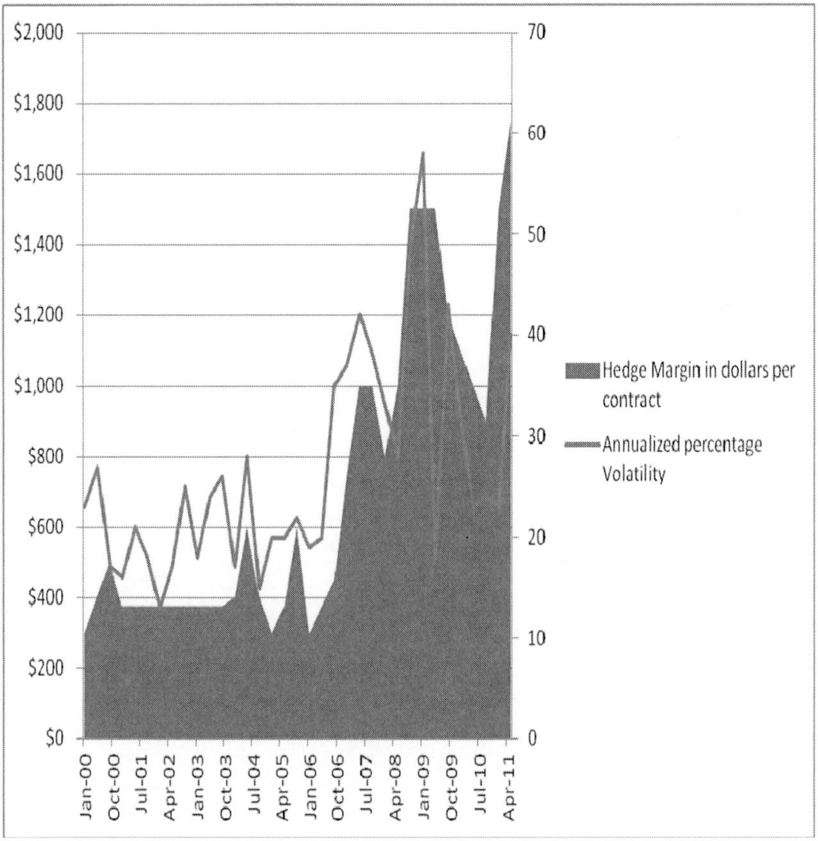

The problem with this traditional risk management approach rests on the fact that huge amounts of working capital may be needed to finance the elevator's hedged position during periods of extreme price volatility when the price spikes after the grain elevator has hedged. While the grain elevator remains fully hedged, there remains and implicit cost associated with the technique which is not readily apparent and is the cause of the current elevator liquidity crisis. In the case of volatility, or more directly large price increases, elevators incur margin calls from the futures exchange. Figure 1 illustrates the relationship between annualized historical corn price volatility and hedging margin requirements of CBOT. The figure clearly shows the higher recent levels of price volatility have resulted in higher margin requirements needed to hedge grain.

Using the previous scenario, assume shortly after the grain elevator hedges the corn in the futures market on April 1 2008 for $5, the price increases to $5.30 per bushel. Since hedging is a financial transaction, and delivery is not expected, from the exchange's perspective the grain elevator's account has a negative $0.30 per bushel exposure that must be covered. The elevator's futures broker (as a member of the exchange) will serve the grain elevator with a $0.30 per bushel margin call to balance the margin account. The size of margin calls will vary as the price level varies daily. If the price decreases to a level below $5, excess funds will flow to the margin account and will be returned to the grain elevator. It is important to note that margin calls do not affect the net profit position at the time the futures position is offset. As long as the elevator maintains the required level of margin money, it is always fully hedged at the time the cash grain is delivered and the futures position offset, irrespective of the level of price volatility and the potential for large margin calls.

Maintaining the margin account and the hedge position in times of price spikes requires large capital reserves on the part of grain elevators. The grain elevators may use their own reserves, or more likely borrow capital with bank support. However, for the duration of the futures contract, margin call money could be sitting idle (from the grain elevators perspective) in the margin account. Note that US Treasury Bills may be used to post the initial hedging margin, but all subsequent losses to the account in the form of margin calls must be paid in cash. The recent extreme volatility in commodity markets has increased the size of margin calls, putting strain on the system. Banks, in light of their own liquidity issues in 2008, were less willing to finance margin calls which further increased tension on the grain marketing system. The resulting decrease in liquidity increased the financing cost of margin calls and threatened elevator viability. Even if the grain elevator was willing to assume the increased financing cost, the lack of access to capital and reluctance of banks to lend caused a liquidity shortage.

New Market Alternative

If liquidity is not a concern, the current system of utilizing the futures market provides a simple, low cost method of hedging and minimizing risk. However, with high price volatility now commonplace in commodity markets along with higher margin requirements (see figure 1), a new liquidity crisis could again threaten the operation of grain elevators, which in turn could bring further disorder to grain markets.

If one is to assume that futures markets provide elevators with an excellent hedging tool to manage price risk, focus should be concentrated on low cost methods to improve this hedging technique. This can be achieved by utilizing the self interest of market participants and allowing market mechanisms to efficiently redistribute from parties least able to those parties most able to accommodate the risk and associated cost. McKenzie and Kunda, (2009), advocate the creation of a secondary market where the margin call risk associated with particular futures contracts can be freely traded. They note that the Merchant's Exchange has explored the potential viability of such a market, which would trade a financial instrument called a Margin Credit Swap (MCS).

Using the prior example, and assuming the availability of a MCS, the grain elevator would purchase the farmer's December 2008 grain for $5 per bushel (assuming a zero basis), and sell the grain on the futures market at $5 per bushel for December 2008 delivery. At the same time, if the grain elevator wishes to abdicate the margin call risk, the grain elevator can offset the margin risk and liquidity requirements by buying a MCS on the newly created secondary market. The grain elevator will pay a fee (e.g. the price of the MCS) to the seller of the MCS, (a bank or speculator), who will in turn fund the margin account and subsequent margin calls and assume potential counterparty risk. Thus the price of a MCS will be determined by the number of sellers (speculators and banks), willing to supply MCS contracts, and by the number of buyers (elevators and other short-hedgers) willing to demand MCS contracts. In turn, the willingness of speculators and banks to sell MCS contracts, will be dependent upon their assessment of counterparty risk and the potential profits generated from financing the cost of providing margin monies to cover the hedging period.

As noted by McKenzie and Kunda, MCS contracts inherently contain various counterparty risks for both MCS sellers and buyers. From the sellers' perspective, counterparty risk takes the form of elevators potentially defaulting on their MCS payments. At an equilibrium price, the bank or speculator agrees to absorb the margin call risk and provide any needed capital requirements. If the futures market price for grain decreases every day over the hedging period (life of the MCS), no margin calls will be required and the MCS seller captures the initial fee or MCS price as profit. If the market for grain moves higher, the bank or speculator forwards the required margin call capital and loses the time value of this money.

Utilizing this market structure, the grain elevator can go into the market at anytime to reduce margin call liability. The fee or MCS price will change each day, based on the current futures contract price, the current expectation of price volatility over the remaining life of the contract and inherent counterparty risk. An actively traded MCS market would be able to ease any liquidity crisis that may reappear in future commodity markets by redistributing the liquidity needs of hedgers (grain elevators) to those parties (banks and speculators) most able to afford the liquidity commitments and associated risk. The equilibrium found in the market will establish the most efficient allocation of margin call risk capital and thereby ease potential future liquidity problems.

Expected Margin Call Cost

Before the first trade on the newly established exchange can be generated, a price (or fee) must be developed which will reflect the cost of bearing the margin call capital requirements and risk. This price measure must be considered fair and unbiased by all market participants. Even if price is to be bid upon, and the final price is a function of market equilibrium, the participants must be able to accurately assess the expected returns and risks associated with a MCS and from such assessments arrive at a rational initial price.

Several issues complicate the price calculation. These factors include, but are not limited to the variation in commodity prices, the daily variation in the size of margin calls, and the need to calculate the compounded or cumulated interest costs of financing the margin account. Margin call risk vests the day after implementation of the futures contract. We assume the MCS seller is (1) responsible for all margin calls; (2) only receives the initial MCS price (fee) at time of sale; and (3) is returned the initial margin amount at the time of MCS purchase. Thus, in this case, the agreed upon interest rate, under the terms of the MCS, is applied to the margin call amount to determine the cost or financing basis each day, and is financed by the MCS seller[1]. Rolling forward period to period, this dollar amount is compounded. Note that the MCS contract could be re-traded by the seller at any point in time prior to maturity (the end of the hedging period). In this case the original seller of the MCS could offset their position by in effect buying the contract from another (bank or speculator) who would then become the new seller. At this point the price of the MCS would reflect the cost of the accumulated interest on margin payments already made and the expected cost of future interest and margin payments, and initial margin, for the remaining life of the contract. At the time of MCS contract expiration, the price will reflect all of the accumulated margin interest payments and the initial margin.

The complexity of the problem arises because of the daily price variation of the underlying commodity, and the resulting daily variation in the size of the margin account. The commodity price variation complicates a direct measurement of margin call cost. However, pricing the MCS is possible if we draw upon commodity futures option theory to formulate an expected margin call cost over the life of the contract. The expected margin call cost would provide a benchmark price for the MCS. With this in mind, let us first consider Black's (1976) model to price European call options on futures contracts.

The Black option pricing model:

$$C(FP, K\sigma, r, T) = FPe^{-rT}\Phi(\delta_1) - Ke^{-rt}\Phi(\delta_2)$$

$$\delta_1 = (\ln(FP/K) + (\sigma^2/2)T)/\sigma(T^{0.5})$$

$$\delta_2 = \delta_1 - \sigma(T^{0.5})$$

Where Φ is the standard normal cumulative probability function
FP = Current Commodity Futures Price
K = Exercise Commodity Price
T = Exercise Time (in Years)
r = risk-free interest rate (in Annual Terms)
σ = Commodity Volatility
(standard deviation of continuously compounded annual returns)

Black's model implies that the price of a call option on a futures contract will reflect the present value of the expected payoff of the option at maturity. If the option is at-the-money (i.e. the exercise price *K* is equal to the current futures price *F*), then the option price *C*, will reflect the market's expectation of the amount by which the futures price is likely to exceed the exercise price at maturity time T. Thus, the option price will proxy the likely size of a margin call at the time the MCS matures.

Of course in our case, we must value an option which takes account of the present value of all cash flows over the life of the MCS. Recall from our discussion above, the MCS seller will receive an initial price based upon the expected costs at time T (the expected costs in terms of cash flow expenditures to cover the frequency and size of margin calls over the life of the MCS). Given that the value of such an option is path dependent (i.e. the path of the futures contract as well as its value at maturity time T is important in determining cash flows), there is likely no analytical solution available, such as in Black's model. However, the value of the MCS contract is similar in nature to the value of an exotic option, such as an Asian option, which makes a payment based on the arithmetic average of a stock price over the life of the option. Such path dependent options are best valued using Monte Carlo simulation. In our case, our exotic option, and hence the MCS, could easily be priced using Monte Carlo valuation, and its price will depend upon the average expected cumulative interest payments.

For example, the first step would involve simulating sequences of daily prices for the relevant December corn futures contract at the time of pricing. Following McKenzie and Kunda, the discrete sequence of daily futures price may be written as:

$$\text{(1)} \qquad \ln FP_{t+\Delta t} = \ln FP_t - (\sigma^2 / \sigma)\Delta t + \sigma\sqrt{\Delta t}\varepsilon,$$

where, $\ln FP_{t+\Delta t}$ is the natural logarithm of the December corn futures settlement prices observed in a sequence of daily increments (Δt), the term σ is the annualized standard deviation of daily futures prices and the term $\sigma\sqrt{\Delta t}$ is the standard deviation of daily futures price changes, and ε is a random drawing from the standard normal distribution with a mean of zero and a standard deviation equal to one.

To implement the simulations, σ, the expected volatility per annum, could be estimated from Black model implied volatilities derived from observed options prices on December corn futures contracts. Each sequence of prices could be simulated 1000 times to create a distribution of potential price paths over the life of the MCS. Once the potential price paths have been simulated, the cash flows associated with margin calls across each sequence i and each daily time period t may be calculated as:

$$(2) \qquad MCC_{it} = (\max[FP_{it} - K, 0]) ,$$

where, MCC_{it} is the daily margin call cost in terms of capital requirements to fund the margin account across each price path or sequence. In terms of the financing charge, the cumulative margin costs $CMCC_{iT}$ associated with each sequence or price path could then be calculated based upon the agreed interest rate specified under the terms of the MCS.

$$(3) \qquad CMCC_{iT} = \sum_{t=1}^{T} MCC_{iT}$$

The average $CMCC_{iT}$ could then be discounted at the risk-free interest rate to arrive at the present value of the expected margin call costs and hence estimate an appropriate initial value (sale price) for the MCS.

$$(4) \qquad P_{MCS} = e^{-rT} E(CMCC_{iT})$$

Given the speed of today's computers, computation time to conduct the simulations would not be a problem, and a new MCS price could easily be generated on a daily basis. The perceived level of counterparty risk would influence the negotiated interest rate (financing cost) under the initial terms of the MCS. The greater the perceived risk and the higher the risk aversion of the MCS seller, the higher would be the financing cost.

To make the theoretical concept of pricing the MCS more concrete we extend the simulation analysis presented in McKenzie and Kunda (2009). Using historical daily corn futures settlement prices over the 2006-2008 bull market period McKenzie and Kunda estimated annual corn price volatility to be 30%. Note from figure 1 above that this volatility level is relatively high in comparison to pre 2006 levels. However, as figure 1 also shows, over the last several years volatility has reached even higher levels. Assuming a 30% volatility level McKenzie and Kunda then used equation (1) above to simulate 100 possible pre-harvest price sequence iterations and so determine the likely margin requirements for an elevator entering a short-futures hedged position over 170 days. Their results with respect to the 6 "worst" case scenarios – with the largest margin requirements – and which would be expected to occur 5% of the time are presented in table 1 (table 3 in McKenzie and Kunda, 2009). Columns 4, 5, and 6 show the cumulative amount of dollars per contract, the cumulative interest payment in dollars and the cumulative interest in cents per bushel needed to maintain the margin account over the 170 day period and assuming a 5% annual interest rate.

Figure 2. Probability distribution of expected cumulative MCS interest in cents/bu based on 100 iterations of Monte Carlo simulation. Dashed lines indicate 95% confidence bands around the mean.

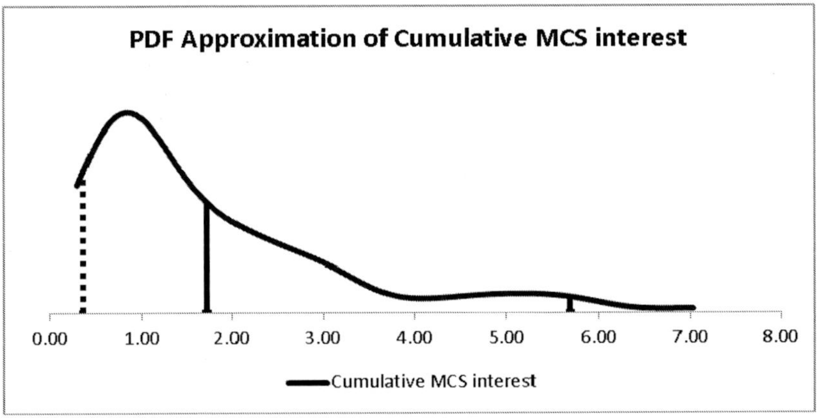

The average cents per bushel financing charge ($CMCC_{iT}$) is of most interest in calculating the MCS price. Over the six "worst" case scenarios this charge is on average 5.71 cents per bushel. Of course to estimate the MCS price (P_{MCS}) the average $CMCC_{iT}$ across all 100 potential price sequences would have to be calculated. Using the same assumptions and simulations as Kunda and McKenzie (2009) and a 5% risk-free interest rate we estimate the P_{MCS} would be 1.66 cents per bushel or $83.17 per contract. Figure 2 shows the probability distribution associated with the Monte Carlo simulation of the cumulative margin interest payments. The negotiated P_{MCS} in an actual trade would also be based upon relative counterparty risk and the financing requirements of the MCS selling firm. The higher the risk, the higher the financing or interest rate payment attached to the MCS, which would result in a higher P_{MCS}. Similarly, the higher the level of market volatility the higher would be the P_{MCS}. Monte Carlo simulation could take into account both of these factors when measuring a fair P_{MCS}.

Conclusion

The liquidity crisis which affected the grain markets in 2008 was the result of vulnerabilities in current hedging practices employed by grain elevators. The crisis was the result of liquidity issues arising and the need for capital requirements to defend the hedging positions. Rather than try to eliminate the margin call risk, we argue for the creation of a secondary market which allows for trading of this risk.

The creation of a secondary market to trade margin call risk efficiently combines the interests of financial credit lenders, speculators and traditional grain hedgers such as elevators. The grain elevator pays a fee (price) in an effort to reduce margin call liability. The financial lenders or speculators gain the MCS price or fee to compensate them for their risk and the time value of their capital. By each party pursuing their own self-interest, the efficient distribution of liquidity risk is achieved by the market mechanisms. The equilibrium of the newly established market is achieved where margin call liability is shifted from those of limited capital reserves, to those parties most capable of affording and accommodating the margin call risk. By freely trading the margin call risk, the tension of liquidity in the commodity markets will be eased.

The margin call risk market will only function properly and efficiently if all parties are provided accurate information. In this instance, a good price approximation from which to assess the risk and generate market trading could be derived from Monte Carlo simulation techniques. Calculating the value of the margin call risk to be traded, and providing this information to all market parties is crucial in ensuring that the market functions properly.

Table 1: Liquidity measures for 6 "worst" scenarios assuming 30% volatility

Scenario	Total Margin Calls $ /contract	Total Margin Withdrawals $ /contract	Cumulative Margin Credit $ /contract	Cumulative MCS Interest $ payment	Cumulative MCS Interest Cents/bu	Maximum Margin Credit level in $	Largest Daily Margin Credit $ Increase	Largest Weekly Margin Credit $ Increase	Largest Cumulative Margin Credit $ Increase[1]
1	42,143.73	22,642.71	21,001.02	283.87	5.68	21,102.56	1,165.28	3,313.46	3,798.69
2	39,417.36	23,693.74	17,223.62	284.48	5.69	17,223.62	1,789.76	2,917.90	5,026.89
3	41,258.29	28,418.64	14,339.66	351.61	7.03	15,738.35	1,624.55	2,729.19	4,334.11
4	38,449.92	27,489.91	12,460.02	254.72	5.09	12,513.24	1,511.95	2,161.42	2,671.85
5	37,551.43	28,056.87	10,994.56	284.59	5.69	14,393.47	1,440.39	1,998.66	3,005.71
6	36,358.16	27,630.28	10,492.93	254.89	5.10	17,036.73	1,407.97	1,913.91	4,938.46
Average	39,196.48	26,322.02	14,418.63	285.69	5.71	16,334.66	1,489.98	2,505.76	3,962.62
Std Dev	2,204.80	2,487.01	4,053.98	35.38	0.71	2,923.80	211.22	565.36	983.01

1. This refers to the largest cumulative margin credit increase in dollars brought about by consecutive daily futures price increases.

Notes

1. Note that McKenzie and Kunda assume that the MCS buyer makes interest payments (the hedger). The interest rate represents the return for supplying margin credit. On a daily basis, the holder of a positive account balance in the MCS (the hedger) pays the holder of a negative account balance in the MCS (the liquidity provider) an interest payment equal to the interest rate times the margin credit offered.

References

Black, F. (1976). The pricing of commodity contracts, *Journal of Financial Economics,* 3(1/2), 167-179.

Hieronymus, T.A. (1977). *Economics of Futures Trading for Commercial and Personal Profit*, Second Edition. New York: Commodity Research Bureau.

Irwin, S.H., Sanders, D.R., and Merrin, R.P. (2009). Devil or Angel: The Role of Speculation in the Recent Commodity Price Boom (and Bust), *Journal of Agricultural and Applied Economics*, 2 (41).

Masters, M.W. (2008). Testimony before the Committee on Homeland Security and Government Affairs, U.S. Senate. Available at: [http://hsgac.senate.gov/public/_files/052008Masters.pdf]

Masters, M.W. and White A.K. (2008). The Accidental Hunt Brothers: How Institutional Investors are Driving up Food and Energy Prices. Available at: [http://accidentalhuntbrothers.com]

McKenzie, A.M., and Kunda, E.L. (2009). Managing Price Risk in Volatile Grain Markets, Issues and Potential Solutions. *Journal of Agricultural and Applied Economics*, 2 (41).

Peck, A.E. (1979). Reflections of Hedging on Futures Markets, *Food Research Institute Studies*. 17, 327-349.

Peck, A.E., and C. Budge. (1947). The Effects of Extraordinary Speculative Margins in the See also: Grain, F., M. (1987). *Food Research Institute Studies*. 20, 165-180.

Stulz, R.M. "Rethinking Risk Management. (1996). *Journal of Applied Corporate Finance*, 9, 8-24.

Working, H. (1960). Speculation on Hedging Markets, *Food Research Institute Studies*,
1, 185-220.

CHAPTER FOUR

STANDARD OF LIVING IN THE EUROPEAN UNION

JANA STÁVKOVÁ, PAVEL ŽUFAN AND NAĎA BIRČIAKOVÁ
MENDEL UNIVERSITY, BRNO, CZECH REPUBLIC

Abstract

This chapter focuses on the measurement of standard of living and on the factors influencing its level. Specific attention is paid to the indicators of standard of living, and the frequent employment of GDP is discussed and compared with possible alternatives. Household income is also a factor of central importance in determining standard of living, and the chapter assesses this factor in terms of household income distribution, the setting of poverty limits, the measurement of income disparity and the causes and effects of poverty. The situation is monitored in five selected EU countries: the Czech Republic, Finland, France, Spain and the United Kingdom.

Keywords: *Standard of living, Indicators, Income situation, Disparity, Poverty.*

Introduction

The meaning of the term "standard of living" seems quite clear at a first glance: however, upon closer attention one finds that the situation is much more complicated, and possible solutions to these complications are being considered in the literature. Understanding the complex factors involved in measuring standard of living forms the basis for establishing comparative relations as regards the level of advancement for individual states and population satisfaction (which influences consumer behavior). In the present chapter, some basic issues relating to standard of living and what influences it are described, and a range of indicators used to measure and quantify standard of living are considered.

A person's standard of living is determined by levels of psychological and material need, as well as the living conditions under which those needs can be satisfied. It is clear that standard of living is closely connected with the social status of an individual within society. Each social class (higher, middle and lower) has a different standard of living and the worst problems are often presumed to arise within the lowest social class. If individuals or groups are excluded from institutions or communities, this leads to a **process of social exclusion**, involving economic, social, political or cultural factors. Isolated individuals move towards poverty, and it is extremely difficult for these individuals to reintegrate within society. Furthermore, the risk of social exclusion is increasing, due to prevailing socio-economic developments and other related structural changes in society.

The process of social integration is based on the so-called 'welfare triangle', which consists of the following three mutually related categories: **state** (the legislature), **market economy** (the labor market) and **civic society** (especially the family). These categories are used to determine the extent to which individuals or groups are integrated within society (Krebs, 2005).

The most significant risk factor in terms of social exclusion is **unemployment**. This category includes not only those who are unemployed, but also those with a low quality of employment. Those within this category are often classified as being members of an 'endangered group' and are often socially excluded. The group also includes the long-term unemployed, who may lose their work habits, their self-confidence and their willingness to search for work. As a result, their employment prospects become increasingly remote. The unemployed receive financial support solely through social benefits, and the primary consequence of unemployment is a loss of income, which leads to a related decline in standard of living.

A further factor leading to social exclusion is **low income on a long term basis,** or inappropriate income. People in this category are unable to satisfy their basic needs and thus become socially isolated. Further factors causing social exclusion include the following: low levels of education and academic qualifications, leaving school prematurely, disability, poor health and advanced age, low quality of accommodation and homelessness, gender inequality, migration and racism, marital break-up, raising children in broken families and living in a disadvantaged area. These individual factors are often cumulative and their negative consequences can intensify very quickly. In order to prevent further social exclusion, it is essential to prevent problems experienced in the past from recurring. Policy is very important in this regard, and should seek to prevent the above-mentioned problems from being passed from one generation to the next (Kotynkova & Nemec, 2003).

The measurement of standard of living can be considered from two points of view. The first emphasizes consumption, and uses a range of possible methods in order to obtain an objective measure of the level of goods and services consumed. The second focuses on the satisfaction of needs and desires, and involves a comparison between people's actual status and their desired status. This second approach is used by sociologists, who seek to determine how people evaluate their own standard of living in terms of such factors as the following: a person's prospects for satisfying their needs; whether they feel they lack sufficient finances to spend on their needs; their perceptions about the level of job security, healthcare and education received; how safe they feel within the society in which they live and, finally, their level of satisfaction with the environment.

To determine an objective measure of standard of living, its individual segments have to be specified. These include the following, each of which may be quantified and numerically expressed.

- Personal consumption
- Social needs
- Standard of accommodation
- Leisure time activities
- Security of livelihood
- Work conditions
- Environment

The two basic approaches to the measurement of standard of living discussed above may be combined. Such a combinational approach is desirable, as one-sided investigations into yield false results. The objective quantification of consumption does not result in greater precision in the measurement of standard of living, and subjective perception does not necessarily offer a distorted view of the situation.

The public perception and evaluation of standard of living always reflects objectively measurable facts, strongly influenced by a number of further factors. These factors are themselves subjective and have individual impact. They include the following: perception of the political and economic situation, confidence and future expectations, the influence of the media, life experiences and family background and, last but not least, social-economic status (education, income, property and power).

An objectively discovered measure of financial and material security does not necessarily play a decisive role in the formation of people's opinions concerning their standard of living, and subjective opinions concerning levels of satisfaction of expectation are very significant. Thus, research into standard of living based on subjective opinions and the views of respondents must play an integral part in the research into standard of living, and can be used to supplement the results of objective surveys.

Economic crisis in society and its social impact raise a number of questions concerning the correctness of the emphasis on the dynamics of economic growth, if its inconsistency with the dynamics of social development is taken into account. Based on economic theory, the generally accepted indicator of economic growth evaluation is **gross domestic product (GDP)**, which is the most frequently used indicator of macroeconomic performance. The measure may be broken down into the following components: private consumption (C), investments (I), government spending (G) and net export (NX). Its value is considered to be an indicator of the success rate of social development, as well as a guarantee of growth in the standard of living. This is why GDP is monitored not only by the professional public, but also by political parties, institutions and the media.

The definition of GDP and its calculation indicate that economic success is measured by market output volume, regardless of social benefits. The volume of GDP shows growth even in cases where the final effect of growth is socially undesirable, or where it has a negative impact upon society-wide interests. Typical examples of this are those investment activities which lead to worsening of the environment and to a deterioration in the quality of life.

GDP recalculated per capita of a country's inhabitants is the most commonly used indicator of standard of living. It enables easy comparison within individual countries and thus gives an indication of quality of life, and lists of countries are supplied by the World Bank and the International Monetary Fund. According to these sources, the countries with the highest GDP per capita are Qatar, Luxemburg, Singapore and Norway, and those with the lowest are Congo, Zimbabwe and Liberia.

The society-wide impacts of financial crisis have proved that GDP per capita is not a sufficiently reliable indicator of either development or the stability of the economic environment generating this development. Typical examples are found among new European Union (EU) member countries; these were classified as highly progressive economies due to their economic dynamics, but the parameters of their social environments did not confirm these results. This was particularly apparent with respect to indicators such as environment quality, education levels, healthcare and care for senior citizens and families with large numbers of children. High dynamics of GDP growth have become "demonizing" and considered as the sole indicator of a "sound" economy. GDP per capita has become an unambiguous indicator of growth in the standard of living.

Investigation into household income and the general public's perception of the level of standard of living shows that GDP as a general indicator of economic success is not sufficient. This issue has recently been discussed by Stiglitz, Sen and Fittoussi (2009).

Arguments concerning the significance and utilization of GDP as an indicator of social development can be divided into the following three categories:

1. The first is connected with the unsuitable utilization of the indicator for the purposes of evaluating the results of social development on society, and claims that the GDP indicator does not contain such information.
2. The second is methodological, and claims that the evaluation of economic growth in terms of GDP does not distinguish between the positive and negative effects of economic activity. Lack of information concerning the consequences of irresponsible utilization of limited natural resources and lack of information concerning environmental pollution as side effects of economic growth are very important.
3. The third and final line of argument concerns the lack (or very restricted amount) of information concerning the economic effects of publicly beneficial activities and charitable activities, which do not impact upon the market environment.

Based on these arguments concerning the imperfections of GDP per capita as a basic indicator of standard of living, the following questions arise: what should a proper indicator of standard of living include, and what are the alternatives to GDP?

Efforts to identify a precise and quantifiable measure of standard of living have resulted in the formation of various indicators that either extend or replace GDP per capita. There are a number of such indicators, and each incorporates different aspects based upon a range of methodologies. There are many views in the professional literature concerning this issue, which suggests that arriving at truly objective results is very demanding.

The **Human Development Index** (HDI), formed in 1990 within the United Nations Development program, is one of the most important and most frequently used indicators. It is based on three factors: health, education and standard of living. Fixed minimum and maximum values for the following individual components have been established (Syrovatka, 2008):

- Average life expectancy at birth (25-85 years),
- Literacy of population older than 15 (0-100 %),
- Combined share of population (in the relevant age ranges) attending the first, second and third levels of education (0-100 %),
- Gross domestic product per capita in purchasing power parity (100USD-40,000USD). According to UNDP (2011), standard of living is measured by means of gross domestic product per capita.

HDI can reach value between 0 and 1, where 0 is the lowest standard of living and 1 is the highest.

It has been queried (Sherman et al., 2008) whether GDP is a suitable indicator for the purposes of reflecting individual human welfare or social well-being. Some goods and services are not included in GDP, e.g., housework. Capitalism itself is the reason for this, for services can be assigned a value only if they are bought and sold on the market. GDP also includes items that clearly have a negative effect (or at least do not have a positive effect) on welfare, e.g., cigarettes. These are some of the many reasons which suggest that a new measure of standard of living is needed to replace (or at least to supplement) GDP. Such an indicator would incorporate housework and unvalued benefits and deduct unvalued costs, i.e., pollution resulting from industrial production and transport, and would also deduct other harmful products. **Genuine Progress Indicator,** which includes the above-mentioned measures, meets these requirements.

Quality of Life Index determines standard of living on the basis of nine factors. The first of these is material welfare, measured by means of GDP per capita, followed by health (life expectancy at birth), political stability and safety, family life (divorce rate per 1000 inhabitants), community life (a dummy variable relating to the degree of religious practice or membership of trade unions), climate and geographic conditions (warmer or colder climate), job certainty (measured according to the unemployment rate), political freedom (measured as an average of indices of civil and political freedom on a scale between 1-7, where 1 means complete freedom) and, last but not least, gender equality, which is measured as a ratio of average salaries of men and women (The Economist, 2005).

More recent indicators include **Sustainable Society Index** (in existence since 2006), which includes human, environmental and economic welfare. A constantly sustainable society is a society which meets the needs of the contemporary generation and does not endanger future generations. In such a society, individuals have the opportunity to develop, to be free and to live in harmony with others in their community (Kerk & Manuel, 2008).

A further life situation indicator was created by the Legatum Institute, **Legatum Prosperity Index**. This indicator defines prosperity by means of wealth and welfare. It does not only take money into account, but also considers quality of life. This index consists of eight sub-indices which represent fundamental aspects of prosperity. These include economy, enterprise and opportunities, public administration, education, health, safety and security, personal freedom and social capital. Each of these indices provides two important analyses of a given country: economic evaluation and evaluation of subjective well-being.

Quality of Living Survey is a yearly research survey conducted by Mercer. This tool takes into consideration 39 factors which influence people's life situation, divided into the following ten categories: consumer goods, economic environment, housing, medical and health considerations, natural environment, political and social environment, public services and transport, recreation, schools and education and socio-cultural environment (Mercer, 2012).

Gross National Happiness is a particularly interesting measure. This official indicator was created in the Kingdom of Bhutan, for the purposes of bringing about better awareness of the government and implementing suitable measures. The nine key areas of GNH are psychological well-being, health, education, time use, cultural diversity and resilience, good governance, community vitality, ecological diversity and resilience and living standards. GNH consists of indices ranking these nine areas in terms of their importance. It includes indicators of mental health, family relationships, financial safety, healthy days in a month, physical condition, education level, air and water pollution, home possession and, last but not least, human rights and government performance. Pilot research into GNH was conducted in 2006 (International Monetary Fund, 2010).

Quality of life in relation to the environment is measured by **Happy Planet Index** (HPI), introduced in 2006 by The New Economics Foundation, London. HPI places the emphases on responsible resource consumption. The essential input concerns resources which sustain life and support all areas of human activities. The final output is a long and happy life.

According to Eurostat, quality of life is defined as a nine-dimensional structure, including material life standards (income, consumption, and property), health, education, personal activities (including paid work and volunteer work), commuting, leisure time and housing. Another dimension includes such factors as political opinions and governmental power, social contacts, environmental conditions, personal security and economic security (Juhascikova & Stukovska, 2011).

An indicator called **Actual Individual Consumption** (AIC) should also be mentioned. This indicator concerns real individual consumption, and was created on the basis of Stiglitz-Sen-Fitoussi report. It includes all products and services consumed by households, such as consumables, services bought directly and services provided by non-profit organizations and government for individual consumption, e.g., healthcare and education. Although GDP per capita is the most widely used indicator of economic welfare, consumption per capita can be useful for the purposes of comparing the relative welfare of consumers in different countries. AIC per capita usually correlates with GDP per capita, as AIC amounts to the major part of GDP expenditure (European Commission, 2011). Based on the Lisbon meeting of the European Council, a statistical infrastructure was established in 2000 in order to analyze the incomes and life conditions of the EU as a whole (Frick & Krell, 2010). The goal of the European Union Regulation 1177/2003 (on statistics concerning incomes and life conditions) was to determine a common framework for systematic analysis, to ensure that a sufficient amount of data was available based upon selective research, in order to obtain results, on a yearly basis at both a national and a European level, concerning household income, level of poverty and social exclusion.

Selective research by **EU SILC** (European Union—Statistics on Income and Living Conditions) was conducted on the basis of an integrated methodology established by the EU, under the title “Life Conditions”. It enabled the acquisition of comparable and representative data on income distribution in individual types of household, the quality and financial demand of accommodation, the economic effectiveness of inhabitants, the social situation of inhabitants, the number of people living in each household, in addition to a range of other factors. The basic variable used was monthly disposable income per household member, calculated on the basis of equalized income per household. This made it possible to compare the results among individual EU member countries, on the basis of equalized income value. The outputs obtained were used to establish EU social policy tools.

Socially adverse effects result in income disparity, and one of the simplest and the most frequently used methods of measuring inequality is the dissimilarity index. This measure classifies individuals and households into categories based on income level. The width of the category may differ in deciles, quintiles, or other statistical measures of categorization. If the income category is divided into quintiles, the range of the category is 0.2 (20 %) and can be marked X_i. There are five categories, each receiving a part of the total income marked as Y_i. The first 20% of the income category can be considered the poorest class and the last 20% the richest. The index can be calculated as a relation $ID=0.5 * \Sigma X_i- Y_i$ and has a value-range between 0 and 1. A value of 0 means absolute equality and value and 1 means complete inequality (Morse, 2004). Based on the data, a **Lorenz curve** can be constructed, expressing the relation between absolute inequality and real inequality in income distribution.

Generally, we can say that the higher the degree of income inequality in a given area, the more poverty there will be in that area. However, the term 'poverty' involves a range of factors which will now be explained.

Inequality and poverty have been troubling almost the whole world for many years, and globalization has worsened the situation. In addition to income inequality, there are a number of other relevant indicators, such as inequality among groups of inhabitants. Improvements in standard of living cannot be supposed to be the result of improvement in economic conditions, and no direct relation between economic growth and the reduction of inequality has yet been proved. On the contrary, it might be argued that inequality increases during times of economic growth, as the poor do not benefit from that growth. Inequality is a problem in poor countries, but in recent years has emerged as a problem in developed countries as well. A country's wealth does not ensure the protection of all its inhabitants from possible poverty (Greig, 2007).

The lack of goods which a society considers to be desirable is commonly called **deprivation**, and is usually defined in relation to material or social conditions. Deprivation was studied by Townsen, who defined it in terms of 12 key indicators. These include social activities, holidays, "luxury consumer goods" (e.g., refrigerators and televisions), frequent meat consumption, etc. Of course, the role of subjective perception must not be forgotten, and although some people might be deprived, they might not necessarily feel that they are. In most cases, when people start to experience material need, the sense of psychical deprivation comes only later. Homelessness is considered to be the most serious deprivation problem (Stavkova, Stejskal & Nagyova, 2011).

Methodology

Based on the meeting of the European Council in Lisbon in 2000, a statistical infrastructure was established for the purpose of analyzing incomes and living conditions in the European Union as a whole (Frick & Krell, 2010). The aim of the European parliament directive No. 1177/2003 (on EU statistics in the field of incomes and living conditions) was to establish a common framework which would ensure the availability of sufficient data on sample surveys of households, and to acquire annually updated results on household incomes, levels of poverty and social exclusion, at both a national and European level.

A sample survey of **EU SILC** (European Union—Statistics on Income and Living Conditions) was conducted, under the title "Living conditions", based on a unified EU methodology. This enabled the acquisition of long-term comparable and representative data in the following (and many other) areas: income distribution in particular household types, quality and financial demands of living, the economic efficiency of inhabitants, social situation and the number of people living in a household. The key variable used was monthly disposable income per household member, calculated on the basis of annual disposable income per household. Based on equalized income value, it was possible to compare results in particular member states of the EU, and to use the outputs to define EU social policy instruments.

In addition to income, basic household characteristics include head of the household, type of household, social group, employment, education and many others. Head of the household requires a more detailed definition. In a complete family, it is always the man, regardless of his economic activity. In incomplete households, the first criterion for determining the head of the household is economic activity; the second is the income levels of particular household members.

The sample survey includes a lot of information which can be interpreted and made available to the public. The data is classified into groups according to various criteria, in order to provide a better analysis of typical characteristics. For instance, original annual income values are recalculated as monthly incomes. As a consequence, from the monthly income of a household, it is possible to calculate income per household member. According to the OECD or EU definitions, it is possible to recalculate the income to one equivalised **household member**, and to enable comparison between selected groups as well as international comparisons.[1]

The subsequent calculations, made on the basis of disposable equivalised income, concern the basic characteristics of position, using modus, mean and median. Modus is the most frequent value and supplements the value of average income. The median is set as the mid-value of the sorted set of data and is decisive for setting the poverty limit of the given group of households. A deeper analysis of household income distribution can be carried out based on the analysis of income deciles.

The Lorenz curve shows the level of income distribution. It is a line which forms a 45° angle with the *x* axis, the so-called "ideal Lorenz curve". All households would have the same income in this ideal case. The opposite extreme of the Lorenz curve is the so-called "absolutely uneven distribution", in which the income of the society as a whole is received by one single household. The real Lorenz curve lies somewhere between these two extremes. The **Gini coefficient** is used for the purposes of representing the real Lorenz curve's deviation from the ideal.

The formula for calculating the Gini coefficient is as follows:

$$G = \left| 1 - \sum_{k=0}^{k=n-1} (X_{k+1} - X_k)(Y_{k+1} - Y_k) \right|$$

X_k and Y_k represent cumulated population and pension variables. The Gini coefficient is not applied solely to the basic aggregate, but to individual segments as well. To obtain a more detailed evaluation of the social situation, it is possible to differentiate households according to individual regions, social groups or education.

The Gini coefficient is the best known and most frequently used tool for measuring inequality. It determines how the real differentiation of incomes differs from the case in which everybody has the same income. The value of the Gini coefficient varies between 0 and 1, and in the case of a value of 0, this represents the extreme of absolute equality, where incomes are equally divided. If the coefficient value is 1, this represents the opposite extreme, absolute inequality (lack of income diversification), with the total income going to just one single household. In the case of coefficient values ranging from 0.44 to 0.6, this means high inequality, and is typical in many developing countries. Relatively low inequality is represented by values ranging from 0.2 to 0.35 (Todara & Smith, 2009).

The disadvantage of the Gini coefficient is that it does not show precisely how inequality is distributed across society as a whole. The coefficient does not say anything about the standard of living, and its calculation requires really high-quality data (Morse, 2004).

Poverty is defined on the basis of the poverty limit, which according to the Eurostat methodology represents 60% of the median of equalized incomes. Household incomes which (per equalized member) fall below this level are considered income endangered.

Depth of poverty is measured using Sen coefficient values, which range from 0 to 1. Values near 0 represent moderate poverty, and values near 1 represent significant poverty.

$$\text{Sen index} = \frac{\text{A} - \text{a}}{\text{A}}$$

In the present chapter, the living conditions and income situation in five European Union countries will be compared. The countries were selected on the basis of the zones of culturally allied countries, as defined by Svetlík (2003). One representative country from each zone was chosen: Finland (for Sweden, Norway, Denmark and Finland), France (for Austria, Switzerland and France), Spain (for Italy, Spain, Greece and Portugal) and the United Kingdom (for the United Kingdom and Ireland). One country from outside these zones was selected (the Czech Republic). The names of these countries will be abbreviated as follows: Czech Republic (CZ), Finland (FI), France (FR), Spain (ES) and the United Kingdom (UK). The monitoring period is 2005 to 2010.

In order to compare incomes and other financial indicators internationally, it is necessary not only to convert the values to the same currency (USD is used most often and EUR is used for comparisons within the EU) but also to clean up the differences in price levels due to the different inflation rates in individual countries. The Purchasing Power Standard (PPS), which creates an artificial currency, is used for these purposes.

Results

The traditional way of determining standard of living in a given country is to use GDP, recalculated per individual inhabitant. GDP is calculated on the basis of personal consumption, investment, government spending and net exports. The average EU member state GDP per capita in 2010 was 24 400 PPS. Across the five selected countries, it was lowest in the Czech

Republic, with a value of 19 400 PPS and highest in Finland, where it reached 28 100 PPS.

The recalculation of GDP per capita, as a percentage measure of PPS to EU average, shows that across the selected countries, Finland had the highest living standard in 2010 (in ninth place within the EU as a whole), with a GDP which was 15% higher than the European average. The United Kingdom was tenth and France eleventh. The living standard in Spain was at the level of the EU average, equivalent to thirteenth place. The Czech Republic, which was in nineteenth position, was 20% below the EU average.

The composition of GDP does not cover quality related aspects of a life situation, and the measure thus represents the success of an economy rather than the standard of living. An alternative indicator of well-being, adjusted to represent household situation, can be represented by the Actual Individual Consumption (AIC) per inhabitant, which shows really consumed products and services within households. Table 1 below shows GDP and AIC per inhabitant, as compared with the EU average in the period 2005-2010.

According to GDP per capita, standard of living was highest in the United Kingdom over the first two years, and was highest in Finland from 2007. However, the AIC per capita shows that standard of living remained highest in the United Kingdom for the whole monitored period. There are several differences in the ranking of the countries over the period. In 2010, in terms of GDP per capita, Finland was doing better than France, but according to the AIC per capita indicator, this situation was reversed. However, the two indicators are consistent in showing that the Czech Republic had the lowest standard of living of the five countries over the monitored period as a whole.

Efforts to quantify standard of living (or life quality) as precisely as possible have resulted in the formation of alternative indicators. Table 2 shows the indicators for which values were known in 2010.

For every country, the ranking reached within the particular indicator is shown, and there is a consequent recalculation of final rankings which takes six indicators into account. The results show that Finland had the best quality of life in 2010, followed by France, the United Kingdom and then Spain. The Czech Republic had the lowest living standard of all the selected countries.

Table 1: Percentage of GDP and AIC per capita in PPS in 2005-2010 (calculated by the authors, source: Eurostat)

Country	GDP per capita in PPS, EU 27 = 100						AIC per capita in PPS, EU27 = 100					
	2005	2006	2007	2008	2009	2010	2005	2006	2007	2008	2009	2010
CZ	79	80	83	81	82	80	71	71	73	69	72	71
FI	114	114	118	119	115	115	101	103	107	110	110	111
FR	110	108	108	107	108	108	113	112	112	111	113	113
ES	102	105	105	104	103	100	99	100	100	99	95	95
UK	122	120	116	112	111	112	135	134	130	124	121	121

Table 2: Selected indicators of living standards in 2010 (compiled by the authors)

Country	GDP/cap.	AIC/cap.	HDI	SSI	QLI	LPI	Ranking
CZ	80 (5)	71 (5)	0.863 (4)	6.8 (2)	73 (4)	29.63 (5)	5
FI	115 (1)	111 (3)	0.880 (2)	7.1 (1)	75 (3)	8.38 (1)	1
FR	108 (3)	113 (2)	0.883 (1)	6.8 (2)	82 (1)	19.00 (3)	2
ES	100 (4)	95 (4)	0.876 (3)	6.4 (4)	76 (2)	22.00 (4)	4
UK	112 (2)	121 (1)	0.862 (5)	6.7 (3)	73 (4)	14.63 (2)	3

Note: numbers in brackets represent the country's ranking within a particular indicator.

Table 3 and Figure 1 below show the income development over the years 2005-2010 across the selected EU countries, where each country represents a so-called 'zone of cultural alliance'.

Table 3: Income situation of households (in PPS) in 2005 – 2010 (calculated by the authors, source: Eurostat)

Country	Characteristics	2005	2006	2007	2008	2009	2010
CZ	monthly equivalised income in PPS (MEI)	728	776	835	910	954	910
	median in PPS	637	688	737	810	842	804
	base index – MEI in %	100.00	106.55	114.75	124.95	131.05	125.01
FI	monthly equivalised income in PPS (MEI)	1 318	1 367	1 412	1 534	1 588	1 563
	median in PPS	1 178	1 237	1 270	1 380	1 440	1 418
	base index – MEI in %	100.00	103.71	107.13	116.42	120.54	118.63
FR	monthly equivalised income in PPS (MEI)	1 379	1 415	1 413	1 720	1 739	1 716
	median in PPS	1 208	1 250	1 264	1 464	1 473	1 463
	base index – MEI in %	100.00	102.62	102.49	124.78	126.13	124.51
ES	monthly equivalised income in PPS (MEI)	1 114	1 181	1 240	1 309	1 309	1 257
	median in PPS	968	1 047	1 093	1 162	1 165	1 110
	base index – MEI in %	100.00	106.07	111.33	117.48	117.54	112.85
UK	monthly equivalised income in PPS(MEI)	1 720	1 718	1 837	1 856	1 699	1 708
	median in PPS	1 408	1 462	1 565	1 532	1 424	1 422
	base index – MEI in %	100.00	99.90	106.83	107.92	98.77	99.32

Figure 1: Development of incomes in EUR PPS, period 2005 – 2010 (compiled by the authors, source: Eurostat)

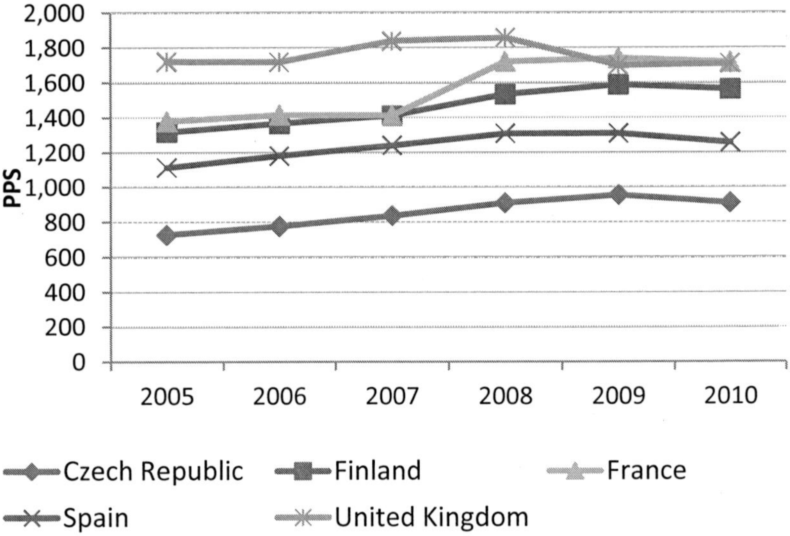

The country with the largest average income growth in 2005-2010 was the Czech Republic (25.01%). A 0.68% decline was noted in households in the United Kingdom. In 2010, French households had the highest incomes (1716 PPS), and earned 1.9 times more than households in the Czech Republic. Households in the Czech Republic had the lowest incomes of all the monitored countries across the period as a whole, in spite of the fact that the country also had the most significant growth. In 2009, incomes in the United Kingdom fell compared to 2008, while they remained equal in Spain.

An important portion of income is represented by social transfers. Every member country of the EU can respond independently to its social problems. The EU only sets out a minimal social standard, the aim of which is to guarantee the best possible level of social protection in all its member countries. Spending on social protection, which aims to moderate the burden upon citizens represented in relation to GDP, is marked in the data as 'social quota'. In each of the selected countries, there was a marked increase from 2005-2010. Spain saw the largest increase in social quota, rising from 20.58% in 2005 to 25.04% in 2010. France, where the social quota was the highest across all the monitored countries, had the lowest growth and in 2010, its social quota stood at 33.06%, having increased from 31.52% in 2005. The quota in Finland increased from 26.7% to 30.26% and, in the United Kingdom it rose from 26.26% to 29.2%. The lowest spending on social transfers in relation to GDP occurred in the Czech Republic, in spite of the increase from 18.36% in 2005 to 20.43 % in 2010.

Figure 2: Gini coefficients in 2005 and 2010 (compiled by the authors, source: Eurostat)

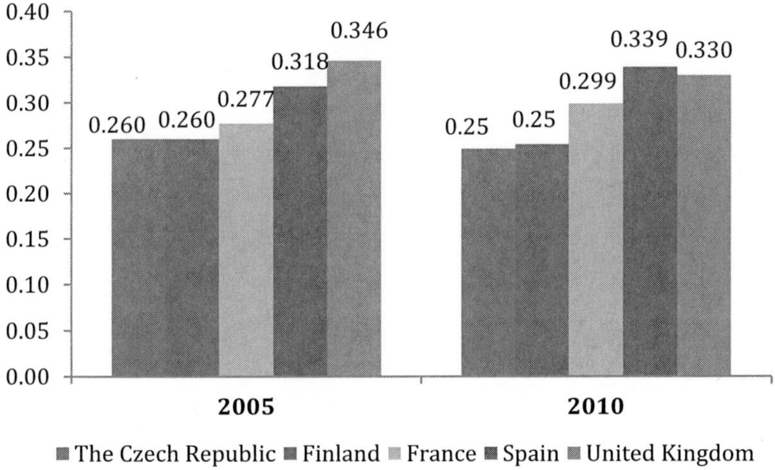

Due to these differing levels, inequality can be found in each of the five countries, and the more significant social problems appear where inequality is greater. The most common indicator of income distribution disparity is the Gini coefficient. Looking at the values of this coefficient as presented in Figure 2, it is possible to state that the selected countries fall within a range corresponding to a relatively low income disparity. Over the monitored period, the values in the Czech Republic and Finland were the lowest. The Gini coefficient reached the highest value (0.346) in the United Kingdom in 2005. This represents a value close to the upper level of relatively low income disparity. On average, the Gini coefficient value in EU member states was 0.306 in 2005, falling to 0.305 in 2010. Spain and the United Kingdom remained above this level across the whole period, which shows that an above-average income disparity prevails in these two countries. In the Czech Republic, a gradual decrease in the coefficient from 0.260 in 2005 to 0.249 in 2010 can be observed, and similarly in Finland (from 0.260 to 0.254). On the other hand, the value increased in France. In the United Kingdom, the coefficient dropped from 0.346 to 0.330, placing the United Kingdom in second place behind Spain, where the coefficient increased from 0.318 to 0.339.

Figure 3 shows the Lorenz curve of income distribution in the Czech Republic.

Figure 3: Lorenz curve (compiled by the authors, source: Eurostat)

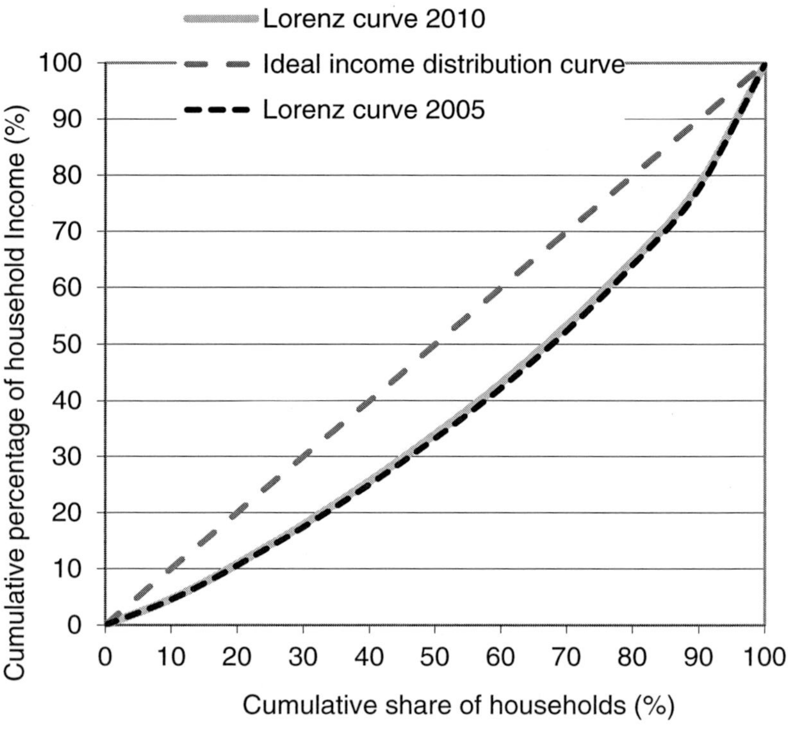

Poverty is a significant worldwide problem and has a variety of causes, including riots in the country or ineffective state power. Nowadays, in a globalized world, poverty exists in developing countries, and is increasing in developed countries as well.

According to the European Commission, the "European Union belongs among the richest parts of the world, nevertheless, 17% of Europeans have low incomes that do not allow them to pay for basic vital needs".[2]

European Statistical Office findings concluded that that "17% of EU citizens were at-risk-of-poverty in 2008".[3] According to this report, the percentage of endangered inhabitants in the current EU 27 has remained relatively stable since 2005.

The EU initiated its orientation on poverty phenomena in 2010, when the European Union Council declared a "European year of combating poverty and social exclusion". One of the main stimuli for this initiative was the fear of the social impact of the economic crisis on economic development.

The findings presented and discussed above suggest that poverty can be understood in two different ways: firstly, poverty can be seen as material hardship and as a lack of basic vital needs (e.g., food, drink) which directly jeopardizes people's lives; secondly, according to a more recent conception, poverty can be understood in terms of the distinctively lower standard of living of an individual, relative to others in the society, even when the individual is not in life danger and has adequate material possessions. Poverty has several causes, and it is possible to distinguish these, in terms of 'outer' and 'inner' causes. Outer causes of poverty include the country's geographical location, its natural resources or size, and the pace of growth of its society. Inner reasons include health and nutrition (famine, AIDS), the level of education, and the country's institutions (government, market).

Extreme households, in which people do not have access to the financial resources necessary to satisfy even basic needs (such as food and accommodation) subsequently enter the so-called 'poverty zone'. There are a number of methodologies available for the purposes of monitoring poverty. A European Union project (SILC) has established a poverty threshold at the level of 0.6 (median of disposable income). This threshold has been set based on knowledge of the theoretical distribution of variable income (log-normal distribution). Households below the threshold are deemed to be in danger of falling into poverty.

In 2010, 16.4% of European households lived below the poverty threshold. Table 4 shows an example of the results concerning poverty in the five selected EU countries in 2010. The results show that the Czech Republic retained its position as the country with the least poverty endangered households in the EU. In 2010, only 9% of Czech households were living in the poverty zone. Spain (20.7%) and United Kingdom (17.1%) were above average, and the values in Finland (13.1%) and France (13.4%) were almost the same.

Table 4: Endangered households, 2010 (calculated by the author, source: Eurostat)

Country	Poverty threshold monthly (in PPS)	Households endangered by poverty (%)	Average income of households endangered by poverty (in PPS)
CZ	483	9.0	364
FI	851	13.1	688
FR	878	13.4	667
ES	666	20.7	3676
UK	853	17.1	610

The depth of poverty is a very important indicator, because it shows the reality in terms of the distribution of financial resources among households. This indicator was defined by Proctor et al. (2002) as the ratio of average household income to the defined poverty threshold. It reveals the financial resources which households or individuals lack, and which would be needed in order to rise above the poverty threshold. In order to be able to calculate the poverty coefficient, the average income of households endangered by poverty must be known (households below 60% of the median), marked as 'a'. This income is subtracted from the value determining the poverty threshold (A) and a so-called poverty depth indicator is determined, which represents the household income deficit. The relative indicator is calculated according to the formula (A-a)/A – Sen poverty coefficient. This calculation is shown in Table 5 below.

Table 5: Calculation of Sen Coefficient, 2010 (calculated by the author, source: Eurostat)

Country	A (in PPS)	a (in PPS)	A-a (in PPS)	(A-a)/A
CZ	504	380	125	0.25
FI	851	684	167	0.20
FR	878	657	221	0.25
ES	666	376	290	0.44
UK	853	610	244	0.29

According to these results, the Sen co-efficient for each country is closer to 0 than 1, so we can say that the depth of poverty in the selected countries is low overall, and is at its deepest in Spain and its most shallow in Finland.

Poverty must also be understood from the point of view of material deprivation. Materially deprived households are those which lack 3 or more of the 9 items defined by the EU Committee for social protection and social inclusion. These items include the following: the ability to cover unexpected costs, the opportunity to eat meat regularly, the opportunity to take a holiday once a year, and owning a color TV set, a refrigerator, a car or a telephone. In cases where the households lack 4 or more of these items, they are considered severely materially deprived. Table 6 gives an overview of the percentage of materially and significantly materially deprived households in particular countries. It is necessary to note the situation of households living under the poverty threshold (UPT).

Life conditions are strongly influenced by state fiscal policy, particularly in relation to the function of redistribution, the goal of which is to establish greater equality among individuals. Redistribution is indirectly guaranteed by means of progressive taxation, and is also related to retirement tax, which might negatively influence work effort. Redistribution is secured by means of financial transfers, such as social credits and family benefits. Within a redistributive framework, household pensions are increased by transfer payments and decreased by taxes, benefits, fees and other contributions to the state. The most important redistribution process is the state's social benefits system. Each state should try hard to decrease the number of inhabitants endangered by poverty.

Table 6: Materially deprived households (calculated by the author, source: Eurostat)

Country	Number of households (in %)	Materially deprived households		Severe materially deprived households	
		2005	2010	2005	2010
CZ	Total	25.7	16.2	15.5	7.9
	UPT	68.2	53.2	50.3	37.0
FI	Total	12.4	9.1	5.6	3.6
	UPT	38.8	30.4	21.7	14.2
FR	Total	15.7	13.6	7.5	6.7
	UPT	42.5	41.9	25.4	25.2
ES	Total	14.5	15.2	5.8	5.6
	UPT	29.6	32.4	14.5	15.0
UK	Total	14.2	20.9	6.5	6.0
	UPT	32.0	31.8	17.1	14.9

Conclusion

The results presented in this study show that those countries with the highest standard of living are those in which incomes are highest (Finland, France and United Kingdom). In comparison with others, these countries have the highest government spending on social protection in relation to GDP. However, in these countries, income disparity and poverty are not the lowest. The United Kingdom has the second biggest share of households living below the poverty level (after Spain), and the country with the lowest number of poor people live in the Czech Republic, even though its standard of living is lower than the EU average. France has the highest purchasing power. Thus, every selected country leads the way in terms of some of the indicators selected.

The Czech Republic has the lowest number of poor people, not only among the five countries compared in the present study but across the EU as a whole. Its depth of poverty is moderate, and it has the lowest standard of living, lowest incomes and lowest social quota. However, its redistribution level, in connection with the minimization of income disparity, is effective. In the monitored period, the income of the unemployed grew at a much faster rate than in the whole set of households, and the number of unemployed people endangered by poverty also fell. In other countries, the incomes of pensioners grew. It remains an open question, though, whether this is the right direction in which to proceed, because strong support for the unemployed has a negative influence on a country's inhabitants as a whole. In spite of the fact that the lowest number of economically weak households are in the Czech Republic, more than half of these suffer material deprivation, which is a sign of the unsuitability of paying attention only to measuring poverty only through border value. It is thus necessary to examine the selected groups in greater depth.

Finland belongs to the countries with the highest living standards and the lowest debt burden. The number of poor people in Finland is slightly higher than in the Czech Republic, but Finland also has the lowest number of materially deprived households in comparison with other countries. Income disparity is also very low and the social quota rather high. Finland can be considered a conscientious nation, with a high provision of government social security and low public debt. Based on these facts, Finland can be considered the country with the highest standard of living.

France has a high living standard and purchasing power, but also has a high level of household debt. Income disparity, poverty and material deprivation are moderate, relative to the other countries monitored. France's social quota is the highest of all the monitored countries, but it is necessary to emphasize its high level of public indebtedness. The needs of French consumers are adequately covered by their incomes, but for a minority of French households, income is insufficient to cover the need for education and equipment. France can be considered a self-confident nation.

The situation in Spain is completely different. Its households have the lowest incomes (after the Czech Republic), the living standard is average and the level of debt is high. The social quota is higher than in the Czech Republic, but social transfers do not prevent a high level of disparity and deep poverty. The Spanish consider themselves rather poor. Accordingly, Spain can be considered the country with the lowest quality of life.

The situation in the United Kingdom is very specific: its inhabitants have a high standard of living and high incomes. The government spends a large amount on social protection, but income disparity is still high, which results in above-average poverty and material deprivation which impacts upon a fifth of all total households. Its ratio of all debts to GDP is the highest of the monitored countries. The United Kingdom was the country in which the development of the financial sphere had the most immediate impact, and this is reflected in its economic decline, which shows up in the analysis of the income indicators across all the selected countries.

These findings show that the issues of poverty and material deprivation which are connected with the risk of social exclusion are very significant, and that they apply to developed EU member states. It seems that poverty levels are at their lowest in the socially oriented and post-communist countries, where indebtedness is low. Social policy is most appropriately oriented in Finland, a country which is not burdened by debts. Here, the number of poor and materially deprived people is low, and more support is directed towards increasing the income of pensioners than towards the unemployed, which is a big mistake in the Czech Republic's redistribution policy. Social policy is a very strong instrument which can significantly decrease poverty levels. However, it is not only how much is spent on social protection which is important, but also towards which social groups the spending is oriented. If social policy is incorrectly focused, this generates economic inactivity and slows down economic growth, and thus decreases the standard of living for a country's inhabitants. Owing to the importance of the role of social policy, it is necessary that particular countries use it effectively. It is more effective to focus on educating groups who are at risk and to generate new employment opportunities.

Household income has a significant influence on consumer behaviour. Consumer behaviour is certainly very different among those who are significantly below the poverty level as compared with those who belong to a higher social class. The extent to which households are willing to incur debt is also important. There are regional differences within every country, but also between countries as a whole. The reasons for this do not lie only in purchasing power, but also in subjective feelings and consumer perceptions, which are strongly determined by particular cultures.

Notes

[1] As a sample EU recalculation, the head of the household is evaluated by the coefficient 1, children of 0-13 years of age have the coefficient 0.3, and other children and household members have the coefficient 0.5).

[2] European Commission pages at http://ec.europa.eu/social/main.jsp?langId=cs&catId=637; cit. 15. 2. 2011. The data are based on the concept of a relative conception of poverty.

[3] http://epp.eurostat.ec.europa.eu/portal/page/portal/product_details/publication?p_product_code= KS-SF-10-009; valid to February 6th, 2011.

References

Bohacova, T. (2007). *Materialni deprivace a chudoba domacnosti v CR*. Available at: http://is.muni.cz/th/102755/fss_b/BKLBohacova_102755.doc

European Commision.Eurostat. (2011). *Glossary: Actual individual consumption*. Available at: http://epp.eurostat.ec.europa.eu/statistics_explained/index.php/Glossary:Actual_individual_consumption_%28AIC%29

Eurostat. (2012). *Statistics*. Available at: http://epp.eurostat.ec.europa.eu/portal/page/portal/statistics/search_database

Frick, J.R., and Krell, K. (2012). *Measuring Income in Household Panel Survey for Germany. A Comparison of EU-SILC and SOEP*. Available at: http://www.diw.de/soeppapers

Greig, A., Hulme, D., and Turner, M. (2007). *Challenging Global Inequality:DevelopmentTheory and Practice in the 21st Century*. New York: Palgrave Macmillan.

Informacni institut. (2010). *Diskrecni zustatek*. Available at: http://www.informacniinstitut.cz/informacniinstitut/Informacni_Institut/Aktuality/Entries/2010/8/31_TZ__Diskrecni_zustatek_lepe_meri_realne_prijmy_ceskych_domacnosti.html

International Monetary Fund. (2010). *Bhutan: Poverty Reduction Strategy Paper*. Available at: http://www.imf.org/external/pubs/ft/scr/2010/cr10180.pdf

Juhascikova, I., and Stukovska, Z. (2011).*Zbornik prispevkov z vedeckej konferencie Statistickeho uradu SR: Kvalita zivota v podmienkach globalizacie*. Bratislava: Štatisticky úrad SR.

Kabat, L. (2007). Prijmova situacia a zivotne podmienky obyvatelstva Slovenska podla statistiky SILC. *Slovenská štatistika a demografia.*

Kerk, G., and Manuel, A.R. (2008). A comprehensive index for a sustainable society: The SSI – the Sustainable Society Index. *Ecological Economics*, 66 (2-3), 228-242. Available at: http://www.sciencedirect.com/science/article/pii/S0921800908000438

Kotynkova, M., and Nemec, O. (2003). *Lidske zdroje na trhu prece*. Havlickuv Brod: Professional Publishing.

Krebs, V. (2005). *Socialni politika*.Praha: ASPI, a. s.

Lapacek, M. (2005). *Ekvivalencni stupnice a prijmova nerovnost*. Available at: http://nf.vse.cz/download/veda/workshops/inequality.pdf

Mercer. (2012). *Quality of Living Reports*. Available at: http://www.imercer.com/products/2011/quality-ofliving.aspx

Morse, S. (2004). *Indices and Indicators in Development: An Unhealthy Obsession with Numbers.* London: Earthscan.

Proctor, B. D., and Dalaker, J. (2003). *Poverty in the United States: 2002. Current Population Reports. Washington, DC:* U.S. Government Printing Office.

Stavkova, J., Stejskal, L., and Nagyova, L. (2011) Income differentiation of households in the Czech Republic. *Acta Universitatis Agriculturae et Silviculturae Mendelianae Brunensis,* 2 (1), 26-52.

Stigliz, J., Sen, A., and Fittoussi, J.P. (2009).*Report by the Commission on the GDP Measurement of Economic Performance*. Retrieved from http://www.stiglitz-sen-fitoussi.fr/en/index.htm

Svetlik, J. (2003). *Marketing pro evropsky trh*. Praha: Grada.

Syrovatka, M. (2008). How (not) to measure quality of life: Critical perspectives on the Human Development Index. *Mezinarodni vztahy*, 43 (1), 9-37.

The Economist. (2005). *The Economist Intelligence Unit's quality-of-life index*. Available at: http://www.economist.com/media/pdf/QUALITY_OF_LIFE.pdf

CHAPTER FIVE

THE QUALITY OF DISCLOSURE IN THE ANNUAL REPORT: ANALYSIS OF DIFFERENT APPROACHES

ALAIN DEVALLE AND FABIO RIZZATO
DEPARTMENT OF MANAGEMENT, UNIVERSITY OF TURIN

Abstract

Disclosure is an important topic both for companies (Douglas W. et al., 1991, Baginski P. et al, 1990) and for investors to permit them to evaluate the reliability of company reporting. The aim of the chapter is to make a literature review on all the methods that have been used for the analyses of the quality of disclosure of the annual report. We have chosen the quality of disclosure of the financial statement, because it is one of the main sources of corporate information (Knutson, 1992) and because annual report disclosure levels are positively correlated with the amount of disclosure provided via other media (Lang and Lundholm, 1993). In particular, we discuss different approaches of research used in evaluating the quality of voluntary and mandatory disclosure of financial statements.

Keywords: *disclosure, index, quality.*

Introduction

The disclosure of the financial statement is an important topic for all the stakeholders of a company. In fact disclosure allows investors to understand the application of the accounting principles used by companies and permits investors to analyse the relevant information (Healy et al., 2001; Graham et al., 2005; Lambert et al., 2007). Users generally rely on information contained in financial statements to make economic decisions (Framework IAS).

In July 2012, the European Financial Reporting Advisory Group (EFRAG) published the discussion paper entitled "Towards a Disclosure Framework for notes" with the objective to "ensure that all and only information is disclosed in an appropriate manner, so that detailed information does not obscure relevant information in notes to the financial statements". The Discussion Paper underlines that there are three main objectives to reach: to identify what disclosures are relevant for the notes of the financial statement, to discuss the meaning of materiality of the information required and to develop a set of principles for a good communication of disclosure.

A relevant and complete disclosure produces economic advantages for companies (Graham et al., 2005) even if it entails investments in information systems (Verrecchia, 1983; Darrough et al. 1990; Skinner D.J, 1994; Botosan C.A., 2000).

Hundreds of studies have been conducted into the analysis of mandatory and voluntary disclosure reported in the financial statement, but there is a huge debate on the relevance and on the requirements that the information disclosed must have. For example, Devalle et al. (2012) demonstrated that the quality of disclosure is very low with reference to the mandatory disclosure of IAS 36 – impairment of assets - and of IAS 40, Investment Properties. In fact, only few groups of the sample analyzed disclosed all the information required by IAS 36 and IAS 40.

International Financial Reporting Standards (IAS and IFRS) and their worldwide application to financial statements are topics of increasing interest for the business and scientific communities involved in the performance evaluation of companies and disclosure. This focus is justified because of different formal and substantial changes that IFRS introduced in the preparation of separate and consolidated financial statements, and because of the recent advances of financial communication brought by national and international rules in response to the financial scandals of the last decade, such as the American Sarbanes Oxley Act or the Italian Law n. 262/2005. As a matter of fact, IFRS are mandatory for the preparation of consolidated financial statements of European listed companies (as stated in the EU Regulation nr. 1606/2002) and other worldwide countries (i.e. Australia). In many countries, such as Italy, IFRS are also required for individual and consolidated financial statements of not listed banks and insurance companies. However, it has been some years since the adoption of IFRS first became mandatory but different events all around the world have highlighted some issues about their application. The 2009 global financial crisis identified some issues of some dominant IFRS principles, such as the application of fair value for the measurement of financial instruments. In past years, the adoption of this measurement model led to relevant increases in the assets value and in the economic performance. The decrease in value of financial assets produced relevant losses in the accounts related to the periods of crisis, which are completely the opposite results if compared to the previous financial periods. These delicate circumstances led to the intervention of the G20 which, in its document for the enforcement of financial markets, highlighted the importance of Standard setters in enhancing the quality of financial statements with particular reference to the valuation of financial instruments, but at the same time simplifying the application of the accounting standards. The IASB and the FASB jointly signed a document, published on 2nd July 2010, where they confirmed their intention to enhance IFRS and US GAAP toward joint convergence. The G20 leaders, at the conclusion of the September 2009 Pittsburgh Summit, asked the Standards setters to increase their efforts to achieve a unique body of high quality accounting standards and conclude their convergence projects before June 2011. Another critical issue is the partial impracticability for investors to compare different European companies, because of the different discretional policies included in IFRS regarding the measurement of single financial statement items. For example, the possibility to measure different assets is alternatively at fair value or at cost. Besides the decrease in comparability, not all the accounting policies allowed by IFRS have the same intrinsic capability to forecast, summarize and influence market values. Some accounting policies include the use of fair value because they are mainly orientated toward investors and present a forecasting perspective, while other policies are based on the cost because they aim at protecting shareholders and creditors' interests through the use of prudential measurements of assets. It is obvious that market based models provide accounting information to be more dynamic and future oriented, and although respecting the going concern principle, the profit/loss of the period acts as a marker of future corporate performance by providing insights and interpretations about future incomes and investment risks. As such, the investor is supported in its financial decision making process.

In order to have this informative purpose, the main measurement basis of the IFRS financial statements is the fair value model, defined as "the amount for which an asset could be exchanged between knowledgeable, willing parties in an arm's length transaction". It represents a model to be applied for different assets of a company.

In some cases, fair value is the only measurement basis allowed: this is the case of some categories of financial instruments (IAS 32 and IAS 39) where the only measurement allowed is the market's value. In other cases, fair value is the suggested measurement model (benchmark treatment) even if it is allowed to continue to apply the cost model (allowed treatment). This is the case of investment property, where IAS 40 suggest the use of fair value while the use of cost is still allowed as a measurement model for these assets. In other cases, fair value is the alternative model allowed when the preferred model is the cost. Intangible assets (IAS 38) and tangible assets (IAS 16) are examples of this treatment. Therefore there is strong evidence of different accounting policies and measurement basis throughout all IFRS which leave financial statement preparers to make the choice. The option of choosing one principle instead of another one is in contrast with one of the objectives of IFRS, namely, the comparability of financial statements. It is so straightforward that whenever preparers have the possibility to choose alternative methods, the final result will be a decrease in the comparability of the data. This decrease in comparability is given by different contextual factors as, for example, the industry sector of the company or factors like culture, which drive companies to apply the same accounting behaviors used in the past. Regarding the influence of culture, several studies show how company financial statements in different countries, prepared according to IFRS, are influenced by the accounting culture of their country. For example, British corporations make a major use of fair value as the main measurement model whereas in other countries, such as Italy, the main measurement model has always been the cost. The only way to achieve substantial and effective comparability of financial data is to impose a common and unique body of accounting standards, by eliminating every possible discretional choice and option.

In this context disclosure is a fundamental topic that must be analyzed by all the stakeholders, and the application of IFRS represents a unique opportunity to improve the quality of disclosure. The analysis of previous studies on the measurement of the quality of disclosure has highlighted that there are many different approaches that researchers have used to assess the quantity and quality of the information reported in the financial statement.

The aim of this chapter is to analyze the literature review on disclosure in order to define the "state of the art" of references on the approach to measuring the quality of disclosure. This chapter focuses, in particular, on the financial disclosure of the consolidated financial statement.

The disclosure: definition

The disclosure of a company "aroused a great deal of academic interest in the past" (Marston C.L. et al., 1991).

The first studies on disclosure refer to the late sixties, for example, Copeland et al., 1968; Mautz R.K. et al 1978; Nair et al., 1980; Gray S.J., McSweeney L.B., Shaw J C et al., 1984, etc, can be quoted.

Disclosure is an important topic (Douglas W. et al., 1991; Baginski P. et al, 1990) because it influences the behavior of an investor and supports economic decisions as, for example, whether to hold or sell their investment in the entity or whether to reappoint or replace the management (Framework).

Groups disclose information through different channels such as annual reports, analyst presentations, investor relations, interim reports, etc. (Hassan O. PP. et al, 2010).

This chapter focuses on the financial disclosure that can be defined as "any deliberate release of financial information, whether numerical or qualitative, required or voluntary, or via formal or informal channels" (Gibbins et al., 1990).

The main source of financial information is the consolidated financial statement of a company. The IAS Framework states that a complete set of financial statements "includes a balance sheet, an income statement, a statement of changes in financial, and those notes and other statements and explanatory material that are an integral part of the financial statements. They may also include supplementary schedules and information based on or derived from the consolidated financial statements, and they are expected to be read with them. Such schedules and supplementary information may deal, for example, with financial information about industrial and geographical segments and disclosures about the effects of changing prices" (Framework).

The transition to IFRS (2005) for European listed companies fuelled the studies on the quality of disclosure related to the financial statement.

Disclosure can be classified in different ways, depending on the obligation to disclose information, the type of information disclosed and on the way it is reported.

For example it is possible to identify:

- mandatory disclosure: mandatory information required by laws, international accounting standards, etc.;
- voluntary disclosure: companies disclose events that are not specifically required by laws, regulations, etc., but whose information

could be relevant for investors (Graham J. R et al., 2005).

Previous research demonstrated that the level of compliance of mandatory disclosure depends on different factors such as control bodies, government authorities, etc. (Graham J. R. et al., 2005; Marston C. L. et a., 1991).

A great deal of research has demonstrated that even if the disclosure is mandatory, its quality is very low. Many companies did not disclose the information requested.

The information disclosed in the notes by companies can be divided also into:

- financial information related to the financial statement of the company;
- non-financial information not related to the financial statement, for example market share, customer satisfaction (Robba W.G. et al, 2001).

Furthermore, in reference to the way information is disclosed we can identify (Marston et al., 1991; Boyatzis et al., 1998):

- quantitative information: based on tables, graphs, numbers, etc.;
- qualitative information: based on texts, diagrams, etc..

Fig. 1 summarizes the different typology of disclosure. When it comes to the measurement of the quality of disclosure, researchers analyzed the degree of all types of information defined in Fig. 1.

The analysis of the quality of disclosure: different approaches

The quality of disclosure analyzed in this chapter refers to the consolidated financial statement even if literature highlighted different documents that are usually used in analyzing the quality of disclosure: interim reporting, management report, etc. (Lang et al., 2003).

The main approaches to study the quality of financial disclosure are the following (Fig. 2):

- content analysis;
- disclosure index;
- subjective rating.

Fig. 1. Typology of disclosure

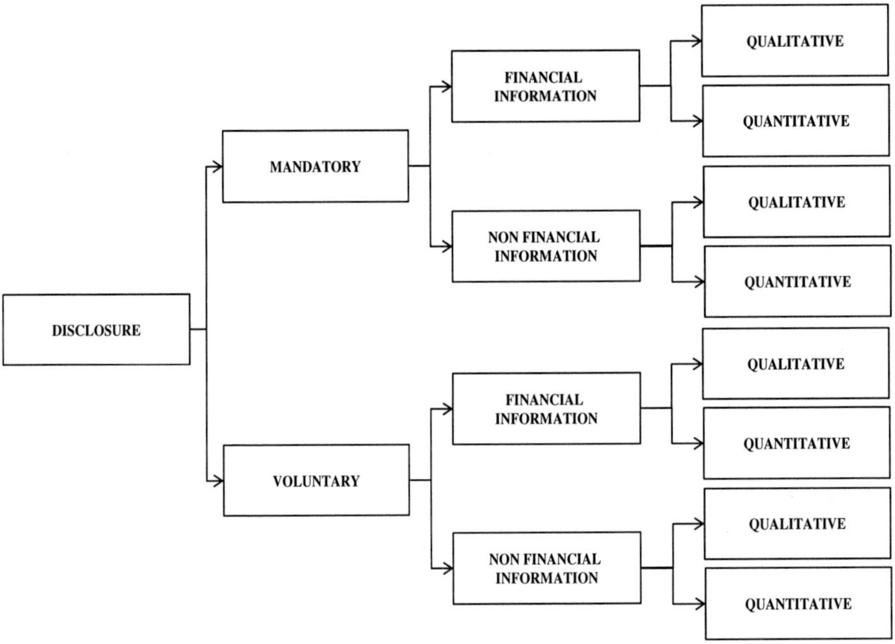

Fig. 2. The approaches to analyze the quality of disclosure

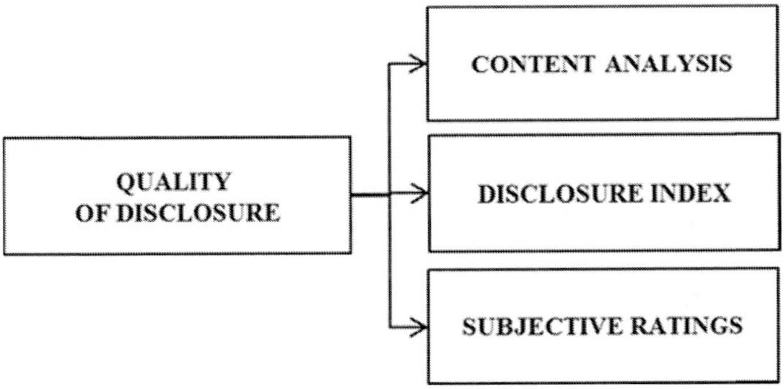

Content analysis

Content analysis is defined as "a set of procedures for collecting and organizing information in a standardized format that allows analysts to make inferences about the characteristics and meaning of written and other recorded material. Simple formats can be developed for summarizing information or counting the frequency of statements. More complex formats can be created for analyzing trends or detecting subtle differences in the intensity of statements" (Krippendorff, 1980).

Through content analysis it is possible to analyze the influence of different phenomena, for instance readability, communication, style, etc. on disclosure (Kerlinger et al., 1964).

Using this methodology it is possible to measure the total amount of information reported in the notes of the financial statement by counting the number of phrases, words, pages, etc. (Hackston et al., 1996).

Content analysis is divided into (Jones M.J. et al, 1994):

1) thematic analysis: which focuses on themes within a text;
2) syntactic analysis: which centers upon the cognitive difficulty of reading the textual message.

Fig. 3. Content analysis

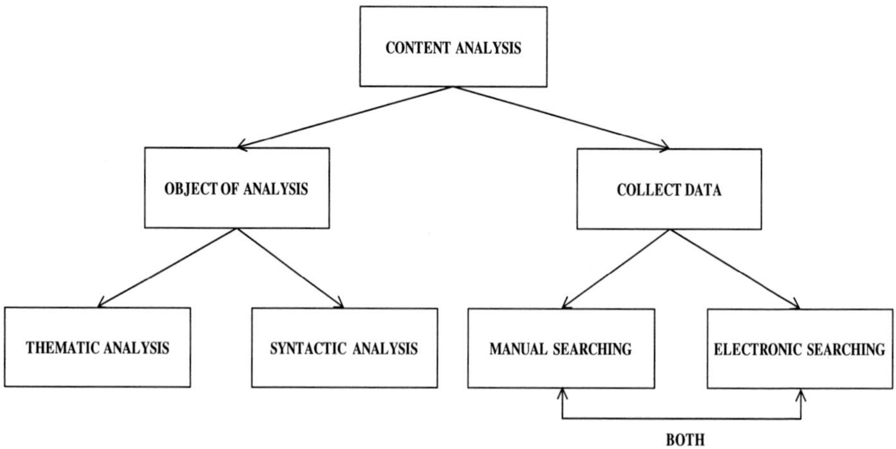

Information is collected by means of checklists (manual searching) (Hackston et al., 1996; Francis J. et al., 1997; Beretta S. et al., 2004; Linsley et al., 2006), by software (electronic searching) (Frazier et al., 1984; Abrahamson, et al., 1996; Rogers et al., 1997; Kothari et al., 2009) or both methods (Hussainey et al., 2003; Beattie et al., 2007).

One of the main limitations of manual studies is the collection of the data which restricts the sample size employed by prior studies (Beattie et al., 2007; Hassan et al, 2010). Electronic searching is simpler to use and costs less than a manual analysis but can generate misleading results. For example, if we search for the words "deferred tax" the results could be positive even if the text states that the information is not present.

Disclosure index

A disclosure index "aims to show the level of disclosure in a set of company accounts" (Marston et al., 1991). A disclosure index which satisfies the requirements of reliability and validity (Marston et al., 1991) is a useful way of measuring disclosure quality.

As the quality of information is hard to measure, the index of disclosure assumes that the quality of disclosure depends on the number of parameters reported, for example, each parameter collected is assigned a score. The total score could represent the quality of disclosure.

An index of disclosure measures the presence of mandatory information, voluntary information or both, reported in the annual financial statements or in the interim reports.

Marston (1991) identified four levels of measurement:

- the nominal or classificatory scale;
- the ordinal or ranking scale;
- the interval scale;
- the ratio scale.

The use of different disclosure indexes depends on the different variables analyzed (Siegel S., 1956). Moreover, in some studies the disclosure index is weighted (Cerf A., 1961; Buzby S.L., 1974, 1975; Botosan C.A., 1997, Richardson A.J. et al., 2001), while in other studies it is not weighted (Cooke T.E., 1989). When it comes to voluntary disclosure this index is usually weighted.

Fig. 4. Disclosure index

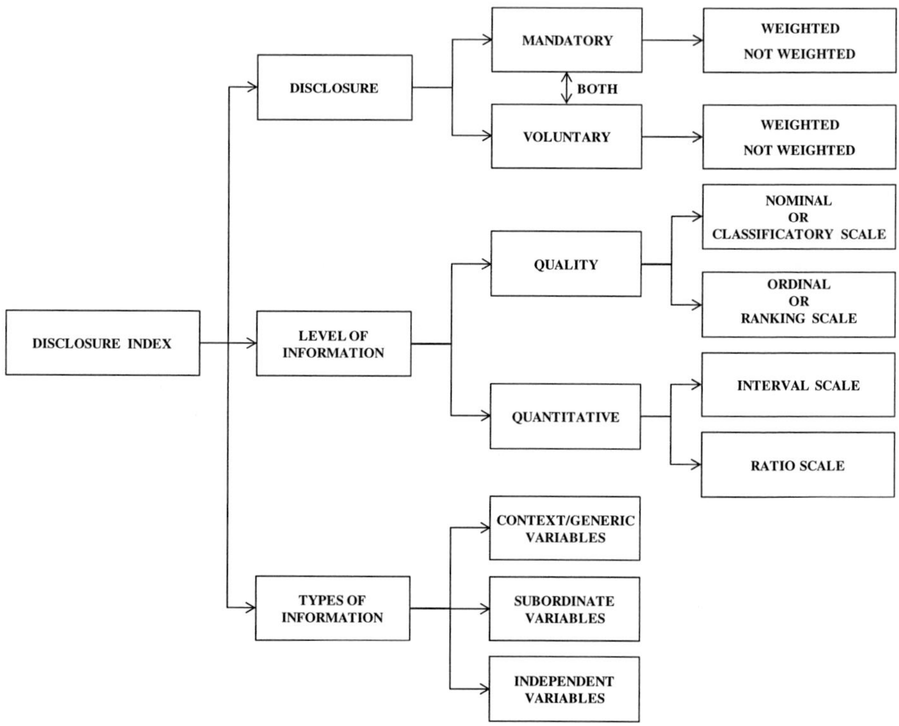

For example, in order to rate the groups analyzed by the degree of the quality of disclosure provided on the impairment of goodwill, Devalle A. et al. (2012) defined an index of disclosure starting from the Botosan model (1997). Thus, if an item of mandatory disclosure of goodwill as stated above was present, they assigned one point. They then proceeded to divide the information into three types:

- context/generic variables: they assigned no score. For example the generic information about the recoverable amount and not the specific data;
- subordinate variables: we assigned one score only if the problem existed. For example, if the group used fair value and it showed the information as it was defined, we assigned one point;

- independent variables: one point for one piece of information. For example, the CGU used for the evaluation of goodwill, or the sensitivity analysis, etc.

An analysis of the literature review suggests that the disclosure index depends on:

- the researcher;
- the number of items analyzed;
- the typology of information analyzed.

With reference to the first point (researcher) there are different indexes:

- indexes defined by the researcher: the researcher defines all the aspects of the analysis;
- indexes defined in previous research: this approach led to a comparison of different studies made by different analysts. Some examples of indexes are the Standard & Poor index, the Security and Exchange Commission Rating of the Management Discussion and Analysis Disclosure, etc.

As far as the number of items analyzed is concerned, the research may focus on a single or few items or a full disclosure.

With reference to the typology of information analyzed we can distinguish between mandatory and voluntary (or both) disclosure.

To summarize, the use of an index of disclosure depends on many variables, and there is a huge amount of studies with different indexes used. In each study a different index is defined depending on the question research.

The definition of an index of disclosure must be reliable and valid in order to be a right methodology to apply in the research. In fact, the definition of the disclosure index could be influenced by the subjectivity of the researcher.

Fig. 5. Disclosure index variables

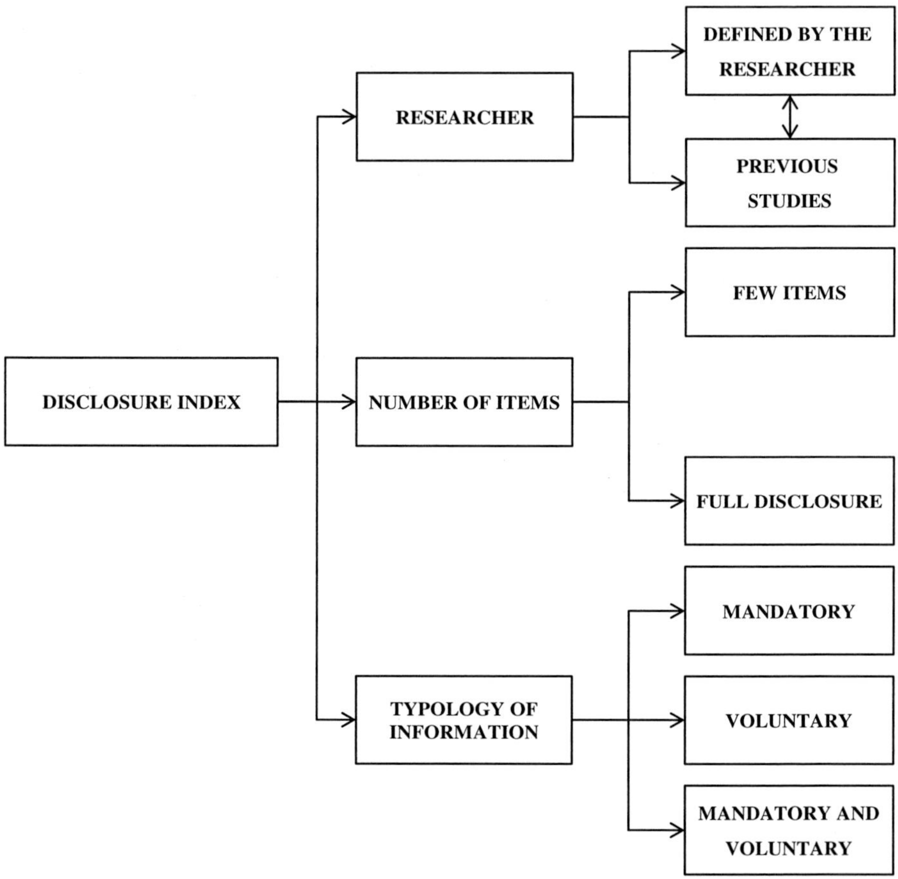

Subjective ratings

The "subjective rating" approach is based on the use of a score attributed by some external entities. This type of analysis is realized by means of questionnaires and interviews carried out by the analyst, investor or other subjects.

For these reasons, the approach is also called disclosure survey (Hassan O.A.G. et al., 2010).

This methodology of research is often used in American studies as in the following papers: see Lang M., et al., 1993; Lang M. et al., 1996; Sengupta P., 1998; Healy P.M. et al., 1999; Botosan C.A. et al., 2002.

These studies are based on the disclosure analyzed by the Association of Investment Management and research (AIMR).

By means of questionnaires the analysis of the quality of disclosure is very simple even if the use of the questionnaire has different limits (see Fink, A., 1995; Gillham B., 2000).

The quality and the reliability of the results depend on the definition of the questionnaire. Finally, this approach is influenced by the perception of the different analysts involved (Lang M.H. et al., 1993).

The limit of this approach is the scarce availability of studies carried out by national and international institutions.

IAS 36 and disclosure index an empirical analysis

The aim of this paragraph is to show an example of the analysis of disclosure under the International accounting standards. The examined sample is made up of the groups listed on the four most important European Continental Union Stock Exchanges (Paris, Frankfurt, Madrid and Milan). The main aim of this empirical research is to analyze the quality of disclosure with reference to the impairment of goodwill. 141 groups listed on the above mentioned stock exchanges were analyzed. The investigation was based on the consolidated financial statements of the entities belonging to the above-mentioned indexes and sectors. In particular, the data of consolidated financial statements regarding 2010 was analyzed.

With reference to disclosure we hand collected the information required by IAS 36 from the notes of consolidated financial statements. We focused our analysis on the annual report as it is the most important report for investors. Knutson (1992) states, “at the top of every analyst's list (of financial reports used by analysts) is the annual report to shareholders. It is the major reporting document and every other financial report is in some respect subsidiary or supplementary to it”. IAS 36 requires that groups disclose the following information on the impairment of goodwill: the carrying amount of goodwill allocated to the unit (group of units), and the basis on which the unit's (group of units') recoverable amount has been determined (i.e. value in use or fair value less costs to sell). If the unit's (group of units') recoverable amount is based on value in use a group shall disclose a description of each key assumption on which management has based its cash flow projections for the period covered by the most recent budgets/forecasts, the period over which management has projected cash flows based on financial budgets or forecasts approved by management and, when a period greater than five years is used for a cash-generating unit (group of units), an explanation of why that longer period is justified. Moreover, IAS 36 requires the indication of the growth rate used to extract cash flow projections beyond the period covered by the most recent budgets, and the discount rate(s) applied to the cash flow projections.

In order to rate the groups analyzed by the degree of the quality of disclosure provided on the impairment of goodwill we defined an index of disclosure starting from the model defined by Botosan (1997). Thus, if an item of mandatory disclosure of goodwill as stated above was present, we assigned one point. We divided the information into three types:

- context/generic variables: we assigned no score. For example the generic information about the recoverable amount and not the specific data;
- subordinate variables: we assigned one point only if the problem existed. For example, if the group used the fair value and it showed the information as it was defined, we assigned one point;
- independent variables: one point for one piece of information. For example the CGU used for evaluation of goodwill, or the sensitivity analysis, etc.

Overall, each piece of information was equally weighted and the maximum total of points was seven. The formula of the "Gscore index" used in this paper is the following:

$$GScore = \frac{\sum_{i=1}^{n} x_i}{x_{tot}}$$

This research shows that the notes are not compliant with IAS 36 regarding the impairment test of goodwill in many cases. Our results are compliant with the findings of Glaum et al. who "pointed out that even when companies formally fulfill IFRS disclosure requirements regarding goodwill impairment tests, the information provided is sometimes not really useful to users. Disclosures are often sparse or vague".

These results are important for the Standard Setters, for Auditors and for accountants, who must verify the transparency of the annual report and the respect of the International Accounting Standard.

Conclusions

The disclosure of the financial statement is a fundamental topic for stakeholders, for academics, professionals, institutions, etc.

We can distinguish between mandatory disclosure, voluntary disclosure, financial information and non-financial information.

The main source of financial information is represented by the annual report that groups have to draw up.

The literature review analyzed in this chapter emphasized different approaches that can be used to assess the quality of the disclosure and in particular the content analysis, the disclosure index and the subjective ratings.

Content analysis is defined as "a set of procedures for collecting and organizing information in a standardized format that allows analysts to make inferences about the characteristics and meaning of written and other recorded material".

An index of disclosure measures the presence of mandatory information, voluntary information or both, reported in the annual financial statements or in the interim reports.

The "subjective rating" approach is based on the use of a score attributed by some external entities. This type of analysis is realized by means of questionnaires and interviews carried out by analysts, investors or other subjects.

The following table shows the strong and weak points of all the methodology analyzed.

Table 1. Characteristics of the different approaches

Methodology	Objective	Strong point	Weak point
Content Analysis	Analysis of the relation between information and its context	1) Electronic analysis: a. Easy to use b. Analysis of all documents c. speed of use 2) Manual analysis: a. Analyst evaluation	1) Electronic analysis: a. Use of keywords 2) Manual analysis: a. Limited sample b. Data collection
Disclosure index	Analysis of the quality of disclosure through the amount of information presented	1) Flexibility	1) Limited sample 2) Data collection 3) Index definition

Subjective rating	Score attributed by some external entities	1) No data collection	1) Based on questionnaire 2) Results influenced by the perception of the analyst

References

Abrahamson E., Amir, E., The information content of the president's letter to shareholders, Journal of Business Finance & Accounting, 1996 (23), 1157-1182

Beretta S., Bozzolan S., A framework for the analysis of firm risk communication, the international journal of accounting, 2004 (39), 265 – 288

Botosan C.A., Disclosure level and the cost of equity capital. The Accounting Review, 1997 (72) (3), 323-349

Botosan C.A., Evidence that greater disclosure lowers the cost of equity capital, Journal of applied corporate finance, 2000 (12), 60-69

Botosan C.A., Plumlee M.A., A re-examination of disclosure level and the expected cost of equity capital. Journal of Accounting Research, 2002, 21-40

Boyatzis R.E., Transforming qualitative information: thematic analysis and code development, Thousand Oaks, CA: Sage Publications, 1998

Buzby S.L., Selected items of information and their disclosure in annual reports, The accounting Review, 1974, 423-435

Buzby S.L., Company size, listed versus unlisted stocks, and the extend of financial disclosure, Journal of accounting research, 1975, 16-37

Cerf A.R., Corporate reporting and investment decisions, Public Accounting Research Program, Institute of Business and Economic Research, University of California, 1961

Clatworthy M., Jones, M.J, Financial reporting of good news and bad news: evidence from accounting narratives, Accounting and Business Research, 2003, 171-185

Beattie V., Thomson S., Lifting the lid on the use of content analysis to investigate intellectual capital disclosures, Accounting Forum, 2007 (31), 129-163

Cooke T.E., Disclosure in the Corporate Annual Reports of Swedish Companies, Accounting and Business research,1989, 113-124

Copeland R.M., Fredericks W., Extend of disclosure, Journal of Accounting Research, Spring, 1968, 106-113

Darrough M.N., Stoughton N.M., Financial disclosure policy in an entry Game, Journal of Accounting and Economics, 1990 (12), 19–243

Devalle A., Rizzato F., Fair value application and disclosure of investment properties (IAS 40). An empirical analysis of European listed companies, GSTF Business Review (GBR), Vol. 1, n. 1, 2011

Devalle A., Rizzato F., The impairment test of goodwill and the quality of mandatory disclosure required by IAS 36, GSTF Business Review (GBR), Vol. 2, n. 1, 2012

EFRAG (2012), Discussion Paper – Towards a Disclosure Framework for notes.

Fink A., How to Ask Survey Question. Sage, London, 1995

Francis J., Hanna J.D., Philbrick D.R., Management communications with securities analyst, Journal of accounting and Economics, 1997 (24), 363-394

Frazier K.B., Ingram R.W., Tennyson B.M., A methodology for the analysis of narrative accounting disclosures, Journal of Accounting Research, 1984 (22), 318-331

Gibbins M., Richardson A., Waterhouse J., The management of corporate financial disclosure: Opportunism, Ritualism, Policies, and Processes, Journal of accounting research, 1990 (28), 121-143

Gillham B., Developing a Questionnaire. Continuum, Real world research, 2000

Graham J.R., Harvey C.R., Rajgopal S., The economic implication of corporate financial reporting, Journal of accounting and economics, 2005 (40), 3-73

Gray S.J., McSweeney L.B., Shaw J.C, Information disclosure and the Multinational Corporation, Chichester, Johm & Sons, 1984

Hackston, D., Milne M.J, Some determinants of social and environmental disclosures in New Zealand companies, Accounting, Auditing and Accountability Journal, 1996 (9) (1), 77-108

Hassan O.PP., Marston C., Disclosure measurement in the empirical accounting literature - a review article, July 15, 2010

Healy P.M., Palepu K.G., Information asymmetry, corporate disclosure, and the capital markets: A review of the empirical disclosure literature, Journal of Accounting and Economics, 2001 (31), 405-440

Healy P.M., Hutton A.P., Palepu K.G., Stock performance and intermediation changes surrounding sustained increases in disclosure, Contemporary Accounting Research, 1999, 485-520

Hussainey K., Schleicher T., Walker, M., Undertaking large-scale disclosure studies when AIMR-FAF ratings are not available: The case of prices leading earnings, Accounting and Business Research, 2003 (33), 275-294

International Accounting Standard Board, Conceptual Framework for Financial Reporting, 2010

Jones M.J., Shoemaker P.A., Accounting narratives: a review of empirical studies of content and readability, 1994 (13)

Kerlinger, F.N., Foundations of behavioral research. New York: Holt Reinhart and Winston, Inc. Kintsch, W. and J.R. Miller, 1964

Kothari S.P., Li X., Short J.E., The effect of disclosures by management, analysts, and business press on cost of capital, return volatility, and analyst forecasts: a study using content analysis. The Accounting Review, 2009 (84), 1639-1670

Lambert R., Leuz C., Verrecchia R., Accounting information, disclosure, and the cost of capital, Journal of accounting Research, 2007 (45), 385-420

Lang M.H., Lins K.V., Miller D., ADRs, analyst, and accuracy: does cross listing in the U.S. improve a firm's information environment and increase market value?, Journal of Accounting research, 2003 (41), 317-345

Lang M., Lundholm R., Corporate Disclosure Policy and Analyst Behavior. The Accounting Review, 1996, 467-492

Lang M.H., Lundholm R.J, Cross-sectional determinants of analyst ratings of corporate disclosures, Journal of Accounting Research, 1993, 246-271

Linsley P.M., Shrives P.J., Risk Reporting: a study of risk disclosures in the annual reports of UK companies. The British Accounting Review, 2006 (38), 387-404

Maddala G., Limited Dependent and Qualitative Variables in Econometrics, Cambridge University Press, New York, 1983

Marston C.L., Shrives P.J., The use of disclosure indices in accounting research: a review article, British Accounting Review, 1991 (23), 195-210

Mautz R.K., May W. G., Financial disclosure in a competitive Economy, New York, Financial Executive Research Foundation, 1978

Nair R.D., Frank W.G., The impact of disclosure and measurement practices on international accounting classification, Accounting Review, 1980, 426–450

Richardson A. J., Welker M., Social disclosure, financial disclosure and the cost of equity capital. Accounting, Organizations and Society, 2001 (26) (7-8), 597-616

Robba W.G., Singleb E., Zarzeskic T., Nonfinancial disclosures across Anglo-American countries, Journal of International Accounting, Auditing & Taxation, 2001 (10), 71-83

Rogers R.K., Grant J., Content analysis of information cited in reports of sell-side financial analysts. Journal of Financial Statement Analysis, 1997

Sengupta P., Corporate disclosure quality and the cost of debt. The Accounting Review, 1998, 459-474

Siegel S., Nonparametric statistics for the behavioural sciences, McGraw Hill, 1956

Skinner D.J., Why firms voluntary disclose bad news, Journal of Accounting research, 1994 (32), 38–60

Verrecchia R., Discretionary disclosure. Journal of Accounting and Economics, 1983 (5), 179 - 194

Wegenhofer A., Voluntary disclosure with a strategic opponent, Journal of Accounting and Economics, 1990 (12), 341-363

CHAPTER SIX

DIVERSITY IN THE BOARD ROOM: A BUSINESS CASE OR RHETORIC?

DANIEL KIPKIRONG TARUS
MOI UNIVERSITY, KENYA

Abstract

Since Hambrick and Mason's (1984) seminal paper on Top Management Team (TMT) demographic characteristics and firm outcomes, researchers have extended the 'Upper Echelons Theory' to predict that TMT characteristics will be reflected in firm performance. However, much of the research to date has focused exclusively on TMT, to the exclusion of boards of directors. Over the last decade, the role of the board of directors has expanded, owing to governance related problems all over the world. Boards are generally expected to perform at least the following functions: monitoring and controlling management, counseling and providing information to TMT, monitoring compliance to laws and regulations, linking the organization to the external environment and providing strategic direction. In the light of these functions, it is clear that the board of directors plays a significant role in the performance of a firm. Although research on demographic diversity has been inconclusive, it is important to consider boards as units of analysis, in order to understand the role of diversity in the boardroom. This is important because in many countries there is a lot of interest from legislators in diversifying the composition of boards of directors. Using various theoretical perspectives, such as resource dependency theory, agency theory, stakeholder theory and upper echelons theory, this chapter reviews whether there is a business case for diversity, or just rhetoric.

Keywords: *Board diversity, upper echelons theory, agency theory, firm performance.*

Introduction

Hambrick and Mason's (1984) 'upper echelons' theory triggered numerous studies on the effect of the demographic composition of decision makers on organizational outcomes. From the upper echelons perspective, organizational outcomes are related to the demographic profiles of teams of top managers, because such characteristics serve as surrogates for cognitive orientation. In particular, the quality of the decisions taken by a firm depends upon managers' personalized interpretations of given situations. The ability to make valuable interpretations depends upon the experiences, values and beliefs of the decision makers.

A review of the literature reveals an increasing emphasis on the effect of top management demographic diversity on firm performance, with little emphasis on boards of directors. Although the literature acknowledges the important role played by executives in decision making (Wiersema and Bantel, 1992), boards of directors have also come under close scrutiny insofar as firms' decision making is concerned. With increasing levels of corporate failure and scandals in publicly listed firms, legislation has been enacted, in both developed and developing economies, in order to address weaknesses in corporate governance. Important provisions in the legislation include empowering board of directors to monitor executives, and engaging boards in strategic decision making. Indeed, there is a growing consensus that boards play three interrelated roles: firstly, a monitoring role, which includes hiring and firing underperforming executives and overseeing internal controls (Jensen and Meckling, 1976; Westphal and Fredrickson, 2001); secondly, the board links the firm to the external environment and enhances the firm's legitimacy (Pfeffer and Salancik, 1978; Hendry and Kiel, 2004); thirdly, boards of directors are expected to be involved in shaping the strategic direction of the firm and to monitor the progress of strategy implementation (Fama and Jensen, 1983; Zahra and Pearce, 1992; Kemp, 2006).

Research has demonstrated a link between diversity in demographic profiles and firm performance (Buyl et al., 2011). The reasons cited in support of this link include the following: the pooling of expertise and skills among diverse teams (Simons et al., 1999), the development of perspectives (Adams and Ferreira, 2009), the provision of necessary networks and linkages (Pfeffer and Salancik, 1978) and greater legitimacy. However, there is scant research on board demographic diversity and firm performance. Given the important role of directors in corporate governance, diversity in board composition adds value to decision making, thereby putting a premium on the value of the firm. The key issue is whether board diversity, especially in relation to gender, ethnicity, education, functional specialization and age and experience, may enhance board competence and thus stimulate firm performance.

There are two possible reasons why researchers have not studied the link between board diversity and firm performance adequately. The first reason is the belief that the decision-making process is dominated by managers and that the support of the board serves merely to rubber stamp these decisions (Lorsch and Young, 1990; Hendry and Kiel, 2004). The second reason is that the selection of board members is controlled by the management, and given the rewards and prestige associated with having a seat on the board, it is unlikely that boards would criticize management decisions. Hence, the board is seen as having a merely passive role in the decision-making process. However, boards often exert a considerable influence on firm decisions, and there are numerous examples of boards of directors hiring and firing members of the management team, engaging in strategic decision making (Tarus, 2011) and approving mergers and acquisitions, as well as in determining the management compensation structure.

The Concept of Diversity

Diversity can be defined as the quality of being diverse, different, varied, or dissimilar. Blau (1977) defines diversity as the degree of population dispersion, in terms of demographic attributes such as race and gender, amongst others. Lau and Murnighan (1998) introduced the concept of 'group faultlines', and suggested that there are dividing lines among group members, by means of which they can be split into sub-groups, based on one or more attributes. Age, for instance, can be used to divide group members into sub-groups of different ages. Using a geological analogy, the authors noted that groups have faults or fractures which are akin to the multiple layers of the earth's crust.

Board diversity can thus be defined in terms of the compositional variety of the board of directors (Kang et al., 2007). The literature distinguishes two types of diversity: the first is observable diversity, which includes the detectable attributes of directors, such as the background characteristics of gender, race, nationality, ethnicity, and age; the second is non-observable diversity, which includes the directors' educational backgrounds, functional backgrounds and industry experience (Kang et al., 2007). Board diversity can arise as a result of differences in director's education, experience, profession, gender, ethnicity and age. The concept of board diversity suggests that boards should reflect the structure of society, appropriately representing gender, ethnicity, and professional background. Boards which are appropriately composed should provide diverse perspectives (Milliken and Martin, 1996), thus enhancing the quality of decisions as well as firm performance.

The Role of Board of Directors

Boards of directors consist of teams of individuals who combine competencies and capabilities that collectively represent the firm's pool of capital. In a dynamic environment, its board of directors is crucial to the smooth functioning of a company. Primarily, boards of directors are responsible for monitoring managerial actions by approving major strategic and financial decisions, such as mergers and acquisitions and changes in capital structure. The board is expected to prevent negative management practices which may lead to corporate failure, but also to ensure that firms act upon opportunities which could enhance firm value. They are also responsible for hiring capable executives and for firing underperforming managers (Hermalin and Weisbach, 1998). By hiring and firing executives, board members are in a position to determine the firm's performance.

Similarly, boards of directors are responsible for determining the strategic direction of the firm (Ingely and van der Walt, 2001). They are expected to initiate organizational change and to facilitate processes that suit the organizational mission (Bart and Bontis, 2003). Although some scholars doubt the strategic role of the board (Henke, 1983), recent research has linked boards of directors to firms' strategic decisions (Rindova, 1999; Stiles, 2001; Tarus, 2011). Boards of directors give advice to executives concerning possible strategic decisions (Demb and Neubauer, 1992; Linck et al., 2008), they set parameters within which strategic decisions occur (Mizruchi, 1983) and they review and ratify these decisions (Jensen and Zajac, 2004). In some cases, boards also participate in the development of the firm's strategy (Johnson et al., 1996).

The board is responsible for connecting the firm with its stakeholders. Most importantly, the board is expected to secure valuable resources for the firm. Some of these resources include linking the firm to providers of capital, suppliers and government. They also provide market intelligence and establish connections and other crucial links with competitors. They bring a diverse pool of information and skills to the boardroom, secure contracts, provide reputational capital and identify business opportunities. In sum, the primary responsibility of the board is to monitor management, to set policy, to secure critical resources and to support the firm in achieving superior performance. Thus, the board's main responsibility is to govern the firm, and this responsibility cannot be delegated.

Theoretical Perspectives

Agency Theory

In their landmark work, Jensen and Meckling (1976) argue that management with no direct or significant ownership stake in a company would neither make the same decisions nor exercise the same care as would the company's owners. Consequently, such a management team may act in their own self-interest. This divergence of interests would incur residual costs, resulting in sub-optimal performance. In order to deal with this, owners must establish controls and reporting systems which regularly monitor the behavior and performance of the management (Jensen and Meckling, 1976; Fama, 1980). Therefore, a central assumption of agency theory is that the separation of ownership and control leads to a potential conflict between managers and shareholders.

Agency theory is often used to explain the role of the board of directors in addressing agency related problems (Fama and Jensen, 1983). The theory is premised on the idea that in a modern corporation, there is a separation of ownership and management. Within this corporate structure, it is likely that the interests of the owners and the management will diverge. When they have the privileged power to make decisions, managers act out of self–interest and pay less attention to the interests of the owners. This pursuit of self-interest increases the firm's costs in such areas as structuring contracts, monitoring and in controlling the behavior of agents, and may lead to losses occasioned by sub-optimal decisions. The board's fiduciary role therefore includes monitoring the CEO, setting compensation levels for top management, approving major strategic decisions and monitoring the implementation of strategies (Boyd et al., 2011).

Resource Dependency Theory

Resource Dependency theory views an organization as an open system. A firm's survival and competitiveness depends upon its ability to procure critical resources from the external environment (Pfeffer and Salancik, 1978). Through the board of directors, the corporation gains access to valuable resources through socializing with representatives of resource providers, or by exchanging other valuable resources such as friendship, networks or information (Boyd et al., 2011). In other words, the theory considers the board as a resource which provides social and business networks and influences the environment in favor of the firm (Carpenter and Westphal, 2001). Directors are viewed as contributing critical resources to the firm, such as establishing links and connections to key stakeholders (e.g., regulators, lenders and suppliers) as well as advice and counsel (Pfeffer and Salancik, 1978; Hillman and Dalziel, 2003; Ruigrock et al., 2006).

Hillman and Dalziel (2003) suggest that the board of directors act as boundary spanners in the environment, securing resources for the firm and providing strategic advice and counsel which help to enhance the firm's performance. Boards of directors reduce uncertainty for the firm by establishing connections with stakeholders, and bringing information, knowledge and skills to the decision-making table. According to Pfeffer and Salanciks' theory (1978), boards of directors provide the following four types of benefits for firms:

- Advice and counsel
- Legitimacy
- A channel of communication between external stakeholders and the firm
- Preferential access to resources.

Stakeholder Theory

Stakeholder theory is an extension of agency theory. Agency theory is premised on the existence of a single constituency of 'shareholders', whereas stakeholder theory postulates that organizations are constellations of cooperative and competitive groups who have an interest in the firm. Donaldson and Preston (1995) argue that organizations need to address the needs of organizational stakeholders by engaging in stakeholder management. In developing the theory, Donaldson and Preston (1995) distinguish the following three aspects: descriptive accuracy, instrumental power, and normative validity. The descriptive aspect of the theory describes or explains specific corporate characteristics and behaviors. The instrumental facet of the theory proposes that firms which pay attention to stakeholder management are comparatively successful and outperform firms without stakeholder orientation (Francoeur et al., 2008). The normative aspect of the theory proposes that attention to stakeholders is a sensible objective, even if it does not necessarily lead to superior performance. Thus, stakeholder management is viewed as being ethical and moral.

There is a lot of pressure on firms to appoint boards of directors from a broad set of groups, arising from the concern with stakeholder orientation. This pressure emanates from institutional investors, diverse shareholders, politicians, labor unions and consumer groups, among others. More importantly, each pressure group is concerned with the issue of representation: for example, affirmative action in most countries now requires that the constitution of boards must take gender balance into account. Similarly, in some countries ethnic minorities, labor unions and young people are agitating for representation on corporate boards. Stakeholder theory suggests that organizations should reflect the diversity of stakeholders, on the grounds that this makes economic as well as moral sense (Donaldson and Preston, 1995). Board diversity is one way of realizing a stakeholder orientation and of translating this orientation into superior firm performance. Thus, the theory makes a strong business case for board diversity.

The Upper Echelons Theory

The upper echelons theory is based on behavioral decision making and bounded rationality. The theory, developed by Hambrick and Mason (1984), hypothesizes that the demographic characteristics of decision-makers have implications for firm outcomes. It proposes that organizational outcomes are related to the particular demographic characteristics of top level decision-makers. In this sense, Hambrick (2007: 334) observes that 'if [one] wants to understand why organizations do the things they do, or why they perform the way they do, [one] must consider the biases and dispositions of the most powerful actors.' In other words, a firm's strategic posture reflects the values, cognitive biases, and perceptions of its top management.

The core assumption underlying Hambrick and Mason's (1984) theory is the belief that demographic characteristics serve as surrogates for cognitive orientations, beliefs, values, perceptions and knowledge. According to Hambrick (2007), executives act on the basis of their personal interpretations of given situations, and these interpretation are a function of their experience. Studies grounded in upper echelons theory contend that demographic characteristics such as age (Wiersema and Bantel, 1992), tenure (Hambrick et al., 1993), experience (Kor and Misanyi, 2008), educational level (Wiersema and Bantel, 1992), functional background (Datta and Rajagopalan, 1998), gender (Carter et al., 2003) and ethnicity (Carter et al., 2010) are important proxies for cognitive bias, and that these characteristics have an impact upon the ability to make decisions that enhance firm performance.

Although upper echelons theory is based on top management, it is important to note that boards of directors are the so-called 'apex of corporate power' (Zahra and Pearce, 1990: 296), and are involved in making decisions which have an effect upon firm performance. Research indicates that the role of the board includes advising and monitoring, hiring and firing management and reviewing, approving, and facilitating strategic decisions (Demb and Neubauer, 1992; Jensen and Zajac, 2004). In the light of these roles, it can be argued that the demographic characteristics of boards of directors may influence the ability to make a meaningful contribution to the deliberations that enhance firm performance.

Board Diversity and Firm Performance

Early discussions concerning strategic management theorized that firm performance is a function of the dispositions, decisions, and choices made by the top decision-makers within the firm (Child, 1972). Board diversity plays an important role in influencing innovation and in signaling the firm's quality to its stakeholders (Certo, 2003; Deutsch, 2005). Hambrick and Mason (1984) note that organizational strategists suffer from bounded rationality, and that limited cognitive abilities may lead to less innovation and creativity, as well as to a potentially depressed performance. Group members who differ in terms of their expertise, perspectives, resources, knowledge and skill base can contribute to greater creativity in group decision-making (Michael and Hambrick, 1992). Thus, greater diversity brings an increase in creative potential.

Among the most important issues currently under discussion in the literature on corporate governance is board diversity and firm value. Although empirical results appear to be mixed, board diversity is considered important because it is seen as a way of broadening the range of new ideas and of enhancing group performance (Knippenberg et al., 2004). Diversity has also been seen as a way of injecting new insights and perspectives (Carter et al., 2003). Similarly, boards are expected to protect the interests of their stakeholders and should therefore be drawn from varied constituencies.

Diverse groups produce a broader range of ideas and information, because of the diversity in their knowledge base (Milliken and Vollrath, 1991). Robinson and Dechant (1997) observe that diversity promotes a better understanding of the market place, enhances creative capacity and results in more effective problem-solving. Rose (2007) argues that higher levels of diversity in corporate boards could serve as a signal to potential job applicants, thereby attracting well-qualified people outside the circles from which board candidates are usually drawn. Board diversity increases competition in the labor market, as minority groups are not excluded from taking up positions in the firm. In other words, board diversity ensures that opportunities are made available based on each person's skills, competence, and qualifications. Board diversity also serves as a signal to its stakeholders—such as suppliers, customers, the public and the community at large—of the firm's inclusiveness, thus improving the firm's reputation and bolstering its performance.

Although some management research suggests that diversity is a source of competitive advantage, other scholars have a different view. For example, it has been argued that it is more likely that in diverse teams there will be barriers to social interaction, leading to increased social differentiation. Further, O'Reilly et al., (1998) argue that demographic diversity decreases the frequency of communication among group members, resulting in reduced group cohesion. Greater diversity has been found to generate more conflict and to provide a fertile ground for disputes (Rose, 2007), thus hampering creativity. In effect, Rose (2007) argues that a higher degree of board diversity may affect problem-solving because the decision-making process may take longer, as the various perspectives on a given matter must be raised and heard in the boardroom. In a diverse boardroom, one cannot ignore the potential for haggling and the possibility that the board might end up being less cohesive and more fragmented as a consequence. In sum, persuasive arguments exist for greater boardroom diversity, yielding both costs and benefits. The costs and benefits of each aspect of boardroom diversity are discussed below.

Gender Diversity

Gender diversity is the most debated diversity issue, not only as regards the boardroom, but also in the more general context of leadership. For example, in recent years, there has been a concerted effort by governments all over the world to legislate for gender diversity in positions of governance. A case in point is Norway, which requires 40% female representation on its boards (Ripley, 2003), and another is Kenya, which demands that one third of its boardroom representatives should be women. Studies have shown the representation of women in the boardroom is rather minimal. According to a Catalyst Census, women directorships stand at only 12.4% in the US and at 6.4% in the UK (Singh and Vinicombe, 2004). Similar results have been observed in developing countries: for example, the representation of women on corporate boards in Kenya accounts for only 8% of their total constitution (Tarus, 2011).

The claim that gender diversity has a positive role in firm performance may be supported from different theoretical perspectives. The first of these is agency theory, which is concerned with the independence of directors and the ability to monitor management. Research shows that gender diversity provides a board with the wherewithal to monitor management (Carter et al., 2003; Konrad et al., 2008; Terjesen et al., 2009). Studies suggest that having more women directors is an effective way of executing monitoring functions (Hillman et al., 2002; Carter et al., 2003). Women are likely to possess managerial skills such as legal, human resources, communication and public relations skills, as compared with men, who are more likely to possess the line functions of marketing and operations (Zelechowski and Bilimoria, 2004). If women directors are known to be effective monitors, then investors will place higher valuation premiums on those firms with greater gender diversity in the boardroom.

Secondly, stakeholder theory argues for the representation of both genders in the firm for the purposes of equity and fairness (Keasey et al., 1997), as a signal of the firm's commitment to gender balance and in order to improve the quality of decision-making. Fancoeuver et al., (2008) used 500 largest Canadian firms to compare financial performance when female representation was either high or low, and found that firms with a high proportion of women tended to outperform their counterparts by a significant margin, thus supporting the claims of stakeholder theory. The same study found that firms operating in complex environments and with a higher proportion of women generate positive monthly returns. This can be attributed to the possibility of women marshaling the goodwill of others in patronizing the company's products, as well as to the role of women in improving the reputation of the firm.

Thirdly, resource dependency theory postulates that an effective board should provide access to linkages and networks. Many scholars now believe that an increase in board diversity leads to better boards and governance, on the ground that diversity allows boards to tap into broader talent pools (Daily et al., 1999; Singh and Vinicombe, 2004). Letendre (2004) suggests that female board members bring diverse viewpoints to the boardroom and provoke lively discussions. Bilimoria and Wheeler (2000) suggest that on an average, a female board member is younger than her male counterparts and that the board therefore benefits from the infusion of new ideas and a new approach to deliberation.

In a study of a sample of 1000 publicly traded firms, Hillman et al., (2007) found that the extent to which a firm is linked to other firms with female directors is closely correlated with the level of female representation on the board. In an earlier study, Hillman et al., (2002) observed that female directors often join the boards they serve after attaining success in their professional careers, and that these directors bring a richness of experience and information to the boardroom.

Adams and Ferreira (2009) found that women directors are less likely to have problems attending meetings and that the overall attendance behavior of directors improves when more women are on the board. Attendance at board meetings is crucial in guiding and providing support for management, and hence in improving firm performance. In the same study, Adams and Ferreira (2009) found that male boardroom attendance improves when there are more women directors. Although the importance of attendance at meetings is not always obvious, it can be seen as a vital aspect of board activity and participation. It has also been found that women are more likely to question conventional wisdom and to speak up when an issue provokes concern (Huse and Solberg, 2006). Although gender diversity might result in disagreements, Latendre (2004) suggests that such disagreements are valuable to the board, as they enhance board dynamics and the effectiveness of decision making.

Research indicates that gender diversity brings both human and social capital to a firm. Human capital includes knowledge and skill bases. Social capital, on the other hand, is the sum of resources such as networks and linkages, which are embedded in social relationships (Burt, 1992). Burt (1997) argues that firms which have well developed links with individuals and organizations outside the firm are more able to innovate and enhance firm performance, as these external links provide decision makers with the opportunity to overcome decision bias and to improve decision quality (O'Reilly, 1983). Coincidentally, research has found that women's social networks tend to be more diverse, as the disadvantages they face along their career paths require them to maintain a wider network of contacts in order to remain competitive (Ibarra, 1992).

It has been argued, on the basis of signaling theory, that having gender diverse boards signals that firms are well positioned to address the needs of a diverse market (Miller and Triana, 2009). Women have a better understanding of consumer behavior, the needs of customers, and of how companies should meet customer needs (Kang et al., 2007). Similarly, research suggests that gender diverse boards can improve firm performance by enhancing reputation (Fombrun, 2004), and it has been found that women are inclined towards charitable giving and philanthropic activities (Wang and Covey, 1992; Stanwick and Stanwick, 1998; Brammer and Millington, 2005). William (2003) suggests that the increase in the number of women on boards has led to a greater degree of attention to socially responsibility business activities.

A study by Miller and Triana (2009) of *Fortune 500* firms in the US found a positive relation between board gender diversity and innovation. Furthermore, the results of this study supported the role of innovation as a mediator in the diversity-firm performance relationship. Consistent with these results, Zahra and Garvis (2000) found that innovation can lead to development of capabilities that enhance firm performance.

Women directors have been found to be effective in executing monitoring roles (Adams and Ferreira, 2009) because they are not part of the 'old boys network' and this allows them to be more independent (Kang et al., 2007). Westphal and Zajac (1995) argue that a demographic similarity between the board of directors and the CEO is associated with higher CEO compensation. This implies that gender diversity on the board acts as a control mechanism insofar as CEO compensation is concerned, resulting in better performance.

Several studies have empirically tested the effect of women directors on firm performance, and have identified a positive effect (Carter et al., 2003; Bathula, 2008). Other studies, such as Bonn's (2004), have identified a positive relationship between a higher ratio of women directors and firm performance, and Bilimoria and Piderit (1994) also examined the effect of women on board committees and identified the positive effects of greater numbers of women on firm performance. However, some studies failed to find any significant relationship between women directors and firm value (Ding and Charoenwong, 2004). Farrel and Hersch (2005) examined gender diversity and found that women board members have no influence on firm performance. They argued that firms include women only in order to build a public image and a reputation for inclusiveness and as a form of token affirmative action or stakeholder representation. In a study of Danish listed firms, conducted between 1998 and 2001, Rose (2007) found that gender diversity does not influence firm performance. One reason advanced to support these results was the possibility of socialization in the boardroom, such that unconventional board members adopt the behavior and norms of conventional board members. Another possible reason is that conformity might be the only way to qualify for re-election to the board. As a consequence, the gains which result from a greater number of female board members are never reflected in performance indicators.

These arguments notwithstanding, other scholars argue that gender diversity is characterized by a reduction in firm value (Tarus, 2011). For instance, Ruigrock et al., (2007) argue that the increased representation of women is not likely to influence the board because they are not members of the 'old boys network', and thus do not sit on executive committees charged with the formulation of strategic decisions, For example, women may not be elected to sit in investment committees. Adams and Ferreira (2009) observed that gender diversity may result in more disagreements and can ultimately fuel conflict. In support of this view, it is argued in Richard et al., (2004) that highly gendered boards encourage stronger identification with the opinions of directors of the same gender, resulting in more conflict. Burke (2000) argues that board members should be appointed to corporate boards on the basis of ability above all else, otherwise inclusion is likely to reduce firm performance. Another perspective is provided by Croson and Greezy (2009), who argue that women are averse to both risk and competition and that, as a consequence of this, their ability to enhance firm performance is curtailed.

Ethnic Diversity

Directors from the same ethnic group are expected to share the same values, beliefs, norms and work culture. The extant literature shows that differences in culture have an influence on business practices. For instance, Marimuthu (2008) studied the top 100 listed non-financial institutions in Malaysia between 2000 and 2005, and found that increased ethnic diversity on the board of directors leads to better financial performance. In the same vein, ethnically monolithic firms have been found to have poor corporate governance practices and greater agency problems (Eichenseher, 1995; CheAhmad and Houghton, 2001).

Diversity has been hailed as vital to corporate governance, especially in terms of board independence. When board members belong to the same ethnic group, there is a high likelihood of developing closer social ties and a greater tendency not to interrogate decisions. In particular, such groups may not hold other members of the group to account. According to Arndt et al., (2002), individuals whose membership of a group is based on ethnicity are likely to face difficulties abandoning the group or in making decisions which are contrary to the group's expectations. People in such groups feel vulnerable and tend to conform to group norms and practices. Consequently, a board of directors drawn from one ethnic group may jeopardize the board's vigilance functions and, at the very worst, the members of such boards may collude to pursue self-serving objectives and personal aggrandizement.

Directors from different social and cultural backgrounds are likely to introduce new perspectives, ideas and problem-solving skills into board discussions and, more importantly, are likely to check the actions of executives and other directors. Despite this, other scholars such as Carter et al., (2010) have found that there is no relation between ethnic diversity and financial performance on US boards. However, they do highlight the caveat that in the US, a board's ethnicity is somewhat unique, because the features that characterize ethnicity, such as language, religion, values and beliefs, are obscure.

Age Diversity

Research indicates that age is an important variable which influences behavior, beliefs, values and attitudes, as well as strategic orientation (Child, 1972; Taylor, 1975; Herrmann and Datta, 2005). In a research review, Hambrick and Mason (1984) hypothesized that age affects behavior relating to risk-seeking, novelty and information-seeking. Some studies argue that older decision-makers are more likely to be inflexible (Grim and Smith, 1991), risk-averse (Vroom and Pahl, 1971; Barker and Mueller, 2000) and conservative in their decision-making, thus hampering their ability to engage in strategies which will improve firm performance. Several reasons have been advanced to explain these findings. For example, Bantel and Jackson (1989) suggest that older decision-makers have difficulties grasping new ideas and learning new behaviors, and have a narrower and more limited knowledge base (Grimm and Smith, 1991). They argue that this affects the ability of older decision-makers to seek new opportunities. Wiersema and Bantel (1992) associate older decision-makers with concerns about financial security and thus risk-taking is considered as a threat to personal security.

On the other hand, younger decision makers are associated with greater mental energy and stamina, novelty, risk-seeking behavior and the promotion of strategic change (Hamrick and Mason, 1984; Wiersema and Bantel, 1992). Child (1972) argues that younger decision-makers expend more physical and mental energy on promoting strategic change and the growth of the firm. He claims that the reason for this is that younger decision-makers are more likely to have been educated recently, and will therefore be more familiar with decision-making and its relation to firm performance (Bantel and Jackson, 1992).

Although studies have focused mainly on young and old executives, it is likely that a board of directors composed of both young and old members is the most likely to facilitate the proper monitoring of executives and to provide meaningful strategic guidance, which may help in enhancing firm performance. Age diversity encourages a wide variety of perspectives on strategic issues, because whilst older board members provide experience and wisdom, younger members bring energy, drive and new information. In other words, older directors bring greater stability and experiential wisdom to the process of deliberation and younger directors bring greater energy and drive to new ventures.

Although it is not unusual to find boards composed of people ranging solely from the middle-aged to those close to retirement, this situation is slowly changing with the increasing demand for the inclusion of younger board members. In effect, age diversity in the boardroom is being actively promoted in the belief that this will encourage boards to reflect the perspectives of people of different ages and to contribute positively to succession planning. The existing literature suggests that while older board members provide experience, wisdom and economic power, younger board members have the energy, the mental stamina and the drive to seek new information and to innovate.

Consistent with stakeholder theory, age diversity helps to ensure that different types of stakeholder are taken care of. For example, companies in the consumer industry may target consumers in different age groups, and the best way to meet the needs of each age group is to have directors who represent diverse age groups and different perspectives (Huse and Rindova, 2001; Kang et al., 2007). Similarly, and consistent with resource dependence theory, Siciliano (1996) used data from 240 YMCA organizations and found that diversity in the age ranges and groupings of board members was linked to higher donation levels.

Tenure Diversity

The ability of directors to engage meaningfully in decision-making and deliberation is not only affected by prior experience, but also by the time spent serving as a director on the same board. Prior boardroom experience provides directors with an understanding of group dynamics and corporate culture, and also with the ability to maintain external networks. Furthermore, long tenure acts as a gauge of a director's reputation in the directorial labor market. Some researchers have advanced the argument that tenure in organizations affects cognitive ability (Hambrick and Mason, 1984; Boeker, 1997).

There are two schools of thought as regards tenure and organizational outcomes. One school believes that long tenure among executives and other decision-makers has a positive influence on firm outcomes. Some reasons advanced in support of this perspective are that long tenure nurtures social cohesion (Michael and Hambrick (1992) and that it reinforces common views, commitments and shared perceptions (Katz, 1982), as well as providing stability and a greater commitment to established routines and policies. It has also been found that long tenure is necessary for firms operating in complex and uncertain environments, because the boardroom team can make reliable predictions concerning the environment as well as reliably assessing the capabilities of the firm (Tihanyi et al., 2000)

However, critics of this school of thought argue that long tenure breeds commitment to the *status quo* (Hambrick et al., 1993), that it affects the ability to process information and that it promotes the tendency to rely on past experiences (Finkelstein and Hambrick, 1990). It is also argued that long tenure promotes risk averseness (Kor, 2006) and inhibits the willingness to make strategic changes (Thomas et al., 1991). Further, it is also believed that as a result of entrenchment, long tenure compromises the board's ability to monitor management (Johnson et al., 1996) because, over time, group members develop 'group think'—a term commonly used to refer to a defensive avoidance of decision-making (Keck, 1997). The 'groupthink' culture may cause board members to succumb to inertia and diminish management vigilance. It may also lead to group members being unwilling to criticize each other's ideas.

The second school believes that short tenure yields positive firm outcomes. For example, Wiersema and Bantel (1992) found that short tenure correlates positively with strategic change. Similarly, board directors who are relatively new to the firm are affiliated to new products and processes (Kor, 2006). Murray (1989) also noted that group members who have been together for relatively short periods of time may explore more strategic alternatives because of the weaker levels of socialization among within the group. Keck (1997) observed that shorter tenure leads to better performance in turbulent environments. Short tenure has also been hailed for enhancing board independence and vigilance (Anderson et al., 2004), which is considered by agency theorists as critical to the survival of the firm (Jensen and Meckling, 1976; Fama and Jensen, 1983).

Although most of the literature on tenure focuses on CEOs and top management, there is reason to believe that board tenure affects the quality of decisions made by the board and, more importantly, that it influences board vigilance. The two streams of research on short versus long tenure have not reached a consensus, and each school criticizes the other. However, there is no doubt that there are strengths and weaknesses on both sides of the debate. It is therefore critical to achieve a balance, such that boards are composed of members of both long and short tenure. In support of this view, Hambrick et al., (1993) argues that boards composed of members of both long and short tenure are more inclined to make strategic changes. Similarly, Kosnik (1990) maintains that a heterogeneous distribution of board tenure is vital for monitoring and executing the strategic functions of the firm.

Drawing upon research in both agency theory and resource dependency theory, it can be seen that diverse boards enhance vigilance, and as a result reduce agency related costs and enhance firm value. In the same vein, diverse board tenure brings different perspectives and resources to the firm: for instance, long tenure brings in experience related resources that are more relevant during periods of environmental uncertainty, while short tenure is more valuable in providing strategic dynamism. Therefore, firms that utilize diverse boards are more likely to benefit from diversity related resources, thus enhancing firm value.

Educational level Diversity

Drawing upon upper echelons theory, Hambrick and Mason (1984) postulated that educational level is a measure of an individual's knowledge, skill base and cognitive skills. Similarly, social scientists have suggested that different educational levels are associated with varied social status, networking and professional development paths (Useem and Karabel, 1986). Evidence from earlier studies interrogating the role of education has established a link between education and innovation levels (Kimberly and Evansiko, 1981; Liebeskind, 1996).

Extending these studies, researchers have subsequently linked increased levels of education with superior information processing capabilities (Hambrick and Mason, 1984; Herrmann and Datta, 2005), greater tolerance of ambiguity (Bantel and Jackson, 1989), the propensity to identify and evaluate new opportunities and alternatives, and greater strategic dynamism (Wiersema and Bantel, 1992). Research has failed to associate higher levels of education with maintaining the *status quo*, but has established a link between education levels and the pursuit of differentiation strategies (Thomas et al., 1991). Bantel and Jackson (1989) found decision-makers with higher levels of education to be more receptive to novel ideas and hence to be more innovative.

There is reason to believe that the level of diversity in education is an important variable in firm performance. For example, Bantel and Jackson (1989) suggest that educational diversity in top management teams enhances creativity and innovation, as a result of the diverse human capital in such teams. In other words, the knowledge embodied in a firm's human capital can lead to a competitive advantage by increasing the likelihood of identifying opportunities for innovation, leading to superior performance.

It is arguable that diverse educational levels provide directors with different perspectives and cognitive paradigms which affect social contacts, the assimilation of information and the capacity for good decision-making. Most studies measuring diversity in educational level have classified directors or team members into categories. For example, Hambrick et al., (1996) and Pegels et al., (2000) distinguish the following five categories: no college degree, college degree (e.g. Diploma), Bachelor's degree, Master's degree and PhD. Thereafter, a Herfindahl Index (Blau, 1977) is used to determine diversity. Using this measurement, scholars have established a significant relationship between educational level and diversity and innovation (Bantel and Jackson, 1989), strategic change (Tarus, 2011) and firm performance. Boards with diverse educational levels are better equipped to enhance the quality of decision making by bringing in different perspectives.

Functional Background Diversity

The question of functional background and its effect on decision-making has received extensive attention in management research. Scholars have tried to discover whether decision-makers exhibit biases in decision making which reflect their functional specializations (Thomas et al., 1991; Barker and Mueller, 2002). Research on top management has shown that executives with accumulated knowledge in a particular functional area develop unique skills relevant to those disciplines which are of strategic value to the firm (Geletkanycz and Black, 2001; Hambrick and Mason, 1984). Functional background has been reported to have an influence on how problems are defined, how information is processed and the nature of the strategic choices adopted (Hitt and Tyler, 1991).

In a study of three tobacco companies from 1950 to 1975, Chaganti and Sambharya (1987) found that functional background has an effect on the individual definition of problems and the formulation of courses of action. These results are consistent with the earlier works of Dearbon and Simon (1958), who observed that decision-makers with differing functional backgrounds differ in attitudes, knowledge and perspectives, and that different strategic choices are made as a consequence. Many studies contend that functional background is manifested in strategic posture: for example, decision makers with a career bias in production and marketing pursue internal development, those in finance, accounting and law pursue acquisition strategies (Song, 1982) and science specialists undertake strategic change (Wiersema and Bantel, 1992).

Although most studies on functional specialization have focused on CEOs and top management, the members of boards of directors also have functional backgrounds which may influence their ability to provide guidance to executives. Boards with more members drawn from a particular discipline are more likely to think and act in a way that is typical of that functional area. Datta and Rajagopalan (1998: 836) observed that "the more specialized the knowledge base, the greater the likelihood that the individual will view problem situations from a narrow, specialized perspective and make choices within their specialized knowledge, while the broader the knowledge base, the wider the range of options likely to be explored". Selecting directors with different characteristics, such as financial industry experience, can help firms connect with investors. Similarly, directors with legal backgrounds are better able to monitor management and to advise the firm on legal issues. Directors with a background in finance and accounting can monitor management by participating in critical monitoring units such as audit committees. In summary, boards composed of directors from diversified functional backgrounds add value to the firm by enhancing monitoring, by supplying a pool of knowledge and skills and, more importantly, by connecting the firm to varied external links.

Business Case or Rhetoric?

A strong board can play an important role in firm performance. I argue that the benefits of board diversity arise from the varied perspectives and talents that group members bring to the boardroom. More specifically, board diversity brings a variety of backgrounds, experiences, skills and talents to the boardroom. According to van de Walt and Ingley (2003), the case for board diversity can be made on a number of grounds:

- ***Theoretical Perspectives:*** There are two main theories in corporate governance that underlie the rationale for board diversity. The first is agency theory, which argues that diversity in the boardroom has the potential to increase managerial control. According to Jensen (1986), managers can expropriate a firm's resources by using corporate assets to their advantage, thus entrenching themselves to the detriment of shareholders. This act of misappropriation may be perpetuated through high levels of executive pay, excessive perquisites, or even investing in less valuable projects. To curb these value reducing actions, managerial safeguards are necessary in the form of a diverse board. Studies support the view that a diversified board curtails board and management entrenchment. A good case in point is the fact that women are known to be good monitors, so their inclusion in the board reduces the social ties inherent in a homogeneous board.

The second theoretical argument is the resource dependency theory, which can be posited in favor of diverse boards. According to this view, diverse boards provide a link between the firm and its external environment, secure critical resources (Hillman et al., 2002) and provide strategic direction (Kemp, 2006). This is a reasonable argument, given the fact that board members drawn from diverse backgrounds are more likely to bring networks and experiences to the boardroom and to improve firm performance as a result. For example, directors drawn from the finance industry are likely to share their experiences and opportunities in financing the firm, while those in the legal sector can provide legal advisory resources in the boardroom. Therefore, firms with directors drawn from diverse backgrounds are more able to make decisions that enhance the value of the firm.

Diverse boards also increase skill complementarities and the experiences of directors, thereby strengthening the boards' capacity to give expert advice, especially in a strategic advisory role. In particular, firms operating in competitive and dynamic environments arguably benefit from the perspectives of diverse boards (Klein, 1998). For example, directors drawn from the information technology industry are more able to guide the firm in responding to competitive pressure, while those from non-competitive sectors help the firm to maintain much needed stability.

• ***The Moral Perspective:*** According to this view, it is moral for the board to represent diversity within the ownership structure of the firm. According to Carver (2000), the only way owners can find a way to govern the firm is by constituting a board that represents their interests.

• ***Philanthropic Perspective:*** The constitution of the board should be seen to be socially responsible. It should not be seen to discriminate against any particular constituency, and the board should reflect the face of the organization's stakeholders (Keasey et al., 1997).

• ***Commercial Perspective:*** There is an abundant literature on the business case for diversity. For example, it is argued that increasing diversity in the boardroom provides a rich source of innovative ideas and practical resources for dealing with difficult business issues (van der Walt and Ingley, 2003). Westphal and Milton (2000) also support this case, arguing that diversity brings together people with different backgrounds and that this wide-ranging expertise can make a valuable contribution to board decisions, by providing unique strategic perspectives. Directors with diverse demographic features such as experiences, backgrounds and skills are more likely to raise questions rather than simply to echo the sentiments of the management (Selby, 2001). In particular, increasing the number of women on the board enriches board information, broadens perspectives and bolsters debate, thereby improving the quality of the decisions made (Burke, 2000).

Conclusion

This chapter has presented different theoretical perspectives that underlie diversity in the boardroom. Although some commentators still advocate homogeneity, the recent literature underscores the importance of diversity in improving the quality of boardroom decisions. As mentioned above, boards provide a platform for effective vigilance and thereby mitigate the reduction in firm value occasioned by poor executive decisions or managerial enrichment. Nevertheless, there are costs or bottlenecks associated with diversity. For example, diversity increases problems of communication and coordination among group members. In particular, bringing diverse perspectives to board deliberations may enhance conflict and slow down decision-making. In sum, the benefits of board diversity outweigh the costs, and demographically diversified boards provide an avenue for value enhancement.

References

Adams, R. B., and Ferreira, D. (2009). Women in the Boardroom and their Impact on Governance and Performance. *Journal of Financial Economics,* 94, 291-309.

Anderson, R. C., Mansi, S. A., and Reeb, D. M. (2004). Board Characteristics, Accounting Report Integrity, and the Cost of Debt. *Journal of Accounting and Economics*, 37, 315-342.

Arndt, J., Greenberg, J., Schimel, J., Pyszczynski, T., and Solomon, S. (2002). To Belong or Not to Belong? That is the Question: Terror

Management and Identification with Gender and Ethnicity. *Journal of Personality and Social Psychology*, 83 (1), 26-43.

Bantel, K., and Jackson, S. (1989). Top Management and Innovations in Banking: Does the Composition of the Top Team make a Difference? *Strategic Management Journal*, Summer Special Issue, 10, 107-124.

Barker, V. L., and Mueller, G. C. (2002). CEO Characteristics and Firm R&D Spending. *Management Science,* 48 (6), 782-801.

Bart, C., and Bontis, N. (2003). Distinguishing between the Board and Management in the Company Mission: Implications for Corporate Governance. *Journal of Intellectual Capital,* 4 (3), 361-381.

Bathula, H. (2008). Board Characteristics and Firm Performance: Evidence from New Zealand. Unpublished PhD Thesis, Auckland University of Technology, New Zealand.

Blau, P. M. (1977). *Inequality and Composition: A Primitive Theory of Social structure*. New York: Free Press.

Bilimoria, D., & Piderit, S. K. (1994). Qualifications of Corporate Board Committee Members. *Group & Organization Management,* 19 (3), 334–362.

Boeker, W. (1997). Strategic Change: The Influence of Managerial Characteristics and Organizational Growth. *Academy of Management Journal,* 40 (1), 152-170.

Boyd, B. K., Haynes, K. T., and Zona, F. (2011). Dimensions of CEO-Board Relations. *Journal of Management Studies,* 48 (8), 1892-1923.

Brammer, S. and Millington, A. (2005). Corporate Reputation and Philanthropy: An Empirical Analysis. *Journal of Business Ethics,* 61, 29-44.

Bilimoria, D., & Wheeler, J. V. (2000). Women Corporate Directors: Current Research and Future Directions. In M. J. Davidson and R. J. Burke, (ed.). *Women in Management: Current Research Issues,* Vol. II, 138 – 163. London: Sage Publications.

Burke, R. J. (2000). Company Size, Board Size and numbers of Women Corporate directors. In R. J. Burke and M. C. Mattis (ed.) *Women in Management: International Challenges and Opportunities,* 239-251. Dordrecht: Kluwer Academic.

Burt, R. S. (1992). *Structural Holes. The Social Structure of Competition.* Cambridge, MA: Harvard University Press.

—. (1997).The Contingent Value of Social Capital. *Administrative Science Quarterly*, 42, 339-365.

Buyl, T., Boone, C., Hendricks, W., and Matthyssens, P. (2011). Top Management Team Functional Diversity and Firm Performance: The

Moderating Role of CEO Characteristics. *Journal of Management Studies*, 48 (1), 151-177.
Carpenter, M. A., and Westphal, J. D. (2001). The Strategic Context of External Network Ties: Examining the Impact of Director Appointments on Board Involvement in Strategic decision making. *Academy of Management*, 44 (4), 639-660.
Carter, D. A., Simkins, B. J. and Simpson, W. G. (2003). Corporate Governance, Board Diversity, and Firm Value. *The Financial Review*, 38, 33-53.
Carter, D. A., D'Souza, F., Simkins, B. J., and Simpson, W. G. (2010). The Gender and Ethnic Diversity of US Boards and Board Committees and Financial Performance. *Corporate Governance: An International Review*, 8 (5), 396-414.
Carver, J. (2000). *On Board leadership*. New York: Jossey-Bass, John Wiley.
Chaganti, R. and Sambharya, R. (1987). Strategic Orientation and Characteristics of Upper Management. *Strategic Management Journal*, 8 (4), 393-401.
Certo, S. T. (2003). Influencing Initial Public Offering Investors with Prestige: Signaling with Board Structures. *Academy of Management Review*, 28, 432-446.
CheAhmad, A. and Houghton, K. A. (2001). The effect of Ethnicity on Audit Pricing", A Working Paper, Universiti Utara Malaysia, Malaysia and University of Melbourne, Australia.
Child, J. (1972). Managerial and Organizational Factors Associated with Company Performance. *Journal of Management Studies,* 11 (3), 175-189.
Croson, R., and Greezy, U. (2009). Gender Differences in Preference. *Journal of Economic Literature*, 47 (2), 448-474.
Daily, C. M., Certo, S. T., and Dalton, D. R. (1999). A Decade of Corporate Women: Some Progress in the Boardroom, None in the Executive Suite: The Path to Prosperity? *Strategic Management Journal*, 20, 93-99.
Datta, D. K., and Rajagopalan, N. (1998). Industry Structure and CEO Characteristics: An Empirical Study of Succession Events. *Strategic Management Journal,* 19, 833-852.
Dearbon, D. C., and Simon, H. A. (1958). Selective Perception: A Note on the Departmental Identifications of Executives. *Sociometry*, 21 (2), 140-144.
Demb, A., and Naubauer, F. (1992). *The Corporate Board*. New York: Oxford University Press.

Deutsch, Y. (2005). The Impact of Board Composition on Firms' critical Decisions: A Meta-analytic Review. *Journal of Management*, 31, 424-444.

Ding, D. K., and Charoenwong, C., (2004). Women on Board: Is It Boon or Bane? *Research Collection Lee Kong Chian School of Business (Open Access).* Paper 737.

Donaldson, T., and Preston, L. E. (1995). The Stakeholder Theory of the Corporation: Concepts, Evidence, and Implications. *The Academy of Management Review,* 20, (1), 65-91.

Eichenseher, J. W. (1995). Additional Factors in Audit Pricing: New Evidence from Malaysia, *Accounting & Business Review*, 2 (1), 1-26.

Fama, E. F. (1980). Agency Problems and the Theory of the Firm. *Journal of Political Economy,* 88 (2), 288-307.

Fama, E. F., and Jensen, M. C. (1983). Separation of Ownership and Control. *Journal of Law and Economics,* 26 (2), 301-325.

Farrel, K. A., and Hersch, P. L. (2005). Additions to Corporate Boards: The Effect of Gender, *Journal of Corporate Finance,* 11, 85-106.

Finkelstein, S., and Hambrick, D. C. (1990). Top- Management- Team Tenure and Organizational Outcomes: the Moderating Role of Managerial Discretion. *Administrative Science Quarterly*, 35 (3), 484-503.

Formbrun, C. (2004). Corporate Reputation as Economic Assets. In Hitt, M. A., Freeman, R. E. and Harrison, J. S. (Eds), *Handbook of Strategic Management*. Oxford: Blackwell, 289-312.

Francoeur, C., Labelle, R., Sinclair-Degagne, B. (2008). Gender Diversity in Corporate Governance and Top Management. *Journal of Business Ethics,* 81, 83-95.

Geletkanycz, M. A., and Black, S. S. (2001). Bound by the Past? Experience- based Effects on Commitment to the Strategic Status Quo. *Journal of Management*, 27, 3-21.

Grim, C. M., and Smith, K. G. (1991). Management and Organizational Change: A Note on the Railroad Industry. *Strategic Management Journal,* 12 (7), 557-562.

Hambrick, D. C. (2007). Upper Echelons Theory: An Update. *Academy of Management Review,* 32 (2), 334-343.

Hambrick, D. C., Geletkanycz, M. A., and Fredrickson, J. W. (1993). Top Executive Commitment to the Status Quo: Some Tests of its determinants. *Strategic Management Journal,* 14 (6), 401-418.

Hambrick, D. C., and Mason, P. A. (1984). Upper Echelons: The Organization as a Reflection of Its Top Managers. *Academy of Management Review*, 9 (2), 193-206.

Hendry, K., and Kiel, G. C. (2004). The Role of the Board in Firm Strategy: Integrating Agency and Organizational Control Perspectives. *Corporate Governance: An International Review,* 12 (4), 500-520.

Henke, J. (1983). Involving Boards of Directors in Strategic Planning. *Journal of Business Strategy*, 7, 447-460.

Hermalin, B. E., and Weisbach, M. S. (1998). Endogenously Chosen Boards of Directors and Their Monitoring of the CEO. *American Economic Review,* 88 (1), 96–118.

Herrmann, P., and Datta, D. K. (2005). Relationship between Top management Team Characteristics and International Diversification: An Empirical Investigation, *British Journal of Management*, 16, 69-78.

Hillman, A. J., Cannella, A. A. Jr., and Harris, I. C. (2002). Women and Racial Minorities in the Boardroom: How Do Directors Differ? *Journal of Management*, 28, 747-763.

Hillman, A. J., & Dalziel, T. (2003). Boards of Directors and Firm Performance: Integrating Agency and Resource Dependency Perspectives. *Academy of Management Review,* 28 (3), 383–396.

Hillman, A. J., Shropshire, C., and Cannela, A. A. (2007). Organizational Predictors of Women on Corporate Boards. *Academy of Management Journal,* 50 (4), 941-952.

Hitt, M. A., and Tyler, B. B. (1991). Strategic Decision Models: Integrating different Perspectives. *Strategic Management Journal,* 12 (5), 327-351.

Huse, M., Rindova, V. P. (2001). Stakeholders' Expectations of Board Roles: The Case of Subsidiary Boards, *Journal of Management and Governance*, 5, 153-178.

Huse, M., and Solberg, A. G (2006). Gender-related Boardroom Dynamics. How Scandinavian Women make and can make Contributions on Corporate Boards. *Women in Management Review,* 21 (2), 113-130.

Ibarra, H. (1992). Homophily and Differential Returns: Sex Differences in Network Structure and Access in Advertising Firm, *Administrative Science Quarterly*, 37, 422-447.

Ingely, C. B., and van der Walt, N. T. (2001). The Strategic Board: The changing role of Directors in developing and maintaining Corporate Capability, *Corporate Governance*: *An International Review,* 9 (3), 174-185.

Jensen, M. C. (1986). Agency Cost of Free Cash Flow, Corporate Finance, and Takeovers, *American Economic Review,* 76 (2), 323-329.

Jensen, M. C., and Meckling, W. H. (1976). Theory of the Firm: Managerial Behavior, Agency Costs and Ownership Structure. *Journal of Financial Economics*, 3, 305-360.

Jensen, M., and Zajac, E. J. (2004). Corporate Elites and Corporate Strategy: How Demographic Preferences and Structural Position Shape the Scope of the Firm. *Strategic Management Journal*, 25, 507-524.

Johnson, J. L., Daily, C. M., and Ellstrand, A. E. (1996). Boards of Directors: A Review and Research Agenda. *Journal of Management,* 22 (3), 409-438.

Kang, H., Cheng, M., and Gray, S. J. (2007). Corporate Governance and Board Composition: Diversity and Independence of Australian Boards, *Corporate Governance: An International Review*, 15 (2), 194-207.

Katz, R. (1982). The Effects of Group Longevity on Project Communication and Performance. *Administrative Science Quarterly*. 27 (1), 81-104.

Keasey, K., Thompson, S., and Wright, M. (1997). *Corporate Governance: Economic, Management, and Financial Issues.* Oxford: Oxford University Press.

Keck, S. l. (1997). Top Management Team Structure: Differential Effects by Environmental Context. *Organization Science,* 8 (2), 143-156.

Kemp, S. (2006). In the Driver's Seat or Rubber stamp? The Role of the Board in providing Strategic Guidance in Australian Boardrooms. *Management Decision*, 44 (1), 56-73.

Kimberly, J. R., and Evanisko, M. J. (1981). Organizational Innovation: The Influence of Individual, Organizational, and Contextual Factors on Hospital Adoption of Technological and Administrative Innovations. *Academy of Management Journal*, 24 (4), 689-713.

Klein, A. (1998). Firm Performance and Board Committee Structure. *Journal of Law and Economics,* 41(1), 275–303.

Knippenberg, D., De Dreu, C. and Homan, A. (2004). Work Group Diversity and Group Performance: An Integrative Model and Research Agenda, *Journal of Applied Psychology*, 89, 1008-1022.

Konrad, A. M., Kramer, V., and Erkut, S. (2008). Critical Mass: The Impact of Three Women or More Women on Corporate Boards. *Organization Dynamics,* 37 (2), 145-164.

Kor, Y. Y., and Misangyi, V. F. (2008). Outside Directors' Industry-Specific Experience and Firms' Liability of Newness. *Strategic Management Journal*, 29, 1345-1355.

Kosnick, R. (1990). Effects of Board Demography and Directors' Incentives on Corporate Greenmail Decisions. *Academy of Management Journal.* 33 (1), 129-150.

Letendre, L. (2004). The Dynamics of the Boardroom. *Academy of Management Executive,* 18 (1), 101–104.

Liebeskind, J. P. (1996). Knowledge, Strategy, and the Theory of the Firm. *Strategic Management Journal,* 17, 93-107.

Lorsch, J., and Young, J. (1990). Pawns or Potentates: the Reality of America's Corporate Boards. *Academy of Management*, 4 (4), 85-87.

Marimuthu, M. (2008). Ethnic Diversity of Boards of Directors and Its Implications on Firm Performance. *The Journal of International Social Research*, 1, 431-445.

Michael, J. G., and Hambrick, D. C. (1992). Diversification Posture and Top Management Team Characteristics. *Academy of Management Journal*, 35, 9-37.

Miller, Y. and Triana, M. C. (2009). Demographic Diversity in the Boardroom: Mediators of the Boardroom Diversity-Performance Relationship. *Journal of Management*, 46, 756-786.

Milliken, F. J., and Martins, L. L. (1996). Searching for Common Threads: Understanding the Multiple Effects of Diversity in Organizational Groups. *Academy of Management Review*, 12 (2), 402-433.

Milliken, F. J., and Vollrath, D. (1991). Strategic Decision-making Tasks and Group Effectiveness: insights from Theory and Research from Small Groups. *Human Relations,* 44, 1229-1253.

Mizruchi, M. S. (1983). Who controls Whom? An Examination of the relation between Management and Boards of Directors in Large American Corporations. *Academy of Management Review*, 8, 426-435.

Murray, A. I. (1989). Top Management Group Heterogeneity and Firm Performance. *Strategic Management Journal,* 10, 125-141.

Lau, D. C., and Murnighan, J. K. (1998). Demographic Diversity and Faultlines: The Compositional Dynamics of Organizational Groups. *Academy of Management Review*, Vol. 23 (2), 325-340.

Linck, J. S., Netter, J. M., and Yang, T. (2008). The Determinants of the Board of Structure. *Journal of Financial Economics,* 87, 308-328.

O'Reilly, C. A. (1983). The Use of Information Decision making: A Model and some Propositions. *Research in Organizational Behavior*, 5, 103-140.

O'Reilly, C. A., Caldwell, D. F., and Barnett, W. P. (1989). Work Group Demography, Social Integration, and Turnover. *Administrative Science Quarterly*, 34, 22-37.

Pegels, C. C., Song, Y. I., and Yang, B. (2000). Management Heterogeneity, Competitive Interaction Groups, and Firm Performance. *Strategic Management Journal*, 21 (9), 11-923.

Pfeffer, J., and Salancik, G. R. (1978), The *External Control of Organizations: A Resource Dependence perspective.* New York: Harper & Row.

Richard, O. C., Barnett, T., Dwyer, S., and Chadwick, K. (2004). Cultural Diversity in Management, Firm Performance, and the Moderating Role of Entrepreneurial Orientation Dimensions. *The Academy of Management Journal,* 47, 255-266.

Ripley, A. (2003), Equal Time, *Time Europe,* 162 (11) www.time.com/time/europe/magazine.

Rindova, V. P. (1999). What Corporate boards have to do with Strategy: A Cognitive Perspective. *Journal of Management studies,* 36 (7), 954-975.

Robinson, G., & Dechant, K. (1997), Building a Business Case for Diversity. *Academy of Management Executive,* 11(3), 21-31.

Rose, C. (2007). Does Female Board Representation influence Firm Performance, *Corporate Governance: An International Review*, 15 (2), 404-413.

Ruigrok, W., Peck, S. I., and Keller, H. (2006). Board Characteristics and Involvement in Strategic Decision Making: Evidence from Swiss Companies. *Journal Management Studies,* 43 (5), 1201-1226.

Selby, C. C. (2000). From Male Locker room to co-ed boardroom: A Twenty Five year Perspective. In R. J. Burke and M. C. Mattis (eds) *Women in Management: International Challenges and Opportunities,* 239-251. Dordrecht: Kluwer Academic.

Siciliano, J. I. (1996). The Relationship of Board Member Diversity to Organizational performance, *Journal of Business Ethics*, 15 (12), 1313-1320.

Simons, T., Pelled, L. H., Smith, K. A. (1999). Making use of difference: Diversity debate and Decision comprehensiveness in Top Management Teams, *Academy of Management Journal*, 42, 662-673.

Singh, V., and Vinnicombe, S. (2004). Why So Few women Directors in Top UK Boardrooms? Evidence and Theoretical Explanations. *Corporate Governance: An International Review,* 12 (4), 479-488.

Song, J. H. (1982). Diversification Strategies and the Experience of Top Executives of Large Firms. *Strategic Management Journal,* 3 (4), 377-380.

Stanwick, B. M., and Stanwick, S. D. (1998). The Determinants of Corporate Social Performance: An Empirical Examination, *American Business Review*, 16, 86-93.

Stiles, P. (2001). The Impact of the Board on Strategy: An Empirical Examination, *Journal of Management Studies,* 38 (5), 627-650.

Tarus, D. K. (2011). Boards Demographic Characteristics and Strategic Change in Kenya. Unpublished PhD Thesis, Moi University.

Taylor, R. A. (1975). Age and Experience as Determinants of Managerial Information Processing and Decision Making Performance. *The Academy of Management Journal,* 18 (1), 74-81.

Terjesen, S., Sealy, R., and Singh, V. (2009). Women Directors on Corporate Boards: Review and Research Agenda. *Corporate Governance: An International Review,* 17 (3), 320-337.

Thomas, A. S., Litschert, R. J. and Ramaswamy, K. (1991). The Performance Impact of Strategy-Manager Co alignment: An Empirical Examination, *Strategic Management Journal*, 12 (7), 509-522.

Tihanyi, L., Ellestrand, A. E., Daily, C. M., and Dalton, D. R. (2000). Composition of Top Management Teams and Firm International Diversification, *Journal of Management*, 26, (6), 1157-1177.

Useem, M. J., and Karabel, J. (1986). Pathways to Top Management, *American Sociological Review,* 51, 184-200.

van der Walt, N., and Ingely, C. (2003). Board Dynamics and the Influence of Professional Background, Gender and Ethnic Diversity of Directors, *Corporate Governance: An OInternational Review*, 11 (3), 218-233.

Vroom, V., and Pahl, B. (1971). Relationship between Age and Risk-taking among Managers, *Journal of Applied Psychology,* 55, 399-405.

Wang, J. and Coffey, B. S. (1992). Board Composition and Corporate Philanthropy, *Journal of Business Ethics*, 11, 771-778.

Westphal, J. D., and Fredrickson, J. W. (2001). Who directs Strategic Change? Directors Experience, the Selection of New CEOs, and Change in Corporate Strategy. *Strategic Management Journal,* 22, 1113-1137.

Westphal, J. D., and Milton, L. P. (2000). How Experience and Network Ties affect the Influence of Demographic Minorities on Corporate Boards, *Administrative Science Quartely*, 45, 366-398.

Westphal, J. D., and Zajac, E. J. (1995), Who Shall Govern? CEO/Board Power, Demographic Similarity, and New Director Selection, *Administrative Science Quarterly*, 40 (1), 60-83.

Wiersema, M. F., and Bantel, K. A. (1992). Top Management Team Demography and Corporate Strategic Change. *Academy of Management Journal,* 35, 91-121.

William, R. J. (2003), Women on Corporate Boards of Directors and their Influence on Corporate Philanthropy, *Journal of Business Ethics*, 42, 1-10.

Zahra, S. A. and Garvis, D. M. (2000). International Corporate Entrepreneurship and Firm Performance: The Moderating effect of International Environmental Hostility, *Journal of Business Venturing,* 15, 469-492.

Zahra, S. A., and Pearce, J. A. (1990). Determinants of Board of Directors' Strategic Involvement. EMJ, 8, (2), 164-173.

Zelechowski, D. D., and Bilimoria, D. (2004). Characteristics of Women and Men Corporate Directors in the US, *Corporate Governance: An International Review,* 12 (3), 337-342.

CHAPTER SEVEN

HUMAN RESOURCE INTANGIBLE ASSETS CONNECTED TO THE ORGANIZATIONAL PERFORMANCE AND PRODUCTIVITY

MARKO KESTI AND ANTTI SYVÄJÄRVI
UNIVERSITY OF LAPLAND

Abstract

Human resource management is one of the most important factors affecting the productivity of organizations, as indicated in a healthcare sector study (Pynes and Lombardi, 2011). In many organizations, operative business capacity results from effective working time. Several action research projects and case studies have indicated that organizational development tends to improve employee competencies. If organizational development has been implemented efficiently, effective working time may increase, which in turn contributes to an increase in human capital productivity. The phenomenon of human capital deepening is essential to effective human resource management. In addition, improvement in an organization's human competences seems to correlate with growth in revenue. In this chapter, these findings are explained with theoretically consistent calculations, and hence it is shown that it is likely that improving competencies leads to better organizational performance. The current study indicates the need for proper human capital and resource data in order to gain advances in corresponding management and development.

Keywords: *Human capital, Tacit knowledge, HCROI, HRM-P, Organization development.*

Introduction

Concern about human resource intangible assets is based on the view that to be effective, productive, and adaptable to rapid change, organizations need realistic information on the competencies, capabilities and talents of their people — in essence, on their human resources. The role of human resources in an organization cannot be understated. Given that human resources are the prime agents, understanding the character of human resources presents challenges for and demands upon the field of organizational performance or productivity (Boxall, 1996). Sustainable development and advantage is typically achieved when an organization's human resource activity is related to its own performance goals. This chapter develops a plausible explanation of the link between human resource intangible assets development, and organizational performance and productivity.

Human capital is concerned with the added value that people provide to organizations. Human capital is one of the key differentiating factors for organizations, and one of the actual bases for organizational performance and productivity. The knowledge, competence and enthusiasm of workers generate a stock of productive capital (Baron and Armstrong, 2007). Thus, human capital can be seen as a people-based factor, which consists of the stocks and flows of knowledge and competences available to an organization. Human capital concerns knowledge, skills, abilities, capacities and the overall competence to develop and produce which the people within an organization possess. These can be regarded as intangible assets which, together with tangible resources (i.e., physical assets), comprise almost the total value of an organization.

In addition, the added value that people contribute to an organization is human capital based, and is thus closely linked to strategic human resource management (SHRM). In this chapter, it is assumed that human capital management is one aspect of human resource management (HRM). This means that human resources are seen both as subjective assets and as rational costs in the context of organizational surroundings. It is important to see both the soft and hard sides of HRM. The latter approach takes human resources to be closely linked to organizational strategy (e.g., business strategy), which regards humans as an instrumental resource, to be managed in the same way as any other resource, in order to generate maximum return (Stone, 2002). The former approach emphasizes that humans are also to be seen and respected as subjects (Syväjärvi and Kesti, 2012).

The fields of intangible assets and strategic human resource management (considered both individually and as a whole) present us with opportunities and challenges, in terms of organizational productivity. In seeking to explain the value of intangible assets, there is a growing demand for better understanding and more information. A considerable number of organizations are beginning to understand that in an increasingly knowledge-intensive and competitive environment, the key to good performance and productivity lies in the human resource management. Guest (1987) has argued that one of the key policy goals of human resource management is the strategic integration of HRM issues within broader organizational settings. Human resource management is an issue which is simply too important to be disregarded or to be given relatively little attention. Hence, by studying the utilization of human capital in healthcare organizations, the present chapter highlights the importance of strategic human resource management. The chapter introduces some thematic findings and offers a plausible theoretical explanation of why the organization and development of human competence can generate better organizational performance and productivity.

Theoretical background

The value of human resource intangible assets depends on a general potential to contribute to the core competence or the competitiveness of an organization (cf. Lepak and Snell, 1999; Baron and Armstrong, 2007). Strategic human resource management refers to both the understanding and the implementation of human resources activities, policies and practices, and to making the ongoing changes which are necessary in order to support or improve the performance objectives of an organization. It has been argued that strategic human resource management fails to integrate the mechanisms through which HR practices influence the performance of a firm (see Guest, 1997; Becker and Huselid, 2006; Fleetwood and Hesketh, 2010). One of the most important functions for human resource management is to add competitive value to the organization (Pfeffer, 1994; Ulrich, 1997; Guest, 1997; Becker and Huselid, 2006). Furthermore, interest in human resource management and its connection to performance (HRM-P) has increased, as a result of research into business scorecard metrics and their link to HR scorecards (Kaplan and Norton, 1996, 2004; Becker et al., 2001; HCROI of Fitz-Enz, 2000; IIP of Cascio and Boudreau, 2008). There are multitudes of HR practices which have been shown to support a positive correlation with organizational performance. These, to mention only a few, include the following:

Ichniowsky et al., (1997): innovative HRM practices raised worker productivity.
Huselid (1995) and Becker & Huselid (1998): High performance work practices improved employee performance.
Guest (1997): HR practices which have a good fit with strategy, policy and context seem to be associated with superior performance.
Kesti and Syväjärvi (2010): Systematic tacit signal development processes help in the implementation of optimal workplace innovations, which contribute to better performance.

However, although positive correlations between HR practices and performance have been identified, there is still a lack of evidence which might explain the phenomenon. Thus, researchers should attempt to open up the 'black box' of the causal relationship between HR components (X) and units of organizational performance (Y) (Becker et al., 2001, Fleetwood and Hesketh, 2010). Indeed, there is an obvious need for managers and executives to know whether the HR developments in question will produce a change in human capital based performance and, if so, to what extent (e.g., Becker et al., 2001; Syväjärvi et al., 2003). Although configurations of certain bundles of HR practices seem to promote better performance (see Lumijärvi, 2009) there remain several open questions which must be answered in order to successfully explain and to put these research outcomes to further use.

Organizational development is complex, and the attempt to increase performance by copying other organizations' best practices will usually lead to major failures. There seems to be too little effort put into identifying the mechanisms which lead to HRM actually influencing the performance of organizations (Guest, 2001; Pauwe, 2004; Becker & Huselid, 2006; Lumijärvi, 2009; Fleetwood & Hesketh, 2010). There have also been problems in generalizing the HRM-P research outcomes because situations, organizations and their people vary to a great extent (see Ramsay et al., 2000; Guest, 2001; Sila, 2006; Fleetwood and Hesketh, 2010). For example, Ramsay et al., (2000) have tested three models of the High Performance Work System (the High-Commitment Model, the High Involvement Model and the Labour Process Model) and found no adequate or complete account of the outcomes. Thus, much more research is needed in order to find an adequate theoretical explanation of why certain HR practice may create better organization performance. Once these ground phenomena are better understood, it should then be possible to create generalisable and systematic human capital development procedures for organizations.

Investments are sacrifices that decrease existing consumption possibilities, but which are supposed to lead to greater earnings and consumption possibilities in the future (Corrado et al., 2005). For example, if an organization invests in staff training, this will decrease available staff working time in the short term, but may improve work processes in the long term. Maliranta and Asplund (2007) discovered that, on average, recruiting more highly educated employees decreases company productivity for up to two years.

Human capital productivity

It is well known that the link between HR practice and organization (or business) performance should be investigated and demonstrated in many different ways. A wide range of methodologies are required if the causal links between human resources and performance are to be identified. For example, human resource intangible assets need drivers which are able to contextualize the relevant HR versus performance focus. We may, for example, find these drivers in quality and innovation policies, but one promising driver originates in productivity, and it is this function which is the concern of the present chapter. A production function describes production performance as a function from input and output (Keat and Young, 2003; Saari, 2006). Such a function can be seen as a measure of the Gross Value Added (GVA) created by investment in labor and production capital. Gross Value Added is the total production value, once intermediate costs such as raw-materials, energy, components and outsourcing services and supplies needed for production have been deducted (Camus 2007). Finnish National Account Statistics define Gross Value Added as the value generated by any unit engaged in a production activity.

$$\text{Production function} = \frac{\text{Gross Value Added}}{\text{Production input}} = \frac{\text{Production output - Intermediate costs}}{\text{Labor + Capital}}$$

In a microeconomic business account, intermediate costs are variable costs which depend upon the revenue created. Investment in labor intangible assets reduces the value of the production function in the short term, but after a period of improved productivity, production value improves. The same phenomenon occurs in the case of production capital when a company invests in technology, a higher gross value added follows, assuming that the technology is put to efficient use by the organization.

Efficiency is a general measure of economic activity, describing the value created by sacrifices. Thus, improved efficiency is achieved either by creating the same value by minimizing sacrifices, or by increasing the value while making the same sacrifices. Productivity and profitability are specified as concepts relating to efficiency. Saari (2006) points out that efficiency improvement should include both quantity and quality, and this means that efficiency may improve as a result of creating higher quality with the same output and input quantity.

Fitz-Enz (2000) defines HCROI as total revenue — excluding staff costs — divided by staff costs. Since only staff costs are excluded from the initial sum, other fixed costs (rent, for example) are included in the equation. Kesti et al., (2011) introduce HCROI scenario-analysis, where HCROI is an index calculated as the gross margin divided by staff costs. The gross margin is the revenue with variable costs deducted. Variable costs include materials and services that are needed in production, and which therefore include some human based quality costs, in the form of wasted materials or produce. For example, if the organization tries to increase its revenue by selling more, in haste, this may give rise to more quality errors and thus generate extra costs which lead to a decrease in productivity. Variable costs are related to the production volume (revenue), and therefore to productivity, whereas other fixed costs are more closely connected to profitability. For example, operating from a more cost effective site increases profitability but not productivity. Gross margin describes the organizational contribution and is, therefore, also called the contribution margin.

HCROI indicates the human capital return on investment, and shows how much Gross Value Added is made as a result of money invested in employees or their full-time equivalent. HCROI value varies across different corporate branches and depends, amongst other things, on the level of required tangible capital. In most organizational fields, the capacity of personnel determines the revenue capacity. In municipal organizations and service branches, personnel are the most important factor in determining the volume of services produced. Therefore, it is interesting to calculate the human capital revenue factor (HCRF), which is the revenue divided by the number of employees (Fitz-Enz 2000). The number of employees is calculated by full-time equivalent (FTE), the total theoretical yearly man-hours invested in generating the revenue. This includes the total working time of the full time and contingent workforce.

The HCRF (human capital revenue factor) is commonly used, but additional metrics are required in order to analyze an organization's human capital productivity.

Short introduction and examples of HR-based performance and productivity

The connection between human resource management and performance can be illustrated by calculating new employee recruiting payback time (Figure 1). In this simplified example, performance is measured in euro units and calculated as the gross margin divided by the number of employees. New employee recruiting costs, which can be seen as an investment, are € 6100. In this illustrative case, the person hired has an upper level education. Therefore, the recruitment costs are relatively high, and include advertisements, candidate testing, health tests and administrative costs. In this study, the complete work orientation time is 16 months, and the worker achieves his personal performance level when the work orientation period is completed. Figure 1 illustrates two cases: in the first case (depicted by the continuous line), person A achieves a performance of € 10350 gross margin per month, and in the second case (the dotted line), person B achieves a performance of €5175 gross margin per month. In both cases, the worker salary costs are € 3750 per month. The personal HCROI for person A is 2.76 but only 1.38 for person B.

Figure 1. New worker recruitment payback time calculation

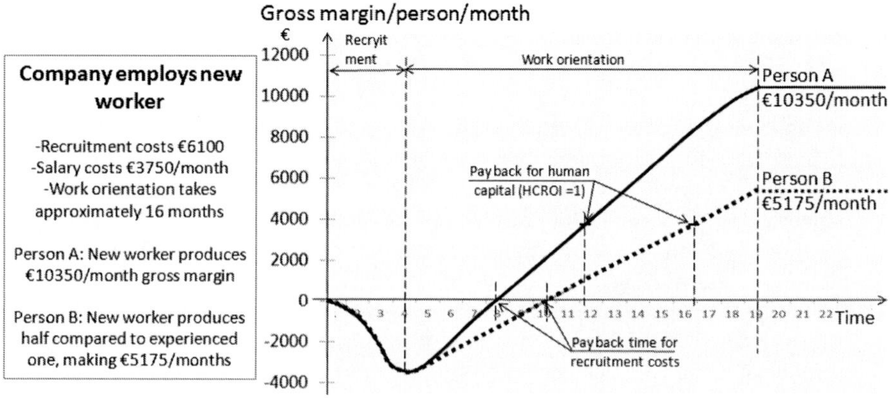

When analyzing the performance of a team as a whole, the human capital productivity can be calculated using the HCROI value, the gross margin divided by staff costs. Figure 2 illustrate the change in the productivity of a team after the recruitment of a new member. Initially, the group is a ten member expert team, and each member has an average performance of € 9000 gross margin per month. In case A, the new member achieves a 15% higher performance (€ 10350 per month) whereas the other members of team's individual performances remain at the same level. This means that nineteen months from the recruitment decision, the team's productivity increases by 1.24% If the new member achieves a performance of only € 5175 per month Gross margin, the performance of the team as a whole decreases by 3.75%, which is a reduction from 2.40 to 2.31 in HCROI.

What if it is supposed that every team member adopts more efficient working methods along with the newly recruited member? Case AK illustrates such a situation, in which the whole team works with the same 15% improvement at efficiency, therefore improving the productivity of the team as a whole by 15%. This productivity increase is the result of the deepening of the human capital intangible assets of the team as a whole, in the form of more efficient collective working methods.

Improving human capital utilization is also possible without new recruitment; either if a team implements more efficient working methods or if work motivation improves. These cases might contribute to a more effective utilization of working hours and therefore to an increase in revenue capacity and team productivity (HCROI).

Figure 2. Team level human capital return on investment in the case of new team member recruitment

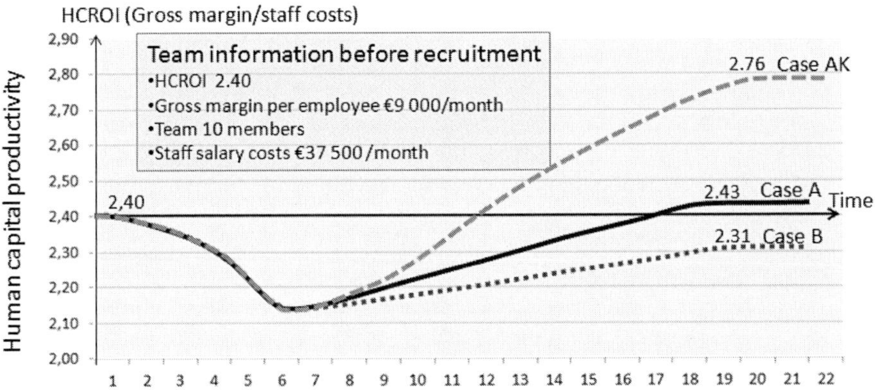

Case A: New team member achieves a 15% higher performance compared to other team members. Team productivity increases by 1.25%.

Case B: New team member performance is half that of other team members. Team productivity decreases by 3.75 %.

Case AK: All team members (N=11) achieve a 15% improvement in performance. Team productivity improves by 15%.

Recent studies on the quality of Finnish companies have indicated that wasted working time is the biggest single reason for the increase in quality related costs (Andersson et al., 2004). For example, it might be argued that as the result of decreased motivation, the quality of work typically decreases, leading to an increase in both mistakes and costs. This leads to the thought that if human competencies (which are an indicator of the quality of working life) improve, this will produce more time for effective work. Increasing the effective working hours of personnel deepens the level of human capital utilization and management (Baron and Armstrong, 2007).

According to Finnish working time statistics, in 2010 the average time spent on actual work was around 82% of the theoretical regular yearly working time (The Confederation of Finnish Industries, 2010). These statistics do not identify the time required for orientating new workers in the workplace, or for time allocated to workplace development, which are included in the total figure of 82%. In a single organization, it is possible to obtain quite accurate data on the distribution of working hours. The time spent on actual work can be calculated by deducting vacancies, absence and other non-working hours from total working time. Working time distribution should also recognize the time needed for the orientation of new personnel and organization development time. Furthermore, to explain the relevant theoretical connections in HRM-P, effective working time and other working time need to be distinguished.

Other working time can be identified using the PAFF classification for quality work (see BS 6143-2), which is not actual operative work. The abbreviation PAFF derives from the classification of work and expenses into preventive actions, appraisal work, handling of internal failures and external failures:

a. Preventive actions

- Organizational work, scheduling, quality systems, preventive maintenance, auditing, cleaning, alarm systems and maintaining order.

b. Appraisal
- Checking, testing, measuring, controlling, piloting, sample taking, analyzing and reporting.

c. Internal failure
- Waste, scrap, redoing, fixing, rechecking, defects finding, correction, repairing and taking care of personal matters.

d. External failure
- Customer reclaims, corrections, returned products and guarantee work.

Labor input capacity grows when the sum total of hours worked increases or if the quality of work increases (Bell et al., 2005). Labor input is the single most important factor in an organization's productivity, and measurement of the hours worked is therefore needed in order to analyze labor productivity (e.g., OECD 2001). The European Commission's employment report for 2002 indicates that better job quality should lead to significantly higher labor productivity. The next section will introduce one possible explanation and analysis of the connection between human capital performance and productivity.

The HRM-P theoretical explanation

For the purposes of explaining the connection between human resource management and performance, an analysis of staff total working hours or FTE is inadequate. Firstly, the total theoretical working hours (paid hours) differ from the total hours spent on actual work. Secondly, each employee makes a different contribution to the organization value-adding process, as described earlier. In addition to physical presence (hours of actual work), this contribution also includes the value of personal human intangible assets — one hour of input by one person is not necessarily the same as one hour of input by another.

It is certainly the case that hours spent on actual work are a significant factor in measuring total capacity and productivity. However, measuring only total actual working time does not take intangible assets and the deepening of human capital into account. The actual time spent at work can be divided into effective working time and other working time (PAFF). On this approach, revenue capacity is achieved through total effective working time. The problem lies in measuring the division between other working time and effective working time. Accurate measurement is not possible in real life, since the process of measuring alters the distribution and because working time registration would increase the Appraisal part of PAFF. Furthermore, employees tend to cover up some aspects relating to internal failure (e.g., taking care of personal matters).

The HRM-Performance improvement phenomenon could proceed as follows: workers are aware of their development needs, because they feel that their contribution gets somewhat wasted. Fundamentally, if the organization and working community are appreciative and provide proper working conditions, every worker wants to give his/her best performance. Employees have tacit knowledge concerning their development needs. Human resource development processes will help teams to implement optimal improvements, by increasing human competencies and removing the obstacles which stand in the way of effective work. These improvements would reduce wasted working time and thus increase effective working time. However, the abovementioned would succeed only if workplace development was efficient. Increasing effective working time would make it possible to generate more revenue with the same cost construction, leading to improved productivity. These conclusions are logical and sensible, based on the action research findings.

The example calculation below explains how productivity improves as a result of human resource intangible assets development. For the purposes of the example, we suppose that a company makes € 100M revenue, that company variable costs are € 60M (60% from revenue), that staff costs are € 15M and that other fixed costs are € 15M. The case is a simplification: for instance, changes in staff turnover and number of personnel are not considered in the calculation. The company's employee quality of working life (QWL) is measured as standing at a level of 70%. Here, the QWL is based upon the collective human competencies of leadership, team culture, working skills and processes. If these competencies are validated for the organization's human drivers of performance, they should correlate with the efficiency of work, thus distinguishing the share of effective working time from the total time available for work.

In this illustrative example, the company improves QWL-competencies from 70% to 75%. Obviously, this requires some additional working time investment on effective HRD. Thus, the organization invests 1.3% units more in HRD, including training, orientation and workplace development. Team level workplace development efficiency can be estimated by evaluating the practical workplace innovations which are implemented to improve QWL-competencies. The HRD correlation with optimal workplace innovations will be studied later, in a section dealing with effective human resource development.

Figure 3. Example illustrating human capital connection and its relation to performance.

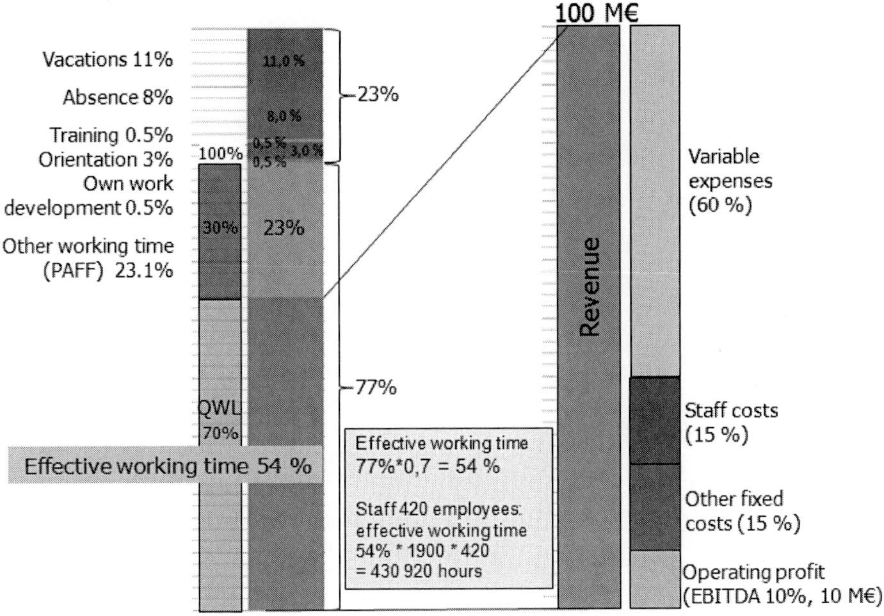

The improved situation is analyzed in figure 4. The cost structure remains the same, although there is a slight improvement in the variable costs percentage, as a result of the improved quality of work. The monetary value of the variable costs has increased, as these are dependent on revenue. If revenue increases, so do the cost of materials and other purchases. It is likely that that HRD processes will reduce absence and thus also staff costs, although these cost savings are not included in this simplified example. With this in mind, it is relatively easy to calculate the HRD effect upon the business, in terms of revenue and EBITDA (earnings before interests, taxes, depreciation and amortization).

Figure 4. Example company's HRD effect on revenue (REV) and gross margin (EBITDA).

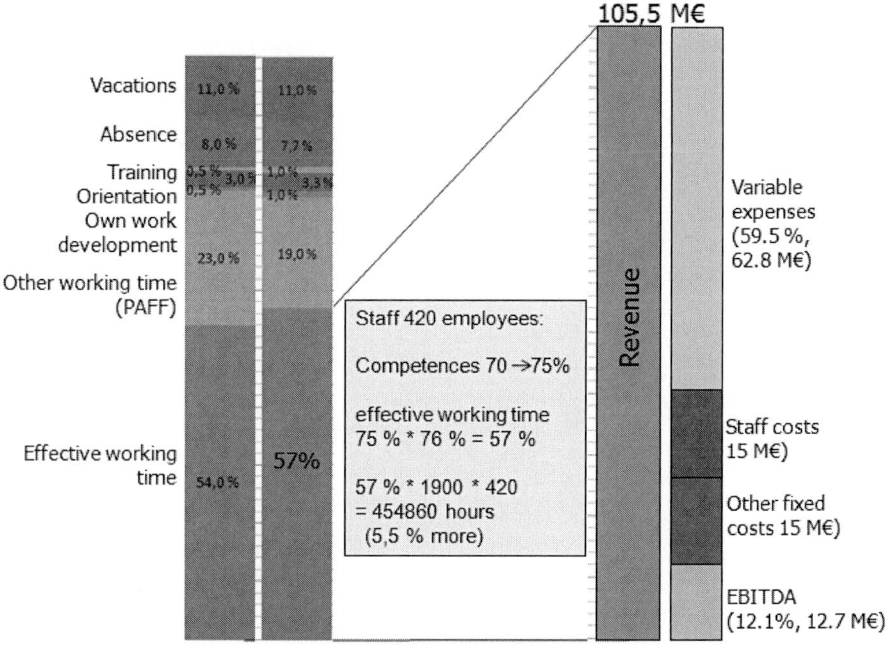

The example company improves its QWL-competencies by 7%. The additional working time invested for HRD (+1.3%) reduces working time from 77% to 76%, due to the fact that absences have simultaneously been reduced by 0.3%. The organization implements workplace innovations for each working team, which reduces PAFF and increases competencies and, eventually, effective working time. As a result, the company reduces PAFF by 4% and gains 5.5% in effective working time. Assuming that the organizational situation is favorable, the company can increase revenue by the same extent, meaning € 5.5M more revenue and, eventually, € 2.7M more EBITDA. This will be possible if the company utilizes the excess in effective working time to generate revenue growth. The company will release hidden human powers by removing the obstacles which are preventing effective work.

Fitz-Enz (2000) argues that while employee development is one of the most important issues concerning the future of organizations, it is one of the worst managed. This may be due to the fact that many HR professionals are not experienced in mining administrative data for the purposes of evaluating HR development efficiency (Cascio and Boudreay, 2008; Syväjärvi and Stenvall, 2010). HR experts are seldom business oriented enough when conducting human resource development to proceed effectively in evaluating development. They tend to focus on behavioral objectives, based on the participants' reactions to the training or the intervention (Wang and Wilcox, 2006). Regardless of improved information systems, evaluation can be a very time-consuming and rather unpleasant exercise for HRD practitioners (Mankin, 2009). Several studies reveal that the impact of HRD investment is not properly evaluated, and that management decision-making proceeds in the absence of information relevant to human capital development possibilities (Wang and Wilcox, 2006; Swansson, 2005; Bunch, 2007; Kim and Cervero, 2007).

Healthcare branch as a case and HRM-based performance evaluation

Nowadays, public and private healthcare organizations are probably subjected to more scrutiny than ever before. This is due to the fact that the health care sector typically represents a large percentage of the national economy, and that the sector is also very knowledge-intensive and human-based or professionally resourced (Pynes & Lombardi, 2011). The performance evaluation of the healthcare branch can be described and, for instance, the difference in human performance and human capital productivity can be illustrated by means of statistics. For example, an analysis of Finnish healthcare services in the private sector (SME not included) reveals a degree of healthy growth from 2006 to 2008. Staff salaries increased (HCCF) and revenue per employee improved to an even greater extend, leading to a steady increase (see Figure 5) in human capital productivity (HCROI). Due to Finland's ageing population, the country's healthcare demands are growing steadily. As a result, the total revenue and personnel levels in the sector have been increasing. However, it seems that healthy levels of growth were disturbed, after 2008. The growth in revenue per employee stabilized in 2009, and underwent a significant reduction in 2010. Human capital costs continued to increase in 2009, causing human capital productivity (HCROI) to decline. Although HCROI improved slightly in 2010, the healthcare sector in Finland is clearly not operating at optimal performance levels, because human capital revenue factor (HCRF) has decreased by 4.9%.

Figure 5. Statistics for human performance and human capital productivity in the Finnish private healthcare business sector (SME not included) (Statistics from StatFin service).

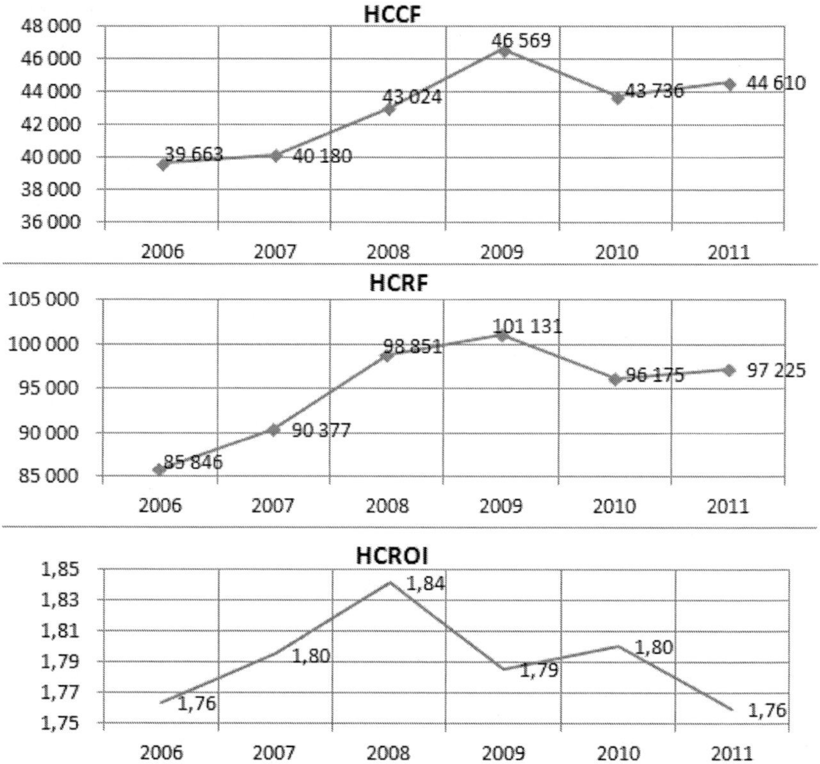

Labor input capacity grows when the total hours worked or the quality of work increases (Bell et al., 2004). Labor is the single most important factor in organization productivity, and it is therefore necessary to measure the number of hours worked in order to analyze labor productivity (OECD, 2001). In the present study, theoretical yearly working hours are relatively stable, ranging from 1876 to 1893 hours between 2006 and 2010. From 2009 to 2010, there was a reduction of 0.7% in the number of theoretical yearly working hours, from 1890 to 1876. Thus, this factor does not fully explain the 4.9% HCRF decrease. Furthermore, the service business branch working time distribution indicates that working time improved in 2010, contrary to the HCRF decline, as shown by the statistics in Table 1 below.

In fact, yearly working hours (see Table 1) increased by 4.1% in 2010, as there was a reduction in vacancies, absence, travelling and training. Vacancies reduce when the percentage of new workers increases. Travelling and training are typical areas affected by cost cutting, where expenditure is minimized when the strategic aim is to improve productivity. The healthcare business sector in this study increased personnel by 36.8% in 2010, but at the same time cut training time by half. As a result, HCRF decreased by 4.9%, despite the 4.1% total increase in time for work. The human intangible capital utilization within the total time for work may explain this negative change in human resources performance. It also seems evident that the strategy of cutting costs, in a growing and labor intensive business sector, has not been the most optimal management decision. One could argue that investing in human resources development would have been more profitable.

Table 1. Working time distribution in the social and healthcare service sector (Statistics from Confederation of Finnish Industries).

	2006	2007	2008	2009	2010	2011
Theoretical yearly working hours	1893	1884	1890	1890	1876	1899
Vacation	10,10 %	11,10 %	11,90 %	11,50 %	10,20 %	9,80 %
Short absence	2,68 %	2,62 %	2,75 %	2,56 %	1,77 %	3,05 %
Long absence	1,72 %	1,68 %	1,76 %	1,64 %	1,13 %	1,95 %
Accidents	0,10 %	0,10 %	0,10 %	0,20 %	0,10 %	0,10 %
Other absence	1,60 %	1,30 %	2,00 %	0,90 %	1,00 %	0,90 %
Maternity leave	4,70 %	4,70 %	3,60 %	2,30 %	2,50 %	2,20 %
Overtime work	0,30 %	0,30 %	2,60 %	0,30 %	0,30 %	0,30 %
Lay-off	0,00 %	0,00 %	0,40 %	0,60 %	0,00 %	0,10 %
Travelling during working time	0,30 %	0,50 %	1,50 %	0,50 %	0,20 %	0,20 %
Training	1,00 %	1,10 %	0,90 %	1,00 %	0,50 %	0,40 %
Time for work	**78,10 %**	**77,20 %**	**77,70 %**	**79,10 %**	**82,90 %**	**81,60 %**

Kesti (2012) introduced the HCROI scenario-analyzing tool, which combines business scorecards, human resource data and the organization of human competencies, for the purpose of forecasting business performance and human capital productivity over a five-year perspective. This more sophisticated method of analysis is needed because an organization is a complex system, consisting of multiple and simultaneously interacting factors. Scenario-analyzing is not based on statistical predictions, but upon estimating the future by calculating values on the basis of evidence based rules. Scenario-analyzing is based on the following basic meta-principles:

Revenue is created from effective absolute working time of human resource
Staff costs are related to the number of employees
Staff costs include costs relating to absence and additional labor costs
Staff activities cause a certain amount of variable costs in the form of quality costs

In addition to these meta-principles, scenario-analysis utilizes a number of simultaneously active sub-hypotheses:

Effective human resource development will improve human competencies
Human competencies determine the share of effective working time and other working time (PAFF) on the basis of the time available for actual work (time for work)
Human competencies have an impact on absence, staff turnover and quality costs
Organizational structural changes tend to decrease human competencies
New employees require work orientation before they achieve the same work efficiency as experienced workers

Scenario-analysis defines the human intangible assets of an organization on the basis of five human competencies: management, leadership, operating culture, working skills and processes (Kesti et al., 2011). These competencies are validated performance drivers for each organization and, considered as a package, can be seen as constituting an organization specific quality of working life (QWL).

When a HCROI scenario-analysis is conducted for the healthcare sector, using the initial starting data from the year 2006, the significance of human intangible assets can be illustrated. In addition to the initial data for the starting year, there are fixed factors (such as the number of employees) which accord with the statistics. These scenario-data are shown in the following table. The aim is to find out how human competencies have developed and to identify which other factors explain the development of HCRF, HCCF and HCROI.

Table 2. HCROI scenario-analyzing datasheet.

Health care business branch (SME not included)	2006				
Organization size (FTE)	6137	pcs			
Revenue	526 835 000	€			
Sales Margin	429 273 000	€			
Employee costs	243 409 000	€			
Estimated quality costs from revenue	6,0 %				
		2007	2008	2009	2010
New worker average work orientation time	4,0	4,0	4,0	4,0	4,0
Labour cost index	2,0 %	1,5 %	3,5 %	11,8 %	-5,3 %
Material and service cost index	2,0 %	25,0 %	0,0 %	-27,0 %	3,0 %
Business branch index	2,0 %	2,0 %	2,0 %	0,0 %	3,3 %
Theoretical yearly working time	1893,0	1884,0	1890,0	1890,0	1876,0
Additional labour costs from total costs	21,5 %	21,5 %	21,5 %	21,5 %	21,5 %
Increase of personnel-%	10,00 %	12,50 %	5,66 %	5,69 %	36,84 %
Organization change factor	5,00 %	5,00 %	0,00 %	0,00 %	10,00 %
Family and training vacancies	4,70 %	4,70 %	3,60 %	2,30 %	2,50 %
Layoffs	0,00 %	0,00 %	0,40 %	0,60 %	0,00 %
Overtime working	0,30 %	0,30 %	2,60 %	0,30 %	0,30 %
Effective personnel training	0,50 %	0,65 %	0,55 %	0,55 %	0,34 %
Effective workplace development	0,50 %	0,65 %	0,55 %	0,55 %	0,34 %
Average personnel absence (%)	6,10 %	5,70 %	6,50 %	5,20 %	3,90 %
Personnel annual turnover (%)	8,00 %	8,74 %	8,66 %	8,59 %	8,82 %
Management competence	75,0 %	77,6 %	80,1 %	82,0 %	77,6 %
Leadership competence	75,0 %	77,6 %	80,1 %	82,0 %	77,6 %
Operating culture competence	75,0 %	77,6 %	80,1 %	82,0 %	77,6 %
Skills competence	75,0 %	77,6 %	80,1 %	82,0 %	77,6 %
Process competence	75,0 %	77,6 %	80,1 %	82,0 %	77,6 %
Outsourced services	55 140 000	64 781 685	75 281 792	81 611 293	106 145 502
Revenue change %		17,5 %	16,2 %	8,4 %	30,1 %
Summary of initial data	**2006**	**2007**	**2008**	**2009**	**2010**
Personnel (FTE)	6137	6904	7295	7710	10550
Personnel transfer (pcs)	613,7	767,1	390,8	415,1	2840,4
Number of new employees (pcs)	1104,7	1370,4	1022,9	1077,6	3771,1
Number of terminated employment (pcs)	491,0	603,3	632,1	662,5	930,7
Absence days per employee (days)	15,4	14,1	16,0	12,8	9,6
Training time per employee (days)	1,3	1,6	1,4	1,4	0,8
Performance improvement per employee (days)	1,3	1,6	1,4	1,4	0,8
Revenue	526 835 000	618 956 461	719 279 706	779 754 911	1 014 166 947
Staff costs	244 504 341	277 866 008	313 249 465	357 708 181	463 028 519
Sales Margin	429 273 000	495 133 752	577 342 599	644 891 245	834 528 747
HCROI	**1,76**	**1,78**	**1,84**	**1,80**	**1,80**

The scenario-analysis includes new workers' orientation time, which is analyzed information and is thus not included in the working time distribution statistics. Orientation time increased significantly in 2010, due to the sharp increase in healthcare personnel. In addition, the sharp increase in personnel (36.8%) probably caused structural changes in the organization which increased development needs and which thus decreased the quality of working life competencies. This is shown as a scenario-analysis in Figure 6. The phenomenon depicted is also described as human capital scenario-analyzing.

Figure 6. Scenario-analyzing estimation for the quality of working life and working time distribution

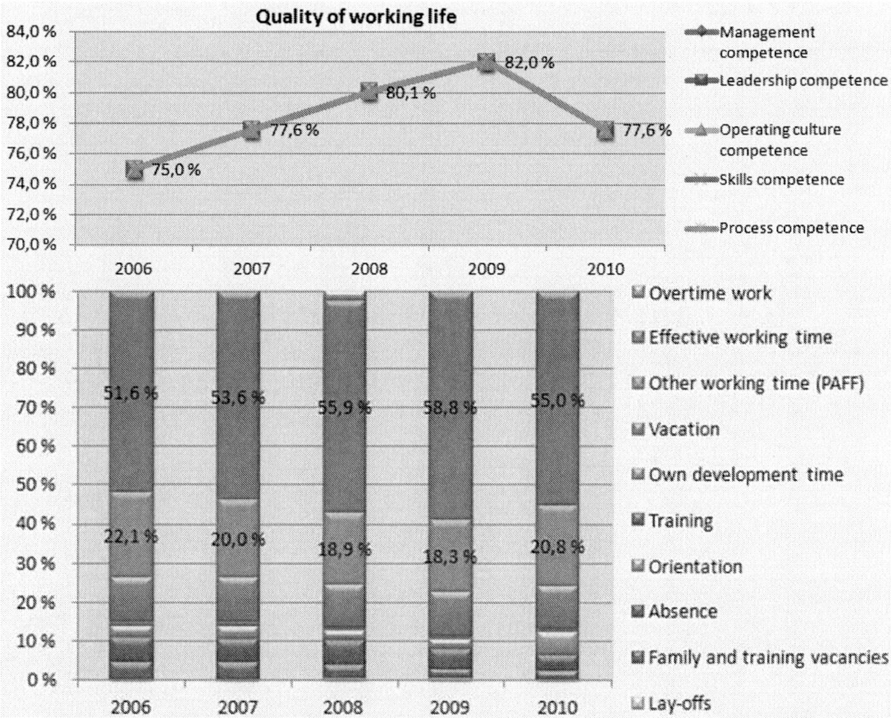

Competencies developed positively until the year 2010, and then reduced significantly. It seems that the level of organization development during a period of steady growth is not enough to lead to improved competencies during more turbulent times. Moreover, working time statistics indicate that human resource development actually diminished in 2010, as staff training time was decreased by 50%. Although the scenario-analysis includes variables (e.g., effective workplace development) which are not easy to verify, it seems evident that human intangible assets utilization explains the healthcare sector data. Furthermore, these results indicate that scenario-analyzing can be applied to the forecasting of human capital performance and productivity in the healthcare business sector.

In order to further consider the possibility of improving business performance through human resources development, we can analyze scenarios by means of some examples. Figure 7 below depicts a practical case study for a healthcare company of 255 employees. The statistics indicate that HR development decreased after 2009. How would the business have performed if the company had not reduced HRD investment but had instead continued to invest in HR development? Two scenarios are analyzed: the first (case STAT) follows the healthcare statistics presented above, and the second (HIGH) follows a scenario in which HR development activities rose steadily, from a 1.2 % rise in 2007 to a 1.8% increase in 2010. These HR developments include training and effective workplace level development. The scenario-analysis comparison in Figure 7 shows that the company revenue could have increased by € 2.6M in 2010, corresponding to the contribution of 30 employees. In addition, the EBITDA would have been €2.6M more, as the business is more labor intensive and the human capital productivity (HCROI) is 7.8% better. During 2010, the EBITDA improvement is € 6070 per full time equivalent, meaning that every worker makes about € 6000 more business profit.

Figure 7. Statistic business case and high road case comparison.

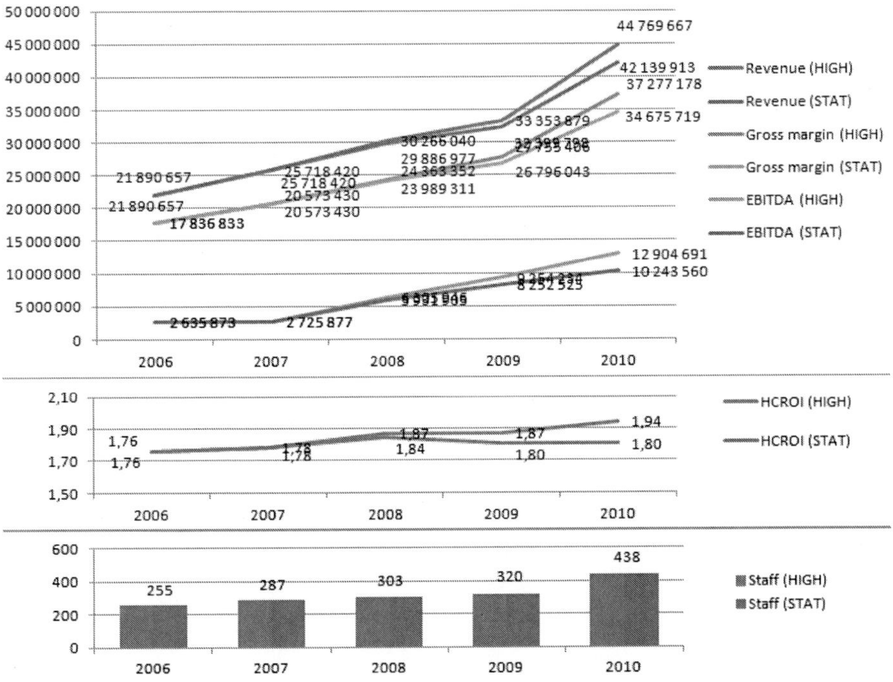

Action research findings

Further research studies using action research should be conducted in individual organizations, in order to identify the components of intellectual capital and productivity. In their case studies, Daveri and Maliranta (2007) made the observation that personnel training will contribute to higher productivity after two years. Action research case studies indicate that organizations could increase their productivity by improving the utilization of human capital (Kesti and Syväjärvi, 2010). In monetary terms, this means that the revenue and gross margins of companies would increase. Kesti and Syväjärvi's (2010) study indicates that systematic human resource competencies development contributes better business performance (see Figure 8).

In this longitudinal action research case study, the effect of human competencies development was observed over a two-year period, using a tacit signals method. In this study, the organization quality of working life was investigated by identifying competencies of leadership and operating culture, measured using HRIS tacit signals measurement. The case study followed fiscal periods over the course of three years (2005-2008). During this time, the overall business sector was steadily growing, the average yearly business sector revenue growth was 5.5%, staff costs increased by 6.1% and gross margin improved by 5.9%. In the company studied, the average yearly revenue growth was 9.6%, staff costs were 8.0% and gross margin improvement was 9.1%. The case company staff costs were higher because personnel increased 71.4% more than an average business branch.

Figure 8 depicts a company analysis in which increase in competencies seems to correlate with business performance improvement. The business units are divided into two sorting groups: units (N=10) that were able to increase competencies, and units (N=9) where competencies decreased. Staff increases are nearly the same in both sorting groups under examination. However, the better sample increased revenue by 10% more than its level of staff increase. This means that the revenue increase is not solely the result of an increase in personnel, but is also the result of other phenomena. It seems that an increase in staff competencies could be the cause of better performance, since competencies improved from 74% to 81% (an increase of 9 percentage units). Furthermore, in the other sample, where the revenue increase was 5% less than the staff increase, the competence decreased from 84% to 79% (a drop of 6 percentage units).

Figure 8. Findings from longitudinal case study.

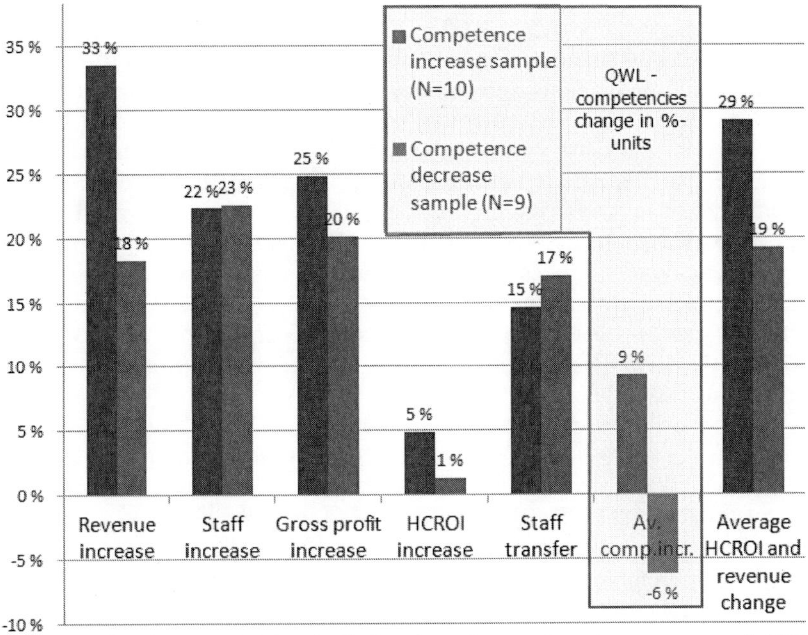

An empirically grounded longitudinal case study was done in a company of 1000 employees, consisting of 19 business units. Each unit applied systematic HRD for a two-year period. The business units applied the same business process at their B2B and consumer sales branch. The HRD process was applied to all BU in the same way.

BUs were divided into two sample groups, according to those where competencies increased and those where competencies decreased. Both groups increased personnel by almost the same amount. The revenue growth difference between the sample groups can be explained by competencies improvement.

Effective human resource development

Human resource development (HRD) is the process of facilitating organizational learning, performance and change. Organized interventions, initiatives and management actions are implemented for the purpose of improving organization performance capacity, capability, competitiveness and renewal (Gilley and Maycunich, 1998). Tacit signals refer to personal guiding opinions, which can be used to improve human competencies (cf. Stone, 2002). In working units, these guiding opinions help to solve problems, and this is also a fundamental element of effective leadership: "The leader who wants to create an emotionally intelligent team can start by helping the team raise its collective self awareness." (Goleman et al., 2008). Collective emotional intelligence seems to be a characteristic of top performing teams (Wheelan, 2005).

Usually, human competences are considered to be so difficult and complex that recognizing and developing them is not easy to achieve. In addition, traditional HRD methods have been repeatedly seen to be too expensive, or too slow, or too complicated in other ways for the purposes of achieving continuous performance improvement. However, to bring about change in a working group change, it is essential to recognize that one is working on dissonant situations (Goleman et al., 2008). A tacit signal development process, with effective IC tools, has been proven to be effective in the continuous development of an organization (Kesti et al., 2009). Leaders can learn to solve team problems and challenges in constructive ways, and team members can learn that problems can be turned into possibilities.

Jack Welch has divided employees into three categories, based upon performance: the top 20%, the middle 70% and the bottom 10% (Welch and Welch, 2005). Our research observation is that the same phenomenon seems to be present in working teams, which may complicate organization level performance improvement. In the case of organizations, roughly 20% of working groups seem to succeed in developing their work practices, but 80% are not able to implement the agreed improvement actions by themselves. Furthermore, our observation is that in many organizations, limited development time is misused, with 80% of the time being spent engaging in non-constructive defensive mechanisms, and only 20% of the time used in actually solving problems. These organization development obstacles are standard in the case of command based management structures, which lack systematic HR development support. Effective HR development with proper tools should enable organizations to transform these common obstacles to their competitive advantage.

Pfeffer and Sutton (2000) say that it is essential to overcome the knowing-doing gap in order to improve organization performance. They point out that organizations should not try to implement the best practices of other organizations but should instead discover their own best value practices. Pfeffer and Sutton are certain that organization employees have ideas for optimal performance improvement. As an example, there are the Welch experiments with Work-Out sessions at General Electric, conducted in order to listen to the development ideas and needs of employees. Welch says that "Work-Outs led to an explosion in productivity" (Welch and Welch, 2005). In the space of a few years, they launched tens of thousands of Work-Outs, until leaders learned that this was a systematic and effective way of bringing about group development.

Senge (2006) has pointed out that, in isolation, employee training does not by lead to improvement. Practical and collective improvement actions are needed in order to make organizational change possible and to create learning organizations. Optimal improvement actions have to emerge on the basis of the knowledge of the team members. As contingency theory implies, these optimal improvement actions must derive from group needs and situations (Hunt 1992). Part of this knowledge is tacit, and part of it is explicit. Tacit knowledge can lead to actions leading to explicit improvement, as the result of social interaction among the group members (Nonaka and Takeuchi, 1995; Nonaka and Konno, 1998). Socially constructive communication, such as dialogue, discussion and observation, speeds up the knowledge creation process, and activates organization learning. It is part of a leader's responsibility to organize constructive team meetings in order to agree upon optimal improvement actions. In this way, leaders can strengthen both the motivation and the commitment to common targets of their team members.

Nonaka (1994) introduced knowledge creation processes, in which shared cognition and collective learning generate organizational knowledge creation. The principle of interrelated and opposing factors affecting organizations is also raised in *The Knowledge Creating Company*, by Nonaka and Takeuchi (1995). They observe that there seem to be a multitude of dichotomies — tacit versus explicit, mind versus body (or matter), self vs. others—which affect organization knowledge creation. These dichotomies are not different coins, but, rather, they are opposite sides of the same coin and are mutually complementary (Nonaka and Takeuchi, 1995).

Kesti (2012) studied the tacit signal method in human competency based organization performance development. The tacit signal method can be described by using the inverted U-curve (Yerkes and Dodson, 1908). The situation in the inverted U-curve can be measured by asking for personal opinions about development needs, in relation to the competence attribute. For instance, "working community meeting practices" could be one competence attribute in a team's competence culture. The person questioned may feel that this competence is not utilized optimally and that there is a need for further development. Therefore, this opinion would fall on the right side of the inverted U-curve.

Figure 9. Figure showing the tacit signal inquiry's connection to the inverted U-curve.

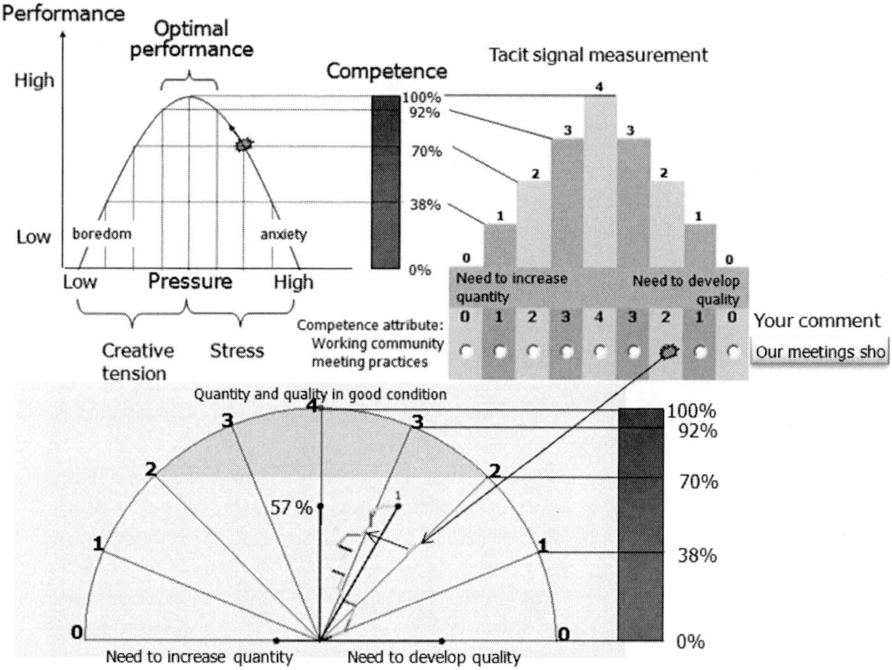

The chosen guiding factors follow the dichotomy principle, where one force guides towards more straightforward action (e.g., quantitative) and the other is more closely related to emotion (e.g., qualitative), thus moving towards a constructive dialogue between the parties and individuals concerned.

Kaplan and Norton have pointed out that the balanced scorecard lacks reliable company specific measures for the perspective of learning and growth. They note that the absence of specific measures indicates that the company is not linking its strategic objectives to its activities as regards re-skilling employees, supplying information, and aligning individuals, teams and organizational units to the company's strategy and objectives (Kaplan and Norton, 1996). Tacit signals measurement and improvement actions follow-up make it possible to measure organization learning and growth perspective in a way that meets BSC needs.

The tacit signal approach seems to generate reliable information for effective organization development (Kesti et al., 2008). Tacit signals provide management with an understanding of human capabilities and of organizations as intelligent systems (Syväjärvi and Kesti, 2012). One case study, which measured several competencies, found that the competencies of leadership and team culture had more development needs than the others (Kesti et al., 2008). These findings lead to the thought that in each working group, there seem to be specific competency attributes that may hinder team performance. Team members have collective tacit knowledge of the human competencies needing development. Therefore, the most effective strategy is to improve the competencies that hinder team performance, as illustrated by the team performance flow model below (Figure 10). After improving the most essential competency attributes, the performance flow will increase, and new issues will emerge for development.

A social consciousness will be created when members of the group compare their own observations with the observations and ideas made by others (Festinger, 1954). Opinions are formed mostly on the basis of feelings, and group interpretations therefore have a great influence. The collective social reality of the group directs individual opinions, especially those which concern interpretative issues, where justification presents a challenge. The members of the group should have a positive mental attitude towards knowledge sharing and the possibilities for open and constructive discussion. Nonaka and Konno (1998) describe this by using a knowledge creating concept (BA). Senge (2006) recognizes three critical dimensions of team learning in an organization environment:

1) Team members are motivated and have the capacity for insightful thought on complex issues.
2) There is a common need for innovative and coordinated action.
3) There is an ability for practices and skills to be shared between teams in the organization.

Figure 10. Team competencies represented in a performance flow model

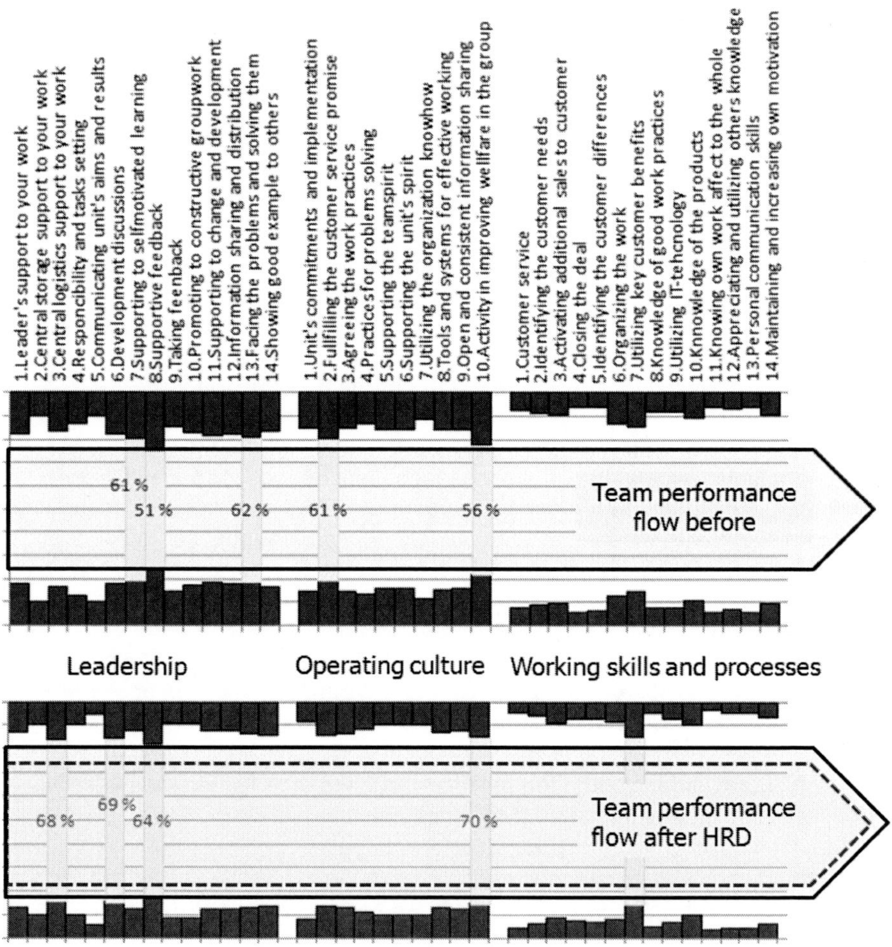

Nonaka and Takeuchi have supplemented Polanyi's (1967) action oriented concept of knowledge with the assumption that knowledge is created through an interaction between the tacit and the explicit. On this basis, they formulate four different modes of knowledge conversion. These are (1) socialization from tacit to tacit, (2) externalization from tacit to explicit, (3) combination from explicit to explicit and (4) internalization from explicit to tacit. In socialization, mental attitudes and skills are shared through social communication, and knowledge is transferred intuitively. For example, the group could build up the mental thrust toward the notion that problems can be shared, not hidden. In externalization, tacit knowledge is transformed into explicit knowledge using words and documented concepts. Typically, this requires dialogue and collective reflection. For example, the group could discuss their feelings and thereby determine their development needs. When knowledge is explicit, for example in a collective agreement concerning an improvement need, it needs to be combined with existing knowledge and practices. For example, the group could decide upon new meeting practices which overcome problems with older practices and which support their needs better. Finally, in the internalization mode, explicit knowledge creates new tacit knowledge, as for example when new meeting practices are implemented, and new experiences are formed by learning through doing.

In his action research studies, Kesti (2012) has used a five-phase development process:

PHASE 1: Management and planning

A development process is planned and organized with the representatives from management, leaders, HR specialists and employees. Targets are set and important human capabilities, as essential competencies, are defined and validated for the purposes of the tacit signal inquiry. Only the competence attributes which are essential for organization strategy and performance management are included.

PHASE 2: The tacit signal collection

Tacit signals are collected from members of each working group in the organization. Results are analyzed by using the tacit signal development semicircle competence analyzing method.

PHASE 3: Strategy development meeting

A strategic HR development focus is chosen, on the basis of the organization's tacit signals.

PHASE 4: Development meetings in working communities

According to the group's tacit signal analysis, each group in the organization agrees upon their own optimal improvement actions with follow-up responsibilities and time-schedule. Ideas and improvement actions are written down.

PHASE 5: Follow-up and support

The implementation of actions is followed and supported by managers, leaders and HR specialists. Leadership forums are held, during which each leader presents the group's improvement actions and problems or successes. The Internet-based innovation management tool is used for action follow-up and for sharing best practices.

To make the organization development process effective from an organization performance point of view, two main factors must be optimized. Firstly, the time consumption of the participants should be minimized, so that the time invested in development gains more value than it consumes in labor capacity. Secondly, the proposed workplace innovations should be implemented as quickly as possible, from the very beginning of the HRD process. This motivates the participants, and the improvement actions pay back the investment in HRD investment rapidly. To summarize, a holistic and appropriately deliberative approach to human resource development is needed, one which combines context, HRD processes, stakeholder satisfaction and management (Garavan, 2007).

Managing organization innovativeness

New forms of work organization aim for the maximum utilization of human potential, and for high levels of learning and problem-solving (European Foundation, 1997). This can be realized by implementing workplace innovations based on the tacit knowledge of members of the organization. It seems that organizations in highly competitive sectors will survive and grow if they can find innovative ways to adapt to a changing market, and to benefit from technological opportunities and new business models. This requires an organization innovativeness which can only be achieved through the systematic development of human competencies. Management should be able to create an attitude that promotes innovativeness, and the ability to capture the tacit knowledge of all employees.

Organization development starts with the management's understanding and commitment to the idea that performance can be improved by utilizing staff innovativeness. Several research studies indicate that organizations which are committed to their employees and allow for the tacit knowledge base to increase are the most successful in the long term (Collins and Porras, 1994; Liker, 2004). Hamel (2007) argues that innovation is everyone's job, as innovation can be described as a knowledge-based initiative for improving performance. He recognizes three essential management innovation challenges:

How to ensure that discomforting information is not ignored or explained away in the organization hierarchy.

How to build an innovative management process that continuously generates hundreds of new strategic options.
How to accelerate the redeployment of resources in initiating future possibilities and not remain stuck in the legacy of the past.

As regards the incremental working group based improvements, the fundamental assumption is that actions for improving recognized development needs are optimal workplace innovations only when they are supported by the whole group, including the leader, and are implemented successfully. In the case studies conducted, it was evident that each organization working team was able to generate several practical ideas for improvement. However, successful implementation was not self-evident, and in fact presented a challenging task for several of the working groups. Successful innovation management typically requires consistent and systematic follow-up methods and integrated tools (cf. Tidd, Beaasant and Pavitt, 2005). These innovation management tools should be as simple as possible, in order to support the innovation management of non-technical HR professionals and operative leaders. Furthermore, the tools should maximize the efficiency of innovation processes. Figure 11 describes an internet based innovation management tool user-interface which supports the HRD process.

Figure 11. An example of internet based innovation management tool.

The innovation management tool was used in SME case studies of nine companies. The average company had 103 employees, divided into five working groups of 21 people on average. Each organization carried out approximately 16 workplace innovations during the development process, which lasted for 12 months. The typical team implemented 3 improvement actions. Most of the teams (47.7%) carried out 1 to 2 improvements, 38.6% of the teams succeeded in carrying out 3 to 4 actions, and 13.6% implemented more than 4 optimal workplace innovations.

Figure 12. Figure showing the average company or business unit development in cases where the Innovation Management Tool is used.

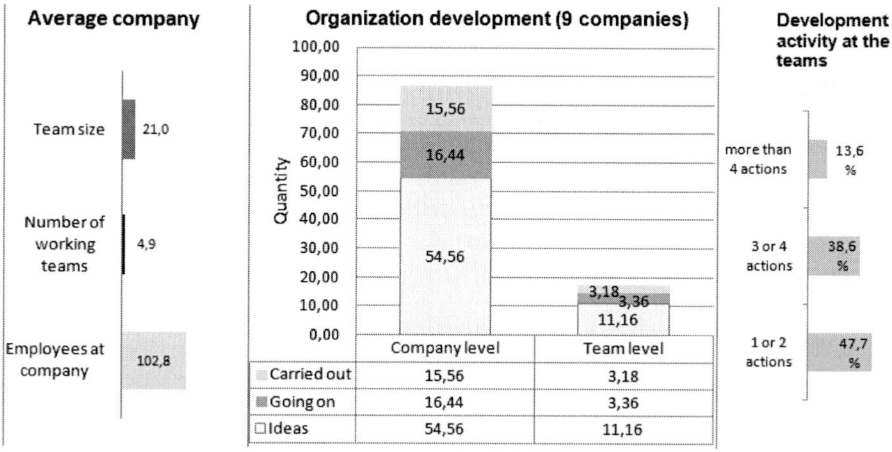

In the group HRD meeting, ideas and selected improvement actions were recorded using the Innovation Management Tool. The basic aim was for each group to select four optimal improvement actions for the project type follow-up, with an agreed upon time schedule. If the agreed time limit was exceeded, the Innovation Management Tool would send a mail-alarm to HR-professionals and to the group leader. Each working group had their own list of potential ideas and accesses to a follow-up blog track the progress of the chosen improvement actions. When the workplace innovation was successfully in place, it was moved to the group's best value practices. This way, the results of the whole innovation process could be surveyed, and best practices could be shared between the organization teams, which are important for team learning and positive experiences (see Senge, 2006; Syväjärvi & Kesti, 2012).

Discussions

Boudreau and Ramstad (1999) point out that a measurement framework is needed for theoretical logic, which will support the inference that investment in human resource development is one of the most important strategic issues. Initially, research results indicate that groups should implement optimal workplace innovations, as this will improve competencies and human performance. If optimal improvement actions are implemented effectively, there will be an improvement in actual effective working time. Thus, workplace innovations will improve human competencies and business performance simultaneously. This is in line with the understanding that improvements (workplace innovations) which are agreed upon collectively can be linked to the organization's collective knowledge sharing, work well-being, values and beliefs. This leads to good competence management and thus to good corporate governance (e.g., Syväjärvi et al,. 2003; Cameron & Quinn, 2006; Kets de Vries, 2006).

There has been recognition that both the public and private sectors are confronting economic and political pressures which are changing human resource practice, as organizational environments and relationships become increasingly complex. For example, Alvesson (2004) notes that many public organizations are indeed knowledge intensive but, without any apparent justification, he chooses to exclude them from his discussion of knowledge work. In contrast, the current chapter has proposed that these pressures and organizational complexities demand new human resource architecture. According to Lepak and Snell (2007), a key challenge for SHRM research is to better understand the nature of knowledge work and the trade-offs among employment options, and to develop human resource systems that are appropriate for managing employees. Thus, adopting an architectural perspective recognizes that organizations have to create an overall picture of human resources, and that they must act according to that picture in order to improve organizational performance and productivity.

The chapter has explained why human resource development may lead to better performance in fiscal organization scorecards. Human resource is one of the most important factors affecting organization productivity, as indicated in healthcare branch studies (e.g., Pynes and Lombardi, 2011). In many organizations, operative business capacity is generated as a result of effective working time. Several action research case studies indicate that organization development has a tendency to improve competencies. If organization development is implemented efficiently, there is the possibility that effective working time will be increased, which will contribute to an increase in human capital productivity. The phenomenon of human capital deepening is essential for effective human resource management. In addition, improved human competences seem to correlate with organization revenue growth. These findings have been explained with theoretically consistent calculations, which have shown that improving competencies is likely to lead to better organizational performance.

The current chapter has also indicated the need for proper human capital and resource data, in order to make advances in management and development. In future organizations, data requirements for human resource assets will play a crucial role, and the better one deals with human capital and resource data, the more effectively these HR contextual goals will be achieved. It now seems fundamental to discover how data mining, concerning human resource intangible assets, could meet organizational information needs that might otherwise be too complex or unclear. The HR information which is needed should, for example, be more future-orientated and combined with performance and productivity. In many cases, the HR data might illuminate past history, explain a present situation, or even predict future trends and behaviors which would allow either public policies or businesses to make proactive and information driven decisions (Syväjärvi and Stenvall, 2010). This human capital or resource information should be connected to activity, performance and added value, but also to more qualitative topics like human experience. To conclude, these viewpoints are important in terms of organization performance and productivity, but also in order to facilitate organizational learning, change and experience (e.g., Bouckaert and Halligan, 2006; Kesti and Syväjärvi, 2010).

This chapter has offered some evidence in support of a plausible interpretation of the relation between human capital and organizational performance and productivity. However, this is only one segment of the organization of human capital performance development research, and further studies are needed. Certainly, as these methods and theories are implemented in organizations with different cultural backgrounds, new and interesting findings will emerge. Finally, it might be useful to obtain results from private and public sector organizations, even though the HR thematic is quite universal. Hopefully, this chapter will encourage further research and case studies in the field of human resource management and organizational performance.

References

Alvesson M. (2004). *Knowledge work and knowledge intensive firms.* Oxford University Press, UK.

Andersson P. H., Hiltunen K. and Villanen H. (2004). *Promoting quality in Finnish companies.* Ministry of Trade and Industry. Edita Publishing.

Baron A. and Armstrong M. (2007). Human Capital Management. Achieving added value through people. Kogan Page, USA.

Becker B. and Huselid M. (1998). High Performance work Systems and Firm Performance: A Synthesis of Research and Managerial Implications. *Personnel & Human Resources Management*, 16, 53-101.

Becker B. and Huselid M. (2006). Strategic Human Resources Management: Where Do We Go From Here? *Journal of Management*, 32, 898-925.

Becker B., Huselid M. and Ulrich D. (2001). *The HR Scorecard: Linking People, Strategy and Performance*. Cambridge, MA: Harvard Business School Press.

Bell V., Burriel-Llombart P. and Jones J. (2005). *A quality-adjusted labour input series for the United Kingdom (1975- 2002).* Bank of England Working Paper No. 280. London.

Boudreau J. and Ramstad P. (1999). Human Resource Metrics: Can Measures be Strategic? *Personnel and Human Resources Management*, 4, 75-98.

Bouckaert G. and Halligan J. (2007). Performance and Performance Management. In Peter B. G. & Pierre J. (eds.) *Handbook of Public* Policy. SAGE Publications, UK. pp. 443-459.

Boxall P. (1996). The strategic HRM debate and the resource-based view of the firm. *Human Resource Management Journal*, 6(3), 59-75.

BS 6143-2 (1990). Guide to the economics of quality part 2: Prevention, appraisal and failure model. London: British Standards Institution.

Bunch K.J. (2007). Training failure as a consequence of organizational culture. *Human resource Development Review*, 6(2): 142–163.

Cameron K.S. and Quinn R. E. (2006). *Diagnosing and Changing Organizational Culture*. The Jossey-Bass Business & Management Series. John Wiley and Sons.

Camus D. ed. (2007). *The ONS Productivity Handbook: A Statistical Overview and Guide*. Office for National Statistics. Palgrave MacMillan.

Cascio W. and Boudreau J. (2008). *Investing In People*. Pearson Education Inc. USA.

Collins J. and Porras J. (1994). *Built to last*. HarperCollins Publishers Inc. New York.

Corrado C., Hulten C. and Sichel D. (2005). Measuring capital and technology: An expanded framework. In Corrado C., Haltiwanger J. and Sichel D. (eds.) *Measuring Capital in the new economy*. NBER, Studies in income and wealth, Vol. 65. The University of Chicago Press: Chicago.

The Confederation of Finnish Industries (2008). Työaikakatsaus. Työajat ja poissaolot EK:n jäsenyrityksissä vuonna 2007. Helsinki.

European Foundation (1997). *New forms of work organization. Can Europe realize its potential?* European Foundation for the Improvement of Living Conditions, Ireland.

Fitz-Enz J. (2000). The ROI of Human Capital: measuring the economic value of employee performance, Amacom. USA.

Festinger L. (1954). A theory of social comparison process. *Human Relations*, 7, 117–140.

Fleetwood S. and Hesketh A. (2010). *Explaining the Performance of Human Resource Management*, Cambridge University Press.

Garavan T. N. (2007). A strategic perspective on human resource development. *Advances in Developing Human Resources*, 9(1), 11-30.

Gilley J. and Maycunich A. (1998). *Strategically integrated HRD*. Perseus Publishing.

Goleman D., Boyatziz R. and McKee A. (2008). *The New Leaders*. Sphere.

Guest D. (1987). Human resource management and industrial relations. *Journal of Management Studies*, 14(5), 503-521.

—. (1997). Human Resource Management and Performance: A Review and Research Agenda. *International Journal of Human Resource Management*, 8(3), 263-76.

—. (2001). Human Resource Management: When Research Confronts Theory, *International Journal of Human Resource Management*, 12(7), 1092-1106.

Hamel G. (2007). *The future of management*. Harvard Business School Press, Boston.

Huselid M. (1995). The Impact of Human Resource Management Practices on Turnover, Productivity, and Corporate Financial Performance. *Academy of Management Journal*, 38(3), 635-72.

Hunt J. W. (1992). Managing People at Work: A Manager's Guide to Behaviour in organizations. Third edition, McGraw-Hill.

Ichniowsky C., Shaw K. and Prennushi G. (1997). The Effects of Human Resource Management on Productivity: A Study of Steel Finishing Lines. *The American Economic Review*, 87(3), 291-313.

Kaplan R. S. and Norton D. P. (1996). *The Balanced Scorecard: Translating Strategy Into Action*. Boston: Harvard Business School Press.

Kaplan R. S. and Norton D. P. (2004).*Strategy Maps: Converting Intangible Assets Into Tangible Outcomes*. Boston: Harvard Business School Press.

Keat G. K. and Yoyng P. K. Y. (2003). Managerial Economics, Fourth Edition, Prentice Hall.

Kesti M. (2012). The Tacit Signal Method in Human Competence based Organization Performance Development. Doctoral dissertation, University of Lapland, Finland

Kesti M., Syväjärvi A. and Stenvall J. (2009). Hiljaiset signaalit HRIS: yksi ratkaisu organisaation inhimillisen pääoman ja henkilöstötuottavuuden kehittämisessä. *Hallinnon Tutkimus,* 28(1), 46-61.

Kesti M. and Syväjärvi A. (2010). Human tacit signals at organization performance development. *Industrial Management & Data Systems,* 110(2), 211-229.

Kesti M., Syväjärvi A. and Stenvall J. and Rivera M. A. (2011). Human capital scenario analysis as an organizational intelligence tool for performance management. *Problems and Perspectives in Management,* 9(1), 46-58.

Kesti M. (2009). *Strategic Human Capital Management*. Talentum, Helsinki (in Finnish).

Kesti M., Syväjärvi A. and Stenvall J. (2008). E-HRM in Competence Recognition and Management - The Tacit Signal HRIS. In Torres-Coronas, T. and Arias-Oliva, M. (eds.) *Encyclopedia of Human Resource Information Systems: Challenges in E-HRM*. Idea Group Publishing Inc, USA

Kesti, M. & Syväjärvi, A. (2012). Human Resource Development Function to both Organizational Performance and Quality of Working Life. *Journal on GSTF Business Review*, Vol. 2(1), 135–141.

Kets de Vries, M. (2006). The Leadership Mystique. Leading Behavior in the Human Enterprise. Second edition. Prentice Hall.

Kim H. and Cervero R.M. (2007). How power relations structure the evaluation process for HRD programs. *Human Resource Development International*, 10(1): 5–20.

Lepak, D. P. and Snell, S. A. (1999). The human resource architecture: toward a theory of human capital allocation and development. *Academy of Management Review*, 24(1), 31-48.

Lepak, D. P. and Senll, S. A. (2008). *Employment subsystems and the 'HR architecture'*. In Boxall P., Purcell J. and Wright P. (eds.) The Oxford Handbook of Human Resource Management. Oxford University Press, UK. pp. 210-230.

Liker J. K. (2004). *The Toyota way*. McGraw-Hill, New York.

Losada M. and Heaphy, E.(2004). The role of positivity and connectivity in the performance of business teams: A nonlinear dynamics model. *American Behavioral Science*, 2(1): 71-87.

Lumijärvi, I. (2009). *Johtamisen vaikutus organisaation tuloksellisuuteen*. Juvenes Print – Tampereen yliopistopaino Oy, Tampere.

Maliranta M. and Asplund R. (2007). *Training and hiring strategies to improve firm performance*. ETLA, Discussion Paper no. 1105, Helsinki.

Mankin D. (2010). *Human resource development*. Oxford University Press.

Nonaka, I., & Takeuchi, H. (1995). *The Knowledge Creating Company*. Oxford University Press. New York.

Nonaka I. and Konno N. (1998). The concept of "Ba": Building a Foundation for Knowledge Creation. *California Management Review*, 40/3 1998: 40–54.

OECD (2001). Measuring Productivity. Measurement of Aggregate and Industry-Level Productivity Growth. Organization for Economic Co-operation and Development: Paris.

Paauwe J. (2004). Human Resource Management and Organizational Performance. Oxford University Press, UK.

Pfeffer J. (1994). Competitive Advantage through People: Unleashing the Power of the Workforce. Harvard University Press, USA.

Pfeffer J. and Sutton R. I: (2000). *The Knowing-Doing Gap: How Smart Companies Turn Knowledge into Action*. Harvard Business School Press, USA.

Polanyi M. (1967). *The Tacit Dimension*. Doubleday, USA.

Pynes, J. E. and Lombardi D. N. (2011). *Human resource management for healthcare organizations*. Jossey-Bass, USA.

Ramsay H., Scholarios D. and Harley B. (2000). Employees and High-Performance Work Systems: Testing Inside the Black Box. *British Journal of Industrial Relations*, 38(4), 501-31.

Saari S. (2006). "Productivity. Theory and Measurement in Business" (PDF). European Productivity Conference, 30 August-1 September 2006, Espoo, Finland. http://www.mido.fi/index_tiedostot/Productivity_EPC2006_Saari.pdf.

Sila I. (2006). Examining the Effects of Contextual Factors on TQM and Performance through the Lens of Organizational Theories: An Empirical Study. *Journal of Operations Management*, 25(1), 83-109.

Senge P. M. (2006). *The Fifth Discipline*. Doubleday, USA.

Stone, R.J. (2002). *Human Resource Management*. Fourth edition. John Wiley & Sons Ltd., Australia.

Swansson R.A. (2005). Evaluation, a state of mind. *Advances in Developing Human resources*, 7(1), 16-21.

Syväjärvi, A., Stenvall, J, Jurvansuu, H. and Harisalo, R. (2003). Management of Technological Health Services Promotes the Organizational Performance and the Quality of Human Life. *American Society on Aging*, 10, 1–28.

Syväjärvi, A. & Stenvall, J. eds. (2010). *Data Mining in Public and Private Sectors: Organizational and Governmental Applications*. Information Science Publishing. IGI Global, USA.

Syväjärvi, A. and Kesti, M. (2012). *Positive Human Tacit Signal Approach and Competence System Intelligence Model in Organization*. In Di Fabio, A. (ed.) Emotional Intelligence – New Perspectives and Applications. Intech Publishing, USA. 139-166.

Ulrich D. (1997). Human Resource Champions, the Next Agenda for Adding Value and Delivering Results. Harvard Business School Press, USA.

Wang G.G. and Wilcox D. (2006). Training evaluation: knowing more than is practiced. *Advances in Developing Human Resources*, 8(4): 528–539.

Welch J., Welch S. (2005). *Winning*. Harper Collings Publishers, USA.

Wheelan, S.(2005). *Creating Effective Teams: A Guide for Members and Leaders*. Second edition. Newbury Park, CA: Sage, USA.

CHAPTER EIGHT

PROMOTING KNOWLEDGE BASED ECONOMY AND MINIMIZING DIGITAL GAP IN ARAB COUNTRIES WITH SPECIAL REFERENCE TO SAUDI ARABIA: A QUALITATIVE STUDY

KHALIL ELIAN ABDELRAHIM
TAIF UNIVERSITY, SAUDI ARABIA

Abstract

The study aims at discussing concepts of knowledge based economy and digital Gap; describing the status of knowledge economy and digital Gap in Arab Countries; investigating challenges and promoting methods of building knowledge economy and minimizing digital Gap in Arab countries. The methodology of the study is descriptive in collection and analysis of data. The study concludes that Arab countries are far away from transferring their economies into knowledge based economies and there is still a digital gap between Arab countries and developed countries and among Arab countries themselves. Arab countries should accelerate moving their traditional economies towards knowledge based economies. The study recommends establishing technology incubators; expanding usage of information technology, internet, innovations, exchange of information, protection of intellectual property rights, modernizing data bases, mass media, TV production and other consultancy services as means of promoting knowledge based economies in Arab countries.

Key Words: *Knowledge-Based Economy, Innovation, Digital Gap.*

Introduction

Knowledge based economy gained momentum in the 21st century, with the world economy moving towards 'knowledge Based Economy and Arab countries are becoming concerned with the significance of knowledge based economy and its role in development.

Knowledge based economy is based on information technology, electronic engineering, nanotechnology, know-how, modern communication, computer processing and their applications in the fields of water desalination, medicine, industry, agriculture, food production and energy.

In the last two decades, development economists concentrated their efforts on moving from traditional economy to knowledge-based economy and narrowing the digital gab between developed and developing countries.

Moreover, knowledge based economy was the subject of international conferences such as the Global Information Technology Conference in Geneva, Switzerland in 2003, besides research initiatives on the role of knowledge based economy in development world-wide.

Knowledge–based economy has become a new branch of economics that may be studied in several universities.

The research problem is that little is known about the extent that Arab economies have been transmitted into knowledge-based economies and about the digital gap that exists between Arab and developed countries in terms of knowledge based economy.

The main research questions to be investigated in this study are: to what extent have the Arab economies been developed towards knowledge -based economy? What is the size of digital gap between Arab and developed countries?

The objectives of the study are to discuss concepts of knowledge based economy and digital Gap; to describe the status of knowledge economy and digital Gap in Arab Countries and to investigate the challenges and the promoting techniques of building knowledge economy for minimizing digital Gap between Arab countries and advanced countries.

As this research is a qualitative study, the author has followed the descriptive methodology in analysis, using mean and standard deviation of the secondary data collected from Arab and foreign sources including periodicals, books, World Bank Development Indicators, IMF publications besides websites and internet.

The study's organizational structure consists of eight sections besides acknowledgements, biography and references. Section 1: introduction. Section 2: the conceptual framework, characteristics and significance of knowledge based economy. Section 3: differences between knowledge based economy and traditional economy. Section 4: indicators of knowledge based economy. Section 5: Status of knowledge based economy and digital gap in Arab countries. Section 6: challenges of knowledge based economy in Arab countries. Section 7: Means of Developing Knowledge Based Economy in Arab Countries and Bridging the Digital Gap. Section 8: Conclusions & Recommendations.

Conceptual Framework, Characteristics and Significance of knowledge Based Economy

Knowledge based economy is an economy that creates, disseminates and uses knowledge to enhance growth and development. A country has an ample scope for exploiting the global information and communication technologies to boost the productivity of agriculture, industry and services to reduce poverty, accelerate growth, improve international competitiveness and join the ranks of developed countries that make successful transition to knowledge economy.

The initial foundation for knowledge economy was first introduced by Peter Drucker in 1966 in his book "The Effective Executive" in which he differentiated between manual worker who works with his hands and produces stuff with a knowledge worker who works with his head and produces ideas, knowledge and information (http://en.wikipedia.org/wiki/knowledge_economy).

The stages of acquiring knowledge include the following (Mariati, 2006):

a- Creation of new knowledge
b-Transmission of Knowledge
c-Distribution of knowledge
d-Implementation of Knowledge

Four critical pillars are recommended for a country to embrace the knowledge based economy (World Bank, 2004):

1-Strengthening the economic and institutional regime.
2-Developing educated and skilled workers.
3-Creating an efficient innovation system.
4-Building a dynamic information infrastructure.

Under knowledge based economy, information and communication technologies (ICT) play a leading role in the process of economic

> development, a source of innovation and accounted for strong investment and employment leading to growth of productivity and minimizing cost of production where USA, European countries and Japan are mostly reaping the benefits of digital economy (UNECE, 2006).
>
> In the new economy, knowledge plays an important role through using the internet, web sites and networks to shape the economy and where information, e-commerce, e-banking and e-learning become the strategic tools in knowledge economy (Elian, 2003).
>
> Knowledge based economy was expressed in deferent terminologies and expressions such as "New Economy", "Information Technology", "Cyber Economy", "Intangible Economy", "Weightless Economy", "Immaterial Economy" and "Virtual Economy" (Ali & Hijazi, 2005)

The characteristics of knowledge based economy include its reliance on intellectual human capital for innovation, continuous education during whole life for individuals and groups, based on digital knowledge, applying quantitative and mathematical models, usage of internet, economies of scale and globalization.

Concerning the significance of Knowledge Based Economy, the world is moving towards knowledge based economy as knowledge becomes the main component in the value added of the economy particularly the advanced information technology (IT) which is playing a vital role in the process of transforming the traditional economy into knowledge economy.

Knowledge-based economy provides vast economic opportunities of investment, job creation, economic value added, innovation and cost effectiveness.

Furthermore, the relation between knowledge and development becomes very clear in contemporary economics as the new development theories link development with new generation of information.

It is estimated that around 50% of GDP in OECD countries is based on knowledge and in the USA around 60% of income comes from information and telecommunication industries. In industrialized countries, the most increases in exports are connected with the increase of export of knowledge based industries to reach 36% in Japan, 37% in USA, 43% in Ireland, 32% in UK. (Mariati, 2006).

The bulk of investments of developed countries are related to information and communication industries, education, training, and research as investment in knowledge increases productivity.

Moreover, most of jobs created in developed countries are concentrated in the fields of information technology, communication technology, nanotechnology, e-commerce and e-learning.

Digital Gap is defined as the breach or space between countries or between people in the same country in having access to computer, internet and information technology. Digital Gap exists between developed and developing countries and insides each country between the poor and rich. It was mentioned for the first time in the literature in 1995 in USA to indicate the digital gab between the white and black inhabitants in USA in acquiring computers and having access to internet. The causes of Digital Gab are technological, economic, political, cultural and social.

Differences between Knowledge-Based Economy and Traditional Economy

Neo-classical economics has recognized only two factors of production: land and capital. This is now changing as information and knowledge are replacing capital and land as the key factor of production. Moreover, human capital is playing a big role in knowledge based economy as global work force with expertise and know-how can be transferred to any place overnight.

The knowledge based economy differs from traditional economy in the following key aspects (www.skyrme,com/insights/21gke.htm):

1. The knowledge based economy is not of scarcity as information and knowledge can be shared and grow through application.
2. The effect of location has diminished with the use of technology and knowledge in the economy as virtual market places and virtual organizations can be created.
3. Laws, barriers and taxes are difficult to apply on solely national bases in knowledge based economy.
4. Knowledge enhanced products and services can command price premiums over comparable products with low knowledge intensity.
5. Value depends heavily on context as the same information or knowledge can have different value to different people at different times.
6. Knowledge locked into systems or processes has higher inherent value than when it can walk out of the door in the people heads.
7. Human capital is a key component of value in a knowledge-based economy.

Knowledge based economy is based on demass production while traditional economy is based on mass production. Other differences are in terms of value, ownership, relation between demand and supply, relation between producer and consumer, evaluation of economic performance and patterns of organization and management as in Table1:

Table 1: Comparison between Knowledge-Based Economy and Traditional Economy

Elements of Comparison	Knowledge-Based Economy	Traditional Economy
Concept of Value	Value of information is lost if they are not used.	Value is not lost if products are not used.
Concept of Ownership	Intellectual property and human capital play an important role.	It is concerned with material capital .
Relation between Demand and Supply	Concentrate on demand increase through plenty of supply to increase value.	Scarcity and low supply increase value. It concentrates on supply.
Relation between Consumer and Producer	Economy is based on reproduction and it is concerned with increasing knowledge.	It is based on national production and consumption.
Bases of Evaluation of Economic Performance	Evaluation is based on probable and available knowledge capacity of networks.	Evaluation is based on actual production and expansion of commodities.
Organization & Management Patterns	A network is based on both central production and non-central control. There is demass production and is concerned with competition and cooperation.	Central hierarchal organization is based on mass production and competitiveness.

Source: Nabil Ali & Nadia Hijazi (2005) *Digital Gap: Arab Vision of Knowledge. Knowledge World Series*. Kuwait.

Indictors of Knowledge - Based Economy and Digital Gab

Performance of Knowledge-Based Economy is measured through the extent of scientific capacity and its ability of expansion and merging with other technologies, besides the extent of availability of networks of internet and communication technologies. The performance of Traditional Economy is measured through its productive capacity, storage and size of the market.

There are several indicators of knowledge-based economy such as availability of appropriate economic and institutional environment, availability of knowledge society, and availability of information infrastructure (Mariati, 2005)

The World Bank has lately adopted the Knowledge Assessment Method (KAM) for rating of knowledge in different countries. Such a method includes indicators of knowledge -based economy which is given 103 points and growth of Gross Domestic Product and human capital which is given 6 points. Components of knowledge- based economy are: economic system (12 points), governance (7 points), education (15 points), labor (24 points), role of women (5 points), Innovation (28 points), information technology (12 points) as shown in Table 2.

Digital gap may be measured through the following indicators (Taif University, 2007):

(i) Tele Density Indicator (TDI)
(ii) Technical Progress Indicator (TPI)
(iii) Technical Achievement Indicator (TAI)
(iv) Network Readiness Indicator (NRI)
(v) Media Usage Indicator (MUS)
(vi) Inform, Intelligence, Quot (IIQ)
(vii) St. No. of Digital Access (SNDA)
(viii) Limit of involvement in globalization

Table 2: World Bank Knowledge Assessment Method (KAM)

<table>
<tr><th>Total Points</th><th>Main Indicators</th><th colspan="4">Evaluation Elements</th></tr>
<tr><td rowspan="2">6</td><td>GDP growth</td><td colspan="3" rowspan="2">Economic Performance Indicators</td><td rowspan="13">Knowledge Assessment Method (KAM)</td></tr>
<tr><td>Human Development</td></tr>
<tr><td>12</td><td>Trade Liberation</td><td>Economic System</td><td rowspan="2">Systems and Incentives</td><td rowspan="11">Knowledge Economy Indicators (KEI)</td></tr>
<tr><td rowspan="2">7</td><td>Quality of Business Environment</td><td rowspan="2">Governance</td></tr>
<tr><td>Security and Judicial system.</td><td rowspan="9">Knowledge Indicators(kI)</td></tr>
<tr><td rowspan="3">15</td><td>Percentage of Educated Youngest.</td><td rowspan="3">Education</td></tr>
<tr><td>Percentage of people registered in Secondary Education.</td></tr>
<tr><td>Percentage of people registered in Higher Education.</td></tr>
<tr><td>24</td><td>No Indicators</td><td>Labor</td></tr>
<tr><td>5</td><td>No Indicators</td><td>Woman role</td></tr>
<tr><td rowspan="3">28</td><td>Number of Published Research per 1 million inhabitants.</td><td rowspan="3">Innovation system</td></tr>
<tr><td>Patents per 1 million people.</td></tr>
<tr><td>Intellectual Licenses per one million people</td></tr>
</table>

12	Number of telephones per 1000 people	Information Technology			
	Number of computers per 1000 people				
	Number of internet users per 1000 people				
109	Total indicators				

Source: Bakry, Said Ali Al-Haj (2011) Towards A Strategy for Innovation in Gulf Cooperation Council. *Altawon Magazine No.73, 2011*

Status of Knowledge Based Economy and Digital Gap in Arab Countries

Most of the economies of Arab countries are still far away from being based on knowledge and information technology. As a result, there is little focus on the role of information, technology, e-learning and e-commerce in the economic performance. However, there should be more recognition and concern of knowledge as a driver of productivity and economic growth and more awareness of the role of information and communication technologies (ICT) in the process of economic and social change in Arab countries. Arab states should have more investment in knowledge as a major source of innovation in Arab communities.

Diffusion of information technology in Arab countries requires better understanding of knowledge networks and national innovation systems to build a knowledge base within Arab communities.

Arab countries should benefit from best practices of knowledge -based economy in the OECD countries, USA, Japan and emerging countries for transmission of knowledge into their traditional economies through information, communication technologies and computer networks. Hence, identifying the best practices in knowledge -based economy should be the focal point of Arab states in the field of science, technology and industry.

There is a need for Arab workers to acquire a range of technical skills that are necessary for acquiring e- learning and knowledge society.

Knowledge indicators of Arab Countries members of Gulf Cooperation Council (GCC) are shown in Table 3.

Table 3 shows that GCC countries have relatively achieved the best results in ownership of telephones (7.82), followed by GDP growth (7.49) followed by rules of the law (7.28), then Human Capital Development(7.18) followed by registration of students in secondary school (7.04) then liberation of trade (6.26). However, GCC countries achieved the least results in knowledge fees (0.34), followed by education for adults (3.97) then registration for higher education (4.18). Moreover, GCC countries achieved higher than average in the rest of knowledge indicators. Within the GCC, Saudi Arabia achieved higher than average in most knowledge indicators compared to other GCC countries.

In term of indicators of knowledge-based economy , innovation, economic incentives, education and ICT, Arab countries have achieved near average results compared to the universal average as shown in Table 4.

Table 3: Knowledge Indicators in Arab Countries Members of GCC in 2009

Evaluation Elements*	Kuwait	Qater	Oman	Saudi Arabia	Bahrain	UAE	Average in GCC
GDP growth (2003-2007)	9٫79	9٫52	3٫31	4٫97	7٫79	9٫59	7٫49
Human Capital Development (2005)	7٫90	7٫69	6٫50	6٫29	7٫27	7٫41	7٫18
Liberation of Trade (2009)	6٫08	6٫36	6٫99	6٫64	5٫45	6٫01	6٫26
Organization Quality (2007)	5٫69	6٫71	6٫92	4٫93	7٫60	7٫05	6٫48
Rules of the Law (2007)	7٫47	8٫08	7٫53	6٫23	7٫19	7٫19	7٫28
Education for Adults (2007)	5٫41	4٫04	3٫08	3٫22	3٫84	4٫25	3٫97
Registered for Secondary School (2007)	5٫83	8٫82	5٫97	6٫74	8٫47	6٫39	7٫04
Registered for Higher Education (2007)	3٫55	3٫26	4٫35	4٫71	5٫14	4٫06	4٫18
Number of Published Research(2005)	7٫15	6٫18	5٫97	5٫28	6٫11	6٫53	6٫20
Patents (2003-20007)	7٫47	6٫71	3٫90	6٫3	2٫47	6٫85	5٫61
Knowledge Fees (2007)	0,34	-	-	0٫34	-	-	0٫34
Telephones (2007)	6٫37	9٫66	5٫96	6٫92	8,08	9,93	7٫82
Computers (2007)	6٫92	7٫33	4٫18	6٫48	7٫04	7٫89	6٫64
Internet (2007)	6٫92	7٫33	4٫18	5٫89	6٫78	7٫95	6٫51

* knowledge indicators index ranges between 0 and 10 where zero is the least value and 10 is highest value.

Source: Bakry, Said Ali Al-Haj (2011) Towards A Strategy for Innovation in Gulf Cooperation Council. *Altawon Magazine No.73, 2011*

Table 4: Position of Arab Countries in Knowledge, Innovation and ICT in Comparison to the Universal Average in 2008

Rank	Countries	Knowledge Based Economy	System of Economic Incentives	Innovation	Education	Information & Communication Technologies (ICT)
	Universal Average	5.992	5.18	8.01	4.16	6.24
42	UAE	6.66	6.95	6.74	4.78	8.18
45	Qatar	6.35	5.44	6.88	6.74	6.33
49	Bahrain	6.02	6.84	4,2	5.82	7.22
50	Kuwait	6.01	7.01	5.05	4.87	7.13
56	Jordan	5.53	5.77	5.66	5.49	5.21
62	Oman	5.37	7.32	4.95	4.3	4.9
70	Lebanon	4.86	4.7	4.69	4.76	5.27
71	Tunisia	4.73	5.26	4.58	4.1	5.0
84	Egypt	4.03	3.57	4.55	4.35	3.66
92	Morocco	3.45	3.8	3.67	2.0	4.32
96	Alger	3.25	2.53	3.48	3.64	3.37
104	Syria	2.9	1.55	3.44	2.91	3.68
112	Mauritania	2.35	3.89	1.75	0.94	2.8
119	Yemen	1.8	1.72	1.68	1.83	1.99

Source: World Bank (2008) *Report on Knowledge-based Economy(KAM),* Washington DC.

Table 4 shows that GCC countries of UAE, Qatar, Bahrain and Kuwait achieved higher than the universal average of indicators, while the rest of Arab countries achieved less than the universal average in innovation. GCC countries within the Arab group achieved better results than the rest of Arab countries in most of the indicators. Syria, Yemen and Mauritania got the least results in most of the knowledge indicators.

In comparison with other regions and countries including Israel, most of the Arab countries achieved lower results in Human Development, culture, and innovation as shown in Table 5.

Table 5 shows that there is still a large digital gap between most of Arab countries and the World Average in knowledge-based economy indicators, such a gap is larger compared with Middle Europe, East Asia, South Asia and Israel.

The status of Saudi Arabia in knowledge-based economy is shown in Table 6.

Table 6 shows that Saudi Arabia is still facing obstacles in its way of transmission to knowledge- based economy, such obstacles include scarcity of technical incubators for promoting small and medium enterprises, little specialization in science and technology branches, insufficient research and development, little expenditure on science and technology compared to developed countries.

In spite of these obstacles, Saudi Arabia has laid down a strategy for promoting knowledge based economy within the 8th Five Year Development Plan which called for building a base for science and technology and establishing promising projects in information and communication technology. King Abdullah University of Science and Technology (KAUST) was established to promote knowledge in the Kingdom. Nowadays, higher education is oriented towards IT, communication technology, internet, e-government, e-commerce, e-learning and electronic university. Moreover, the Government has established several knowledge cities for promoting information and communication technologies in Riyadh and Madina (http://www.saudi chambers.org.sa) Furthermore, Saudi Arabia has got the rank 18 among 144 countries in competitiveness which is a remarkable position according to the competitiveness report of World Economic Forum in Davos, Switzerland (World Economic Forum, 2012)

Table 5: Indicators of Human Development Indicators, Culture and Innovation in Arab countries in Comparison with Other Regions in 2002

Countries And Regions	Rank in Human Development Indicator Index	workers in Scientific Research per a million inhabitants	Expenditure on Research as a Percentage of GDP	Patents per a million person	Internet per a million inhabitant	Mobile Telephone per 1000 Inhabitant	Fixed Telephone per 1000 Inhabitants
Bahrain	40	.	.	.	245,6	579	261
Kuwait	44	212	0,2	.	105,8	518	204
Qatar	47	591	.	.	113,4	433	286
UAR	49	0	.	.	313,2	647	291
Libya	58	361	.	.	22,5	13	118
Oman	74	4	.	.	70,9	183	92
Saudi Arabia	77	.	.	.	64,6	228	151
Lebanon	80	.	.	.	117,1	227	199
Jordan	90	1948	6,3	.	57,7	229	127
Tunisia	90	336	0,5	.	51,7	52	117
Palestine	102	.	.	.	30,4	93	87
Syria	106	29	.	.	12,9	23	123
Alger	108	0	.	3	16	13	61
Egypt	120	992	.	.	68,2	304	107
Morocco	125	.	.	.	23,6	209	38
Moon Island	136	.	.	.	4,2	-	13
Sudan	139	.	.	.	2,6	6	21
Iraq	-	.	.	.	-	-	s-
Yemen	158	.	.	.	5,1	21	28

Mauritania	152	.	.	.	3,7	92	12
Gyboti	154	.	.	.	6,9	23	15
Average of Arab Countries	-	-	.	.	28	85	81
Israel	22	1563	5	75	301,4	453	453
East Asia	-	607	1,6	.	60,9	142	142
Latin America	-	285	0,5	1	81,2	191	166
South Asia	-	160	.	.	14,9	13	41
Africa	-	0	.	.	9,6	39	15
Middle Europe	-	2289	1	30	71,8	189	226
World Average	-	1096	2,5	48	99,4	184	175

Source: UNDP (2004) *Human Development Indicators Report*. New York

Table 6: Indicators of Knowledge Economy in Saudi Arabia

Intermediate Institutions	Private Sector	Research & Development	Scientific and Technical Education
Weakness of technical and engineering Centers	Weak demand of private sector to services of science and technical institutions	Low expenditure on R&D to 0.25% of GDP compared to 3% in Korea and 5% in Israel	Low number of graduates of technical education
Absence of financing and risk funds	Weak relation between private sector and scientific and technical centers	Low percentage of researcher in scientific topics of 13 to 100000 inhabitants compared to 532 in Japan.	Low percentage of students in scientific and technical specializations to 22% compared to 62% in China
Scarcity of technical Incubators	Low number of research in private sector enterprises	Low number of R&D in the advanced scientific fields.	Low number of scientific graduates of higher education to 70 of 100000 compared to 383 in South Korea.
	Reliance on foreign consultative and technical companies	Weak relations among research centers and between them and beneficiaries.	Weakness of educational programs in the field of water, IT, and Minerals .
	Low number of SMEs in technology field.		Weak programs of graduate studies in science and technology to 2.1% of total graduate students

Source: Al-Rasheed, Abdulla (2005) *National Institutions for Science, Technology and Innovation are Necessary for Technology Development.* 2nd conference for Technology Development at King Abdel-Aziz Scientific City. Riyadh

Jordan has geared its economy towards knowledge-based economy through establishing a national information center in 1993, providing schools with a computer for every student, teaching English from the first elementary class, having high education programs in IT, computer processing and communication with more graduates in information technology (Jordan Ministry of Planning and International Cooperation, 2005).

United Arab Emirates (UAE) has achieved the highest achievement in knowledge and innovation according to the rating of World Economic Forum in Davos. UAE has achieved progress in transferring its economy towards knowledge-based economy through more investment in information and communication technologies, e-government, e-commerce and e-learning particularly in Dubai and Abu Dhabi (www.sheik mohammed.co.ae).

Kuwait has also achieved progress towards knowledge- based economy through more investment in information and communication technologies.

In Egypt, several attempts were made towards knowledge-based economy and several symposiums and scientific conferences were held since September, 1999 (Elian, 2005).

Tunisia is concerned with knowledge based economy as it has formed a new council for information and technology and held international conferences on technology, internet and innovation (www.akhbar.tn/ html).

In Morocco, education reform was made with more concentration on information technology in order to increase competitiveness. Morocco has adopted modern approaches for teaching in higher education (Moroccan Ahdath Journal, 2006).

Syria has already started transforming its economy towards knowledge -based economy through promoting science and technology and establishing a virtual university in 2003 for better and continuous high education.

Oman has also taken steps in the process of gearing its economy towards knowledge –based economy by investing in establishment of information and technology centers and holding several international conferences on innovation (www.kom.om/index).

Furthermore, Arab countries have great efforts to integrate their economies in the global economy through having accession to the World Trade Organization and having free trade accords with developed countries as a step towards transmitting their traditional economies towards knowledge- based economy.

Concerning the digital gap in Arab countries, it is noticed that most Arab countries are still behind the developed countries and Israel in terms of advancing information and communication technologies and in their way towards knowledge-based economy as shown in Table 7:

Table 7: Knowledge Digital Gap Between Arab Countries and Israel

Indicators of Digital Gap	Arab Countries	Israel	Digital Gap
Percentage of internet to Total Population.	3%	16%	-13%
Percentage of who have computer to total population	4%	47%	-43%
Rank in Readiness of Website	Tunisia 0.34 Jordan 0.57 Morocco 0.52 Egypt 0.65	12	-11.48
Scientific Research Publication per 10000 inhabitants	0.33	11.7	-11.67
Number of translated books to 1 million inhabitants	3	100	-97
Number of companies working in IT	Less than 2000	2000	N/A

N/A=not available
Taif University (2007) *Digital Gap*. Deanship of Development and Quality Management. Taif

Table 7 shows that Israel is superior to Arab countries in all knowledge indicators particularly in possession of computers, translated books and scientific research.

In sum, transferring traditional Arab economies into knowledge – based economies is still a long term objective to be achieved due to the digital gap between Arab countries and developed countries such as USA, European countries, Japan, South Korea and Israel and among Arab countries themselves. More efforts and investment are required to move towards knowledge-based economy.

Challenges of Knowledge Based Economy in Arab Countries

Arab countries have not bridged yet the digital gap between themselves and advanced countries in term of knowledge –based economy due to weak infrastructure, monopoly in the market by transnational companies, brain drain of human resources, lack of political will, lack of investment in ICT, internet, e-commerce, e-government and e- learning, besides insufficient scientific research and lack of quality of education in most Arab universities. No Arab university is considered within the first 500 top international universities in 2007 (Taif University, 2007), but in 2012, a few Saudi and Arab universities were classified within the first 500 universities in the world.

According to Arab Labor Organization (ALO), lack of knowledge, science and technology in Arab countries is due to the following obstacles (Arab Labor Organization, 2007):

1-Brain drain due to immigration of Arab scientists to developed countries.
2-Lack of legal framework particularly intellectual property.
3-Lack of incentives and the enabling environment for promoting innovation, science and technology.
4-Low expenditure on scientific research in the areas of science and technology.
5-Shortage of human resources and scientists in the field of science and technology.
6-Weak quality of education in most Arab universities.
7-Absence of strategies for development of information and communication technologies.
8-Lack of application and implementation of IT in economic sectors.

Means of Developing Knowledge Based Economy and Minimizing Digital Gap in Arab Countries

To bridge the digital gap in Arab countries, the following policies should be adopted (Al-Saleh, 2009):

1-Adoption of a strategy for moving towards knowledge -based economy.

2-Upgrading education and training programs in the field of information technology.
3-Producing, distributing and implementing knowledge in the economy.
4-Increasing expenditure on scientific research in science and technology.
5-Attracting graduate students to specialize in information and communication technologies (ICT)
6-Providing opportunities for education for whole life.

For promoting knowledge-based economies of Arab countries, several suggestions were proposed such as (Abbass, 2000):

1-Designing an Arab plan for dealing with knowledge economy.
2-Connecting economy with information technology.
3-Supporting training of human resources in the area of knowledge economy.
4-Facilitating transfer of technology from developed countries to Arab countries.
5-Reducing brain drain of Arab scientists in information technology by providing them with incentives to keep them at home.
6-Translating foreign articles on information technology to Arabic.
7-Creating awareness of knowledge economy among Arab society .
8-Having cooperation among Arab scientists in the area of knowledge economy.
9-Having appropriate legislations for organizing legal aspects of knowledge economy.

Conclusions and Recommendations

The study aims at discussing concepts of knowledge -based economy and digital Gap; describing the status of knowledge economy and digital Gap in Arab Countries; investigating challenges, promoting methods of building knowledge economy and minimizing digital Gap in Arab countries.

The study concludes that there is still a long way for Arab countries to transform their traditional economies into knowledge -based economies. Digital gap still exists between Arab countries and developed countries and among Arab countries themselves with UAE, Kuwait, Saudi Arabia taking the lead in acquiring knowledge and information technology.

For promoting knowledge-based economy in Arab countries and narrowing the digital gap with the developed world, the study recommends the following: having appropriate strategies, developing education, establishing technology incubators; expanding usage of information technology, internet, innovation, exchange of information, protection of intellectual property rights of patents, trade marks, industrial designs and geographical indicators besides building data bases, mass media, TV production and other consultancy services for developing knowledge, IT, science and technology in Arab economies.

References

Abbas, Bashar (2000) *Information Technology*, Arab Society for information . Amman, pp: 85-101

Ali, Nabil & Nadia Hijazi (2005) *Digital Gap: Arab Vision of Knowledge. Knowledge World Series*. Kuwait.

Al-Rasheed, Abdulla (2005) *National Institutions for Science, Technology and Innovation are Necessary for Technology Development*. 2nd conference for Technology Development at King Abdel-Aziz Scientific City. Riyadh

Al-Saleh, Mohamed Ben Abdulla (2009) Knowledge-Based Economy the Way for Competitiveness. *Alqassim No.135, February 2009*. P.25

Arab Labor Organization 'ALO' (2007) *Labor Arab conference in its 34 Session held in Egypt during 10-17 March.* Sharm Al-Sheik

Bakry, Said Ali Al-Hajj (2011) Towards A Strategy for Innovation in Gulf Cooperation Council. *Altawon Magazine* No.73, 2011

Elian, Ribhi Mustafa (2005) *Information Society*. Jarir Publishing Co. Amman

Elian, Rula (2003) *Towards Computerized Knowledge Based Economy in Jordan.* Research Paper at College of Administration & Finance. Amman Arab Univerity for Graduate Studies. Amman.

Jordan Ministry of Planning & International Cooperation (2005) *A Reform Project of Education towards Knowledge Economy*. Amman

Mariati, Mohamad (2006) *Knowledge Economy & information Technology in Arab Countries.* ESCWA. Beirut.

Moroccan Ahdath Journal (2006) National Strategy for Use of Digital Techniques in Education. Rabat

Taif University (2007) *Digital Gap*. Deanship of Development and Quality Management. Taif

UNDP (2004) *Human Development Indicators Report*. New York

United Nations Economic Commission for Europe 'UNECE' (2006) *Industrial Restructuring, Energy and Enterprise Development* .Geneva

World Bank (2004) *India and Knowledge Economy: Leverage Strengths and Opportunities.* November 8. Washington DC

World Bank (2008) *Report on Knowledge-based Economy* (KAM) Washington DC

World Economic Forum (2012) *Competitiveness Report.* Davos, Switzerland

Drucker, Peter (1966) "*The Effective Executive*" available at: http:// www. en.wikipedia.org/wiki/knowledge_ economy

Difference between Knowledge based Economy and Traditional Economy Available at http://www.skyrme,com/insights/21gke.htm.

Oman is Gearing its Economy Towards Knowledge –based Economy available at: http://www.kom.om/index.

Saudi Knowledge Cities for Promoting Information and Communication Technologies in Riyadh and Madina available at: http://www.saudichambers.org.sa

Tunisia Council for Information and Technology available at http://www.akhbar.tn/html.

United Arab Emirates Achieved the Highest Achievement in Knowledge and Innovation available at: http://www.sheikmohammed.co.ae

Acknowledgement

I appreciate the guidance of Dr. Abdel-Aziz Al-Ankari, Dean of Faculty of Administration & Financial Sciences at Taif University who gave me the opportunity to contribute to the book entitled " Business Review: Advanced Application" and many thanks to Professor Talal Al-Malki, vice president for Development and Quality Management at Taif University for his sustainable encouragement.

CHAPTER NINE

INFORMATION SYSTEMS AND INTERNAL CONTROL SYSTEMS

FABRIZIO BAVA AND ALAIN DEVALLE
DEPARTMENT OF MANAGEMENT - UNIVERSITY OF TURIN

Abstract

The rules of Corporate Governance are increasingly involving company information systems as a fundamental support to the control system in order to protect data and to ensure the reliability of financial information. Recently, the need to provide the functions of internal auditing with suitable support for the planning activity of internal auditing has led to the necessity to develop appropriate methodologies and software that satisfy the reporting and control criteria oriented towards Corporate Governance compliance. The aim of this paper is to analyze the role of information systems in the internal control system of a company. The conclusions suggest that ERP is able to improve the internal control system of a company.

Keywords: *information systems, ERP, internal control.*

Introduction

The rules of Corporate Governance are increasingly involving company information systems as a fundamental support to the control system in order to protect data and to ensure the reliability of the financial information.

Recently, the need to provide the functions of internal auditing with suitable support for the planning activity of internal auditing has led to the necessity to develop appropriate methodologies and software that satisfy the reporting and control criteria oriented towards Corporate Governance.

In particular, such applications are becoming increasingly important to guarantee the reliability of the data and documentation of the control procedures following events such as the change to new accounting standards, the compliance for firms listed on the stock exchange in the USA to the Sarbanes - Oxley Act of 2002 and the greater attention paid to company risk management oriented towards the compliance with the Italian Law n° 231/01.

Considering this, firms must be committed to guaranteeing the reliability of data and their information systems in the following areas:

- technological;
- organisational.

The technological level is what is guaranteed with methodologies that have already been in use for some time and are aimed at the auditing of the information systems. On the other hand the organisational logistics level regards to what extent the effectiveness of the control actions oriented towards internal and external communication can be shown and the suitable formalisation of the control procedures, depending upon the case, to the supervising authorities of the financial market (Sarbanes Oxley Acts), to the Committee for internal control (Corporate Governance), to the official authorities (for example, Italian Law n° 231/01), to the Board of Directors (Enterprise Risk Management), etc.

The auditing of information systems (also known as information system auditing - I.S.A. -) deals with the analysis and monitoring of the control system that exists within the company information structure, by means of methodologies aimed at obtaining and assessing the established control objectives.

The information system is exposed to numerous risks linked to the malfunction and violation of security, as occurs in the case of accidental loss of data or violations following access to the data by unauthorised people.

Control activities of the information systems can be divided into:

- business audit: a set of controls aimed at analysing the different company processes and the different balance sheet items;
- system audit: geared towards safeguarding the system from the several risks it is subject to as a whole, from the operative system that is necessary for the installation of the information system to the authentication of the passwords and management of the authorisation profiles.

The availability of reliable information, aimed at informing the internal and external needs of the company, depends on the effectiveness of the structure of the internal control system.

Internal control is broadly defined (COSO Report, 1992) as a process, effected by an entity's board of directors, management and other personnel, designed to provide reasonable assurance regarding the achievement of objectives in the following categories:

- effectiveness and efficiency of operations;
- reliability of financial reporting;
- compliance with applicable laws and regulations.

Effectiveness and efficiency of operations.

This category addresses an entity's basic business objective, including performance and profitability goals and the correct use of resources.

Reliability of financial reporting.

This category relates to the preparation of reliable published financial statements, including interim and condensed financial statements.

Compliance with applicable laws and regulations.

This category deals with complying with those laws and regulations which the entity is subject to.

Internal control systems operate at different levels of effectiveness. Internal control can be deemed effective in each of the three categories respectively, if the board of directors and management have reasonable assurance that:

- the entity's operations objectives can be achieved;
- published financial statements are being prepared reliably;
- applicable laws and regulations are being complied with.

While internal control is a process, its effectiveness is a state or condition of the process at one or more points in time.

Internal control consists of five interrelated components. These are derived from the way management runs a business, and are integrated with the management process. Although the components apply to all entities, small and mid-size companies may implement them differently compared to large ones. Its controls may be less formal and less structured. However, a small company can still have effective internal control. The following figure represents the internal control process.

Fig. 1 The objectives of the internal control system.

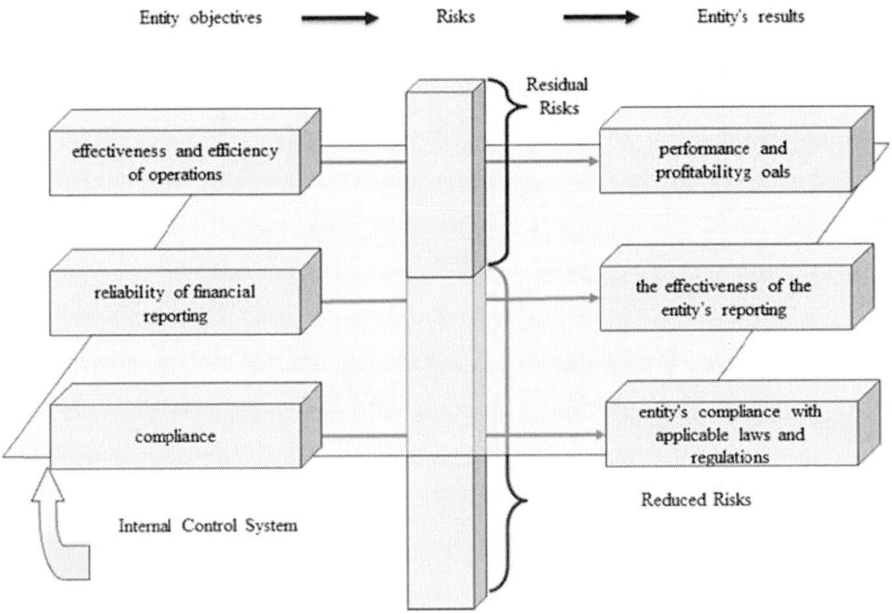

The components are:

1. control environment;
2. risk assessment;
3. control activities;
4. information and communication;
5. monitoring.

1) Control Environment

The control environment sets the tone of an organization, influencing the control consciousness of its people. It is the foundation for all other components of internal control, providing discipline and structure.

Control environment factors include:

- integrity, ethical values and competence of the entity's staff;
- the management's philosophy and operating style;

- the way management assigns authority and responsibilities, and organizes and develops its personnel?;
- the attention and guidance provided by the board of directors.

2) Risk Assessment

Every entity faces a variety of risks from external and internal sources that must be assessed. Risk assessment is the process of identification and analysis of relevant risks for the achievement of the objectives, forming a basis to determine how the risks should be managed. As economic, industry, regulatory and operating conditions will continue to change, mechanisms are needed to identify and deal with the special risks associated with these changes.

3) Control Activities

Control activities are the policies and procedures that help to ensure that management directives are carried out. They help to ensure that necessary measures are taken to address the risks which jeopardize the achievement of the entity's objectives. Control activities include a range of activities:

- approvals;
- authorizations;
- verifications;
- reconciliation;
- reviews of operating performance;
- security of assets and segregation of duties.

4) Information and Communication

Information must be identified, collected and communicated in a form and timeframe that enable people to carry out their responsibilities. Information systems produce reports containing operational, financial and compliance-related information, which make it possible to run an entity.

Information systems deals with:

- internally generated data;
- information about external events, activities and conditions necessary to carry out the business decision-making and external reporting.

Effective communication also must take place in a broader sense, crossing the organization both horizontally and vertically.

All the personnel must understand the importance of their responsibilities as well as their role in the control process and also the interrelationships of their own tasks with those of the colleagues. Communication has an important role both in the relationships with the other members of the staff and in the contact with the external parties, such as customers, suppliers, regulators and shareholders.

5) Monitoring

Internal control systems need to be monitored as a process that assesses the quality of the system's performance over a period of time. This is accomplished through ongoing monitoring activities, separate evaluations or a combination of the two. Ongoing monitoring occurs in the course of operations. It includes regular management and supervisory activities, and other actions personnel usually take when performing their duties. The scope and frequency of separate evaluations will depend primarily on an assessment of risks and the effectiveness of ongoing monitoring procedures. Internal control deficiencies should be reported upstream, with serious matters reported to top management and the board.

There is synergy and linkage between these components, forming an integrated system that reacts dynamically to changing conditions. The internal control system is intertwined with the entity's operating activities and exists for fundamental business reasons. Internal control is most effective when controls are built into the entity's infrastructure and are a part of the essence of the company. These controls support quality and empowerment initiatives, avoid unnecessary costs and make a quick response to changing conditions possible.

There is a direct relationship between the three categories of objectives, which are what an entity attempts to achieve, and the components, which represent what is needed to achieve the objectives. In order to conclude whether the internal control of operations is effective, all five components must be present and functioning correctly.

In conclusion the internal control system is a process, carried out by people, which provides reasonable assurance for the achievement of the above-mentioned objectives.

The definition above underlines that through the internal control system it is possible to lay down conditions to reach a reasonable certainty of company objectives. Among the “structural” components of the internal control system the role of the information systems is significant (Bava, 2003, Devalle, 2006).

The internal control system is represented in the table below.

Fig. 2 The internal control system.

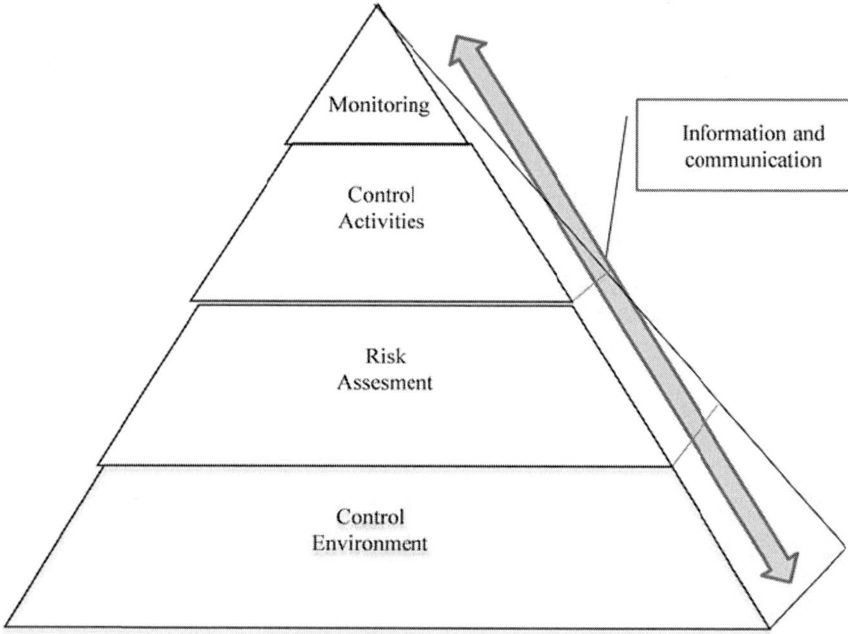

This paper focuses on the different typologies of information systems and their role in the internal control system.

Information Systems Management

The information that is produced by the information system represents the fundamental basis for the reasonable management of the company (Ferrero, 1987, Laudon and Laudon, 2006). The information system is an organized system of elements – IT, people, procedures, etc. – that collects, elaborates, changes and archives data with the aim of producing and distributing information to people in need, at the right time and in the right place.

Considering the information needed by the company, the objective of the information system must pursue the following objectives (Pisoni, 1979):

- to supply every managerial activity with all the information needed with the objective of right decision making;

- to organize data and knowledge to satisfy information needs manifested in the external environment.

To satisfy the information needs described earlier, the following typologies of information systems can be identified:

- *operational;*
- *managerial*;

Operational information systems

The *operational information system* represents an underlying system of the information system of the company in its entirety. In particular, the characteristic of the information system is the drawing up and support of the exchange of the information that is generated:

- inside any operational process (Zappa, 1937; Porter 1987; Stalk and Hout, 1991; Earl and Khan, 1994; Atkinson et al., 1998) of a company: for example the process of the physical transformation of the material into the final product, the process of sales billing, etc;
- among operational processes of the same company: for example the research and the development which involves different business areas;
- among the operational processes of different companies: for example the process of the distribution of goods.

The operational information systems therefore have the objective to draw up data that is related to primary business activities and to create knowledge attributing the foundation of data that is permanently managed by the system.

In particular, the operational information systems can be distinguished in:

- traditional information systems (or not integrated);
- enterprise resource planning.

The traditional information system is made up of a series of applications and of related archives that collect the information for homogenous categories. For example, general accounting uses one specific information system whereas management control uses another one, etc. The scheme of synthesis of different traditional management systems can be the following.

Fig. 3 Scheme of synthesis of different traditional management systems.

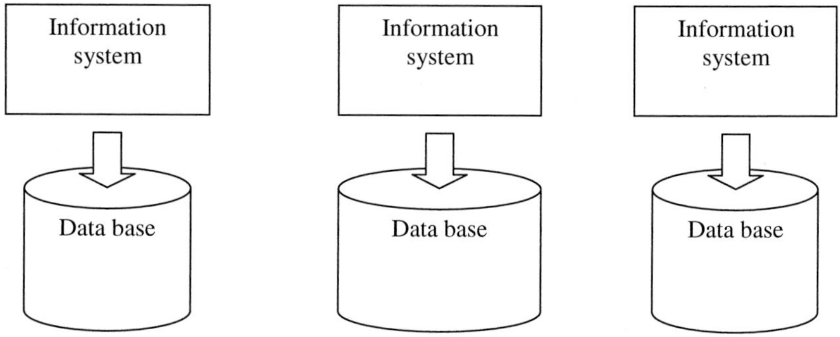

As noted, the different traditional informative systems are developed on the stimulus of particular business requirements (for example General Accounting, Production Management and Human Resources Management, etc.) and they generate specific archives that do not respond easily to the processes of extraction and communication of the data. It is necessary to remember that the information systems evolve and develop following technological waves that generate, in the same system, a stratification formed by numerous applications belonging to various technological eras, thus inevitably conditioning the company as well as the group for many years.

Enterprise Resource Planning represents the most recent global solutions of software application packages, finalized to integrate the principle business functions, such as administration, finance, production and sales, with a guideline to the improvement of the activities of planning, management and control of all the business resources.

The implementation of these information systems allows a complete integration between internal activities and external activities. ERP Packages are information systems that enable the enterprise to automate its own administrative and operating activities more extensively. The advantages of the use of ERP systems are laid down by the rationalization of business processes with the aim of creating greater value for the shareholders and in particular:

- to reduce the processes quickly, both productive as well as administrative transactions.
- to improve performance (constant improvement of the performances), in order to cut the superfluous production costs;
- for greater efficiency of the distribution activity;
- for greater attention to the final customer.

The increment of the installations of integrated information systems (ERP) is the most obvious answer to the needs manifested by the companies to easily and rapidly obtain the great amount of managerial information that the traditional information systems do not supply.

With reference to this, the producers of ERP integrate the traditional administrative modules (for example: general accounting, management control, production management, sales management, etc.) within complete suites of business management that also include the operating part (production, sales, staff, etc).

In some cases, also when the company implements an ERP system, the plan can consider the conservation of traditional information systems (or legacy) of the company that prove to be more functional than the ERP system.

In other cases, the company can develop technological platforms dedicated to managing particular company processes (Best of Breed approach) such as "Customer Relationship Management" (CRM), "Supply Chain Management" (SCM) and "e-commerce.

For this reason, it can be concluded that the real problem is the integration of data among application products, which are relatively autonomous, and which generate transactions and produce information utilized by different company functions. The scheme of the summary of the whole information system can be the following.

As seen in the scheme, every application can be integrated with ERP and for this reason can aliment the DBMS of the company or can directly extract the data from the same company database. The ERP generally makes periodic updates that adjust all the modules to the new condition provided that the customisation of the user has not modified the structure of the software. The adjustment of ERP to the International Accounting standards can be realized with an appropriate module.

Fig. 4 The scheme of the summary of the whole information system.

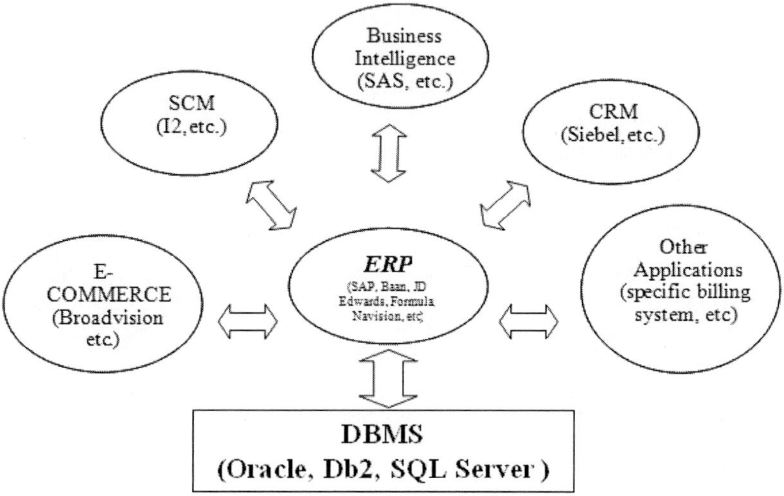

Managerial information system

The *managerial information system* refers to the operational information system and supports the activities of the management of the company or rather the managerial activities that are addressed to the definition of objectives (of long, medium, or short term) and of actions that must be carried out by those responsible. Moreover, it supports the activities which are necessary to reach the objective of a company.

The objectives of the managerial information system are (Anthony, 1985):

- *strategic planning:* management through the strategic planning process defines the long term objectives of a company and the strategy and strategic plans to be followed;
- *managerial control:* high and medium level management through the process of managerial control transform the strategic objectives into a short term objective, often expressed in economic and financial terms. The objective is periodically verified, imposing eventual corrective interferences.

Such managerial information systems are parts of an underlying informative system which have been put together, those that are directed to the production of reporting accounting or non – accounting entries. Reporting supports managerial activities.

The considerations made in the previous point give a different architectural approach to business data which can be divided into:

- the level of transactional data;
- the level of directional data.

Transactional data memorizes single transactions which register managerial events, for instance, the emission of an invoice from a store is documented by one or more recordings and single registry that memorizes the various transaction elements, for example the article code, description, price, etc..

Directional data base picks up information which refers to a data theme, for instance the data concerning the sales for commercial analyses or the accounting data of the financial statement of the company for the editing of the consolidated financial statement.

The information gathered is multi-dimensional and timely, therefore the feeding of the database involves a transformation of the transactional data which determines:

- timing;
- selection of data to register;
- choice of dimensions;
- calculation method.

Below there is a synthesis of the construction of the datawarehouse:

Fig. 5 Synthesis of the construction of the directional database.

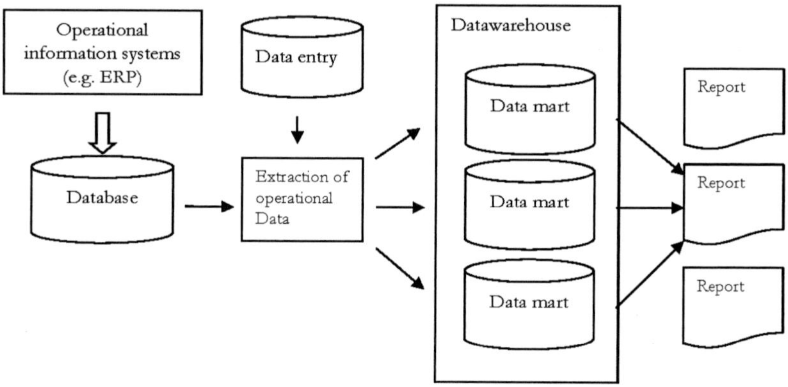

The structure above can be divided into different levels:

- level 0: transactional data;
- level 1: extraction of operational data and transformation for directional uses;
- level 2: memorizing and organization of data of specific directional structures;
- level 3: analysis and presentation of information;
- level 4: access to the information produced.

In particular, level 0 is the level of the operational information system (described above). With its database, (alone if an ERP is used or many if a traditional information system is used) it is the main source of information for the managerial system.

Level 1 is constituted by processes that execute the cycle of extraction of the operational data, and the transformation of the same so as to produce the directional information and load this transformed information into the data warehouse. In this level we also find the data entry application. Level 2 constitutes memorisation and organisational processes in a useful structure to then make the necessary analyses. There are various forms of organisation and memorisation of data: the most important ways to organize data are the Data Warehouse and the Data Mart.

Level 3 is constituted by processes of analysis elaboration and the presentation of the information by the single business users. Across the calculation engine (for example: OLAP Technology) elaborations are made often consisting of multidimensional analyses of the same indicator on the basis of which they can make suitable forecasts and support simulations which can then be given to the managers.

Level 4 is constituted by processes of access to the functionalities of the previous level 3 through tools such as intranet, internet and other electronic channels.

The extraction process produces data mart that makes up the data warehouse which is the data base for the business intelligence instruments.

The Instruments that realize the process of data extraction are called “analytical applications”. The analytical applications:

- provide users with access to a distributed network of unstructured content (text, image and audio data) and structured content (data warehouse and data marts) in a manner that facilitates active user collaboration in the decision-making process;
- address the information needs of every user within the corporation and those external to the corporation which can accelerate effective decision-making and implementation;
- provide information to every user on a “need to know” basis and therefore do not place the information search burden exclusively on the user.

The software houses that produce intelligence business packages have started to offer solutions which can be used to satisfy the needs of administrative managers which choose the second approach to manage the passage to the international accounting standards.

Information Systems Audit

The progressive extension of the information system to all, or almost all, the company processes is the reason why the information system is today a leading component of the internal control system of a company.

Though it is certain that a greater reliability of these systems reduces the frequency of risks, it is necessary to consider that the impact of such risks may be significant, precisely in consideration of the integration of the processes.

The automation and integration of the ERP systems involve numerous effects on the company processes. In particular, the integrated information systems take on the role of "integrator" of the various activities that make up the processes.

The automation and integration of the ERP systems involve numerous effects on the company processes. In particular, the integrated information systems take on the role of "integrator" of the various activities that make up the processes.

The effects produced by the integration of the processes are composed of new risks and elements that strengthen the effectiveness of the internal control system.

The main risks linked to the use of such integrated systems are the following:

- alteration of the programs or data: the possibility that unauthorised personnel may gain access to the programs or data altering them easily;
- wrong application of the principle of task-sharing;
- excessive delegation to information experts: the wrong conviction that in order to solve problems regarding the processing of data it is necessary to have technical knowledge results in giving information experts tasks that are beyond the correct areas of responsibility;
- great economic impact of typing errors: in fact the uniqueness of the data means that on the one hand there are fewer errors and on the other there is a greater impact when there are some.

Consequently, so as to verify the reliability of the information system, it is necessary to develop the control activity of the information systems that can be divided into:

- business audit: set of the controls aimed at analysing the different company processes and different balance sheet items;
- system audit: geared towards safeguarding the system against various risks it is subject to as a whole, starting from the operative system necessary for the installation of the information system to the authentication of the passwords and management of the authorization profiles.

The business audit turns out to be of particular interest, in that it has recently been influenced by many national and international laws that are moving towards the production of documents which show the true reliability of the company processes managed by information systems.

The audit system is particularly important so as to create an entire mapping of the information system as a whole, identifying the main critical areas.

The Business Audit identifies the coordinated set of the activities aimed at verifying the company operations from an accounting and financial point of view, as well as the other aspects that are linked.

The business audit is developed with reference to the following lines:

a) audit system of internal controls in the company;
b) audit of each balance sheet item.

The activity of auditing aimed at the company system of internal controls is a procedural one that concerns the entire internal control system set up and in operation in the various functional areas (accounting, administrative-financial and managerial) of the company.

From the point of view of the practical application of the company audit system of internal controls, the tasks and responsibilities of the Internal Auditing deal with the following areas:

- suitability of the accounting controls, with particular attention paid to the conditions safeguarding the patrimony and the correct supply of the accounting system;
- suitability of the administrative-accounting and managerial controls, paying particular attention to the conditions of functionality and effectiveness of the controls that are part of the planning and programming activities, of the operative system which is used to make a practical and particular execution of the general plans and programs, as well as of the company information system;
- suitability of the general internal control system in terms of the cost-benefit ratio and in relation to the positioning and scope of the real or potential risk areas within the organisational and operative structure of the company;
- reliability and integrity of the information given to the Board;
- congruity of the control procedures.

The balance sheet does not only deal with the formal verification of the normal book-keeping activities but tends to go back to the identification and quantification of each item.

From this point of view the information system turns out to be the subject of control and at the same time the tool with which several reliability tests on the information are carried out.

The controls regarding the audit system can be developed in four different lines:

a) organisational controls;
b) controls of the development and modification of the systems;
c) controls of the systems' hardware and software;
d) controls of security.

a) Organisational controls

The organisational structure affects the internal control system by means of the definition of the organisational units, the assignment of tasks and the identification of relations between the different organisational units.

The assignment of tasks defines the separation of duties aimed at making sure that the activities of authorisation, registration of data and management of goods are carried out by different people.

The use of automated information systems must make the application of the organisational principle of the division of tasks possible.

In some cases the management of activities using the information system can generate a confusion of roles and also the risk that there will be less of a division of functions.

From an operative point of view it is possible to define the degree of division of tasks by means of the definition of different access profiles and the use of passwords that give access to the system, thus making different people carry out incompatible functions.

b) Control of development and modification of the system.

The different programs that have been developed must be adequately documented (by means of manuals, flow charts, etc.) so as to make verifications possible.

Controls aimed at verifying that the modifications to the programs have been correctly authorised are included in the controls of the modifications to the system. During the implementation of the information systems the software must firstly be developed and then tested in a «suitable environment», before being actually utilised by the user, thus entering the «production environment».

c) Controls of the hardware and software of the system.

The verification procedures of the correct functioning of the computers and the entire information system are usually established by the firms producing the hardware and the operative systems beforehand.

The controls of the hardware guarantee that the program instructions are carried out in an appropriate and correct way.

The verification of the correct functioning of the software system and the control of the peripherals can be carried out by means of the analysis of the «logs», that is files that contain information on the different activities carried out by the system.

d) Security controls

The «threats» to the information system, that is to say the risks with negative effects on the physical goods or on the information patrimony of the system, may derive from human or natural factors. Accidental events as well as voluntary ones are amongst the harmful events arising from human intervention.

The threats deriving from human intervention may arise from people operating within the organisation, as is the case with acts of sabotage, or external people, the so-called «hackers».

However, in the past «attacks» to the system often came from within the organisation, the last few years have been characterised by an increase in the number of external attacks, due to the increase in the connections brought about by the Internet.

«Environmental» threats are represented by events caused by natural disasters, such as flooding, earthquakes, fires, etc, which can damage or destroy the information system.

The information basis contained in the information system must be protected with regards to:

- confidentiality (or secrecy);
- integrity;
- availability.

The safeguarding of confidentiality is obtained by reducing to an acceptable level of risk the possibility that any one unauthorised person, either voluntarily or not, may gain access to the system.

Integrity of the information consists of reducing the risk of deletion or modification due to the intervention of unauthorised persons or by phenomena which are uncontrollable, such as deterioration processes of the memorisation support, natural disasters, etc. Availability consists of reducing the risks of non-access to the data and information as a result of various events that could jeopardise accessibility (such as black-outs, natural disasters, external attacks).

Conclusions

The control environment sets the tone of an organization, influencing the control consciousness of its people. It is the foundation for all other components of internal control, providing discipline and structure.

One of the components of the control environment, in the overall control system of the company, is the information system. Some authors have stated that ERP is able to influence all the components of the internal control system as defined by Coso Report (Valipour et al., 2012). The typology of information system adopted by the company influences the reliability of data. ERP seems to guarantee a higher reliability of the internal control of a company even if a successful implementation depends on different factors (see, Ngai et al., 2008, Basoglu et al., 2007, Petter et al., 2008). Consistently with previous research, ERP is able to raise the quality of auditing and internal control systems (Soral et. Al., 2010), and a reduction of risks is perceived by auditors (Saharia et al., 2008).

References

Anthony R.N. (2011). *Planning and Control System*, Harvard University Press, 1985

Atkinson A. Bunker R.D., Kaplan R.S., Young S.M. (1998) *Management Accounting* – Una prospettiva fondata sulle attività, ISEDI, Torino

Basoglu, N., Daim, T. and Kerimoglu, O. (2007) 'Organizational adoption of enterprise resource planning systems: a conceptual framework', Journal of *High Technology Management Research*, Vol. 18, No. 1, pp.73-97

Bava F. (2003). , L'audit del sistema di controllo interno, Milano Giuffrè

Botta, G.V., Millet, P.A., and Grabot, B. (2005). A survey on the recent research literature on ERP systems. *Computers in Industry*, 56, 510–522

Committee of Sponsoring Organizations of the Treadway Commission (1992)., Available from: [http://www.coso.org/publications/executive_summary_integrated_framework.htm]

CoSo, CoSO Report, Available from: [www.coso.org]

—. (2007). *Internal Control- Integrated Framework*: Executive Summary, The.

Devalle A. (2006). *Il sistema informativo aziendale ed il passaggio* agli IAS/IFRS, Giuffrè

Douglas Hackney (Enterprise Group): Analytical Applications Defined. Available from: [http://www.egltd.com/production/resourcesindex.html]

E.W.T. Ngai, C.C.H. Law*, F.K.T. Wat. (2008). Examining the critical success factors in the adoption of enterprise resource planning, *Computers in Industry* 59, 548–564

Earl M., Khan B. (1994). How new is business process redesign? In *European Management Journal,* n. 12

Ferrero G.(1987). , *Impresa e Management*, Giuffrè, Milano

Laudon & Laudon (2006), Management information systems, Pearson

Petter, S., DeLone, W. & McLean, E. (2008). Measuring information systems success: models, dimensions, measures and interrelationships. *European Journal of Information Systems*, 17(3), 236-263

Pisoni P. (1979). *Il sistema informativo aziendale*, Giuffrè, Milano

—. (2000). *Il bilancio consolidato*, Giuffrè Milano

Porter M. (1987). *Il vantaggio competitivo*, Edizioni Comunità, Milano

Saharia, A., Koch, B., & Tucker, R. (2008). ERP Systems and Internal Audit. Issues in Information Systems, 4(2), 578-586

Soral G., Jain M. (2011). Impact of ERP system on auditing and internal control, Research Journal of Social Science & Management, Volume: 01, Number: 04

Stalk G.J. Hout T.M., Competere contro il tempo, Sperling & Kupfer, Milano 1991

Valipour H., Moradi J., Fathed M. (2012). The Impact of Enterprise Resource Planning (ERP) on the Internal Controls Case Study: Esfahan Steel Company, *European Journal of Social Sciences*, Vol.28 No.2, pp. 228-238

CHAPTER TEN

THE IMPACTS OF ICT EXPANSION, LEGAL AND INSTITUTIONAL FRAMEWORK ON FDI FLOWS: A COMPARATIVE STUDY BETWEEN ASIA-PACIFIC AND THE MIDDLE EASTERN ECONOMIES

FARID SHIRAZI
RYERSON UNIVERSITY, CANADA

Abstract

This chapter investigates the causal impacts of Foreign Direct Investment (FDI) and information and communication technologies (ICTs) in the Middle East and Asia-Pacific regions for the period of 1996 to 2010. To investigate such impacts, concomitant determining factors such as the level of educational attainment, the rule of law, institutional democracy, the growth of GDP per capita, the level of trade openness and socio-political stability in each economy and across the regions have been considered. The results of this study show, despite differences in terms of their level of socio-economic and political stability, that educational attainment and the growth of GDP and FDI flows in these economies have been effective in promoting ICT development in these regions. Also, there is a bi-directional relationship between the expansion of ICTs and the flow of FDI (inward and outward) in general. In other words, the development of ICTs has been effective in attracting FDI flows in these regions despite the global economic crises of 2008-2009. Additionally, differences in the level of trade openness, educational attainment, the existence and level of rule of law, and institutional resistance across economies act as both enhancers of and barriers to the relationship between ICT and FDI flow.

Keywords: *FDI, Trade Openness, Stability, ICT, Institutional Resistance, Democracy, Education.*

Introduction

In recent years, a growing number of empirical studies conducted by research scholars as well as the international organizations have found the positive impacts of Foreign Direct Investment (FDI) on the expansion of ICTs on a global scale (Gholami et al., 2006; Shirazi et al., 2010; Soper et al., 2006; UNCTAD, 2007; UNCTAD, 2008; WSIS Forum, 2011). For example, the World Summit on the Information Society (WSIS Geneva 2011) has emphasized that "Progressive liberalization of government policies, rapidly expanding services sector, FDI growth, rising global competitiveness and increasing domestic demand have all contributed to a strong economy" (p.137). FDI becomes an important component of the economic strategies of developing countries (UNCTAD, 2006). In this context, the increased level of FDI flows from emerging economies into other developing nations through so-called South-South FDI has been positively effective toward the expansion of ICTs in host countries (UNCTAD, 2007).

This study extends earlier empirical studies conducted by Shirazi, Gholami and Higon (2010, 2012), which investigated the impact of FDI flow on ICT diffusion in nine Middle Eastern countries (Bahrain, Iran, Jordan, Kuwait, Oman, Qatar, Saudi Arabia, Syria, and the United Arab Emirates (UAE)) and eight Asia-Pacific economies (China, Hong Kong, Indonesia, Malaysia, the Philippines, Singapore, Thailand, and Vietnam). In this study, the author is interested in including other determining factors such as institutional resistance, the level of democratic freedoms, the rule of law, and the level of socio-political stability in each nation, which may influence the relations between FDI flows and ICT expansion in the above economies. The study has also extended the time period of study to include data from the recent global economic crises of 2008-2009 and beyond.

As noted by Shirazi et al. (2010), in recent years, several economies in the Asia-Pacific region have witnessed profound progress in Information and Communication Technology (ICT) and FDI flows (inward and outward). As shown in table 1, the total global share of inward FDI for the Middle Eastern countries of this study has increased from 0.8% in 1996 to 3.6% in 2010, while the global share of Asia-Pacific economies remained almost at the same level (21%) during the same period. However, when it comes to outward FDI, we are witness to a profound performance of FDI

Table 1: Inward FDI (USD million)

Middle East (ME)	1996	1998	2000	2006	2008	2010
Bahrain	2,048	-275	364	2,915	1,794	156
Iran	20	38	194	1,647	1,909	3,648
Jordan	16	310	913	3,544	2,826	1,651
Kuwait	347	59	16	121	-6	319
Oman	61	101	83	1,597	2,952	1,142
Qatar	339	347	252	3,500	3,779	4,670
Saudi Arabia	64	94	183	17,140	38,151	28,105
Syria	89	82	270	659	1,467	1,850
UAE	301	258	-506	12,806	13,724	5,500
Sum (ME)	3,285	1,014	1,768	43,929	66,595	47,040
Asia Pacific (AP)						
China	41,726	45,463	40,715	72,715	108,312	114,734
Hong Kong	10,460	14,765	61,938	45,060	59,621	71,069
Indonesia	6,245	-207	-4,495	4,914	9,318	13,771
Malaysia	7,297	2,714	3,788	6,060	7,172	9,103
Philippines	1,520	1,752	2,240	2,921	1,544	1,298
Singapore	11,432	5,959	15,515	36,700	11,798	48,637
Thailand	2,338	7,492	3,410	9,501	8,455	9,733
Vietnam	2,395	1,671	1,298	2,400	9,579	8,000
Sum (AP)	83,413	79,608	124,409	180,272	215,798	276,345
World	390,900	706,266	1,400,541	1,463,351	1,790,706	1,309,001
Developed Economies	236,035	508,745	1,137,996	981,869	1,019,648	618,586

Source: UNCTAD (2012)

outflow from the Asia-Pacific region, the "South-South FDI outflow." The value of outward FDI in this region has increased from 13% of the total global share in 1996 to 21% in 2010 (see table 2). The increased volume of outward FDI has contributed to economic growth in these nations and the region as a whole. As noted by the UNCTAD report (2006), "Outward FDI from developing countries can also contribute directly and indirectly, to a home economy as a whole. Arguably, the most important potential gain for home countries from outward FDI is the improved competitiveness and performance of the firms and industries involved" (p.28).

For the Middle Eastern region, despite the increased level of outward FDI during the period of this study (see table 2), the FDI outward flow in the region still remains low and accounts for only 1% of the total global outward FDI stock.

Table 2: Outward FDI (USD million)

Middle East (ME)	1996	1998	2000	2006	2008	2010
Bahrain	305	39	10	980	1,620	334
Iran	155	66	22	386	380	346
Jordan	-43	2	9	-138	13	28
Kuwait	1,740	-1,867	-303	8,211	9,091	5,065
Oman	2	-5	-2	276	585	1,012
Qatar	9	21	18	127	3,658	1,863
Saudi Arabia	323	128	1,550	-39	3,498	3,907
Syria	2	2	44	-11	2	0
UAE	129	127	424	10,892	15,820	2,015
Sum (ME)	2,621	-1,486	1,770	20,683	34,666	14,571
Asia Pacific (AP)						
China	2,114	2,634	916	21,160	52,150	68,811
Hong Kong	26,531	16,985	59,374	44,979	50,581	95,396
Indonesia	600	44	150	2,726	5,900	2,664
Malaysia	3,768	863	2,026	6,021	14,965	13,329
Philippines	182	160	125	103	259	616
Singapore	9,196	3,544	6,650	18,637	6,812	21,215
Thailand	932	132	-20	968	4,057	5,415
Vietnam	0	0	0	85	300	900
Sum (AP)	43,323	24,362	69,221	94,678	135,023	208,346
World	397,770	689,700	1,226,633	1,415,094	1,969,336	1,451,365
Developed Economies	331,416	637,994	1,088,321	1,152,034	1,580,753	989,576

Source: UNCTAD (2012)

To investigate the relationship between ICT expansion and FDI flows, this study raises the following research questions: 1) Can FDI flows (inward and outward) provide insights into the differences in ICT expansion between these two regions? And, 2) What are the impacts of other determining factors such as the level of educational attainment, the rule of law, institutional democracy, the growth of GDP per capita, the level of trade openness and socio-political stability on the growth of FDI flow and ICT expansion? To answer these questions, we performed an econometric analysis for a balanced panel[1] of nine Middle Eastern states and eight Asia-Pacific[2] economies.

This chapter is organized as follows: the following section provides an overview of the relationship between FDI flows and ICT expansion in both regions while the following section reviews the literature on the determinants of ICT expansion. Then the research approach is introduced, followed by regression results and findings. Finally, a discussion and concluding comments based on these findings are presented.

FDI and ICT expansion

During the period of 1996-2010, both Asia-Pacific and the Middle East experienced an explosive ICT expansion due to increased investment in this area. As for the Asia-Pacific region, ICTs play an important role in the region's economic development and growth. The ICT industry became not only the largest industry among economies of this region but also the fastest growing industry that attracted the most investors from across the globe. As a result of this investment, many nations in this region became important players in the manufacturing and exporting of ICT goods and services. For example, in 2010, on average the region's share (economies of this study) of ICT goods exports accounted for 29% of their total exports, according to UNCTAD's common database (2012). ICT goods exports from two well-developed ICT economies, namely Hong Kong and Singapore, accounted for 44.16% and 34.33% of these nations' total exports in 2010.

According to one UNCTAD (2007) report, the success of Singapore's ICT industry is mainly linked to the establishment of the country's people-centric and innovation-driven policies in which structured market reform has provided a platform for the growth of an ICT industry. In this context, Singapore fully liberalized its telecommunication market, allowing for competition by lifting all limits on direct and indirect foreign equity investment in the Singaporean telecom market. As a result, currently the nation enjoys easy and widespread access to advanced telecommunication networks and services, powered by highly-skilled human resources, R&D and innovation activities (UNCTAD, 2007).

Hong Kong's role as the world freest economy and Asia's leading logistics, communications and financial hub has made it a natural location for the development of a sophisticated IT infrastructure (Austrade, 2102). Today, Hong Kong is the home of the world's leading IT companies. Particularly, FDI-based companies registered in Hong Kong have many advantages in exploiting the huge potential in mainland China where ambitious goals have been set for advancements in the areas of innovation, technology and information (Austrade, 2012). China's vast market size along with the country's booming economy (GNI per capita doubled between 2002 and 2007) and reform policies allowing FDI flow has resulted in increased consumer demand for ICT products and services (ITU, 2009). As such, the growing ICT industry has allowed ICT operators and manufacturers to supply large amounts of ICT products at competitive prices for the domestic market (ITU, 2009). As a result of ICT investment and development, China's export of telecommunication products increased during the last decade. In addition, China's twelfth five-year development plan has prioritized the development of seven industries including the new-generation of ICT and scientific R&D. It is expected that the total value-added output of China's new industries will account for 8% of the country's GDP in 2015 and 15% by 2020 (Austrade, 2012).

Despite a profound expansion of ICT technologies in the Middle East between 1996 and 2010, the production of ICT goods and services in the region compared to the Asia-Pacific remains insignificant. For example, the highest recorded value in this region belongs to the UAE in 2005, in which the emirate's ICT goods export accounted for 4.3% of the country's total merchandise trade. There are many factors that impede Middle Eastern countries' ability to play a vital role in the production and export of ICT goods and services. One of these factors is due to these countries' heavy dependency on oil and natural gas productions. For example, the export of oil and natural gas to other countries significantly influences the national economies of Bahrain, Iran, Kuwait, Qatar, Saudi Arabia and UAE. Oil and natural gas production accounted for an average of 76% of their total exports. The leading exporter of oil was Saudi Arabia, at 90%, while Bahrain exported the least amount of oil, at 60% (Shirazi et al., 2009). Some countries in the region took initiatives to revert the situation including the liberalization of incumbent national telecommunication sectors and the establishment of "Free Trade Zone" areas to boost FDI flow in high technology sectors such as ICTs. For example, the establishment of the free trade zone called "Internet City" in Dubai, UAE which has played a pivotal role in the growth and development of the Internet in the region and was established to attract ICT investors to the UAE by offering a 100% tax-free zone to all companies participating in this community.

According to the ITU report (2012), over the past five years, the Arab States region has made significant progress when it comes to ICT uptake. In particular, the number of mobile-cellular subscriptions in the region has almost tripled, particularly when it comes to the mobile penetration rate. It has reached a level of 97% which is ten percent higher than the world average (ITU, 2012). However, when it comes to Internet usage, particularly broadband Internet access, less than 30% of the population in the region were online at the end of 2011. The situation for fixed-broadband penetration stood at just above two percent, well below the level of most other regions and the world average of around nine percent (ITU, 2012). However, there is a positive tendency to ICT development in Middle East due to the liberalization of the ICT sector during the last decade. Table 3 shows the competitive environment of the telecom sector among the Arab States of Middle East. As indicated, the majority of these countries have liberalized their telecom market, particularly in the area of Internet services, in which it provides a more comfortable environment for FDI flow into this industry.

There are arguments suggesting that economies with free competition in the telecom sector will have higher Internet connectivity than economies with monopolies in this sector (ITU, 1997; Hargittai, 1999). Using a sample of 2001 data from 45 countries and focusing on variables of regulatory, regime characteristics and price regulation, Wallsten (2005) finds that the more formal and controlled a country's regulatory system, the fewer Internet users and hosts there are (cf. Shirazi et al., 2009).

Table 3: The ICT Regulatory Landscape in the Middle East (reference year 2011)

	Fixed telephony		Fixed Internet		
Country	Regulatory landscape	Number of service providers	Regulatory landscape	Number of service providers	Number of infrastructure providers
Bahrain	Competitive	More than 6	Competitive	More than 11	3 (including 2 WiMAX providers)
Jordan	Competitive	111	Competitive	195	9 (including 5 WiMAX providers)
Kuwait	Monopoly	1	Competitive	4	1
Oman	Duopoly	2	Competitive	2	2
Qatar	Duopoly	23	Duopoly	2	2
Saudi Arabia	Duopoly	2	Competitive	508	3 (including 2 WiMAX providers)
Syria	Monopoly	1	Competitive	12	1
UAE	Duopoly	2	Duopoly	2	2

Source: ITU (2012)

Table 4 shows the classification of economies in both regions with regards to their ICT development as introduced by ITU. ITU measures each country's progress in ICT development through an index called ICT Development Index (IDI). This index evaluates the degree to which a country has been transformed into an information society or a knowledge-based society (ITU, 2010). The IDI index is composed of three main indices: a) *ICT Access*, which captures five infrastructure indicators such as fixed telephony, mobile telephony, international Internet bandwidth, households with computers, and households with Internet; b) *ICT Use* which captures the intensity of ICT usage through indices such as the number of Internet users, fixed broadband and mobile broadband users in each country; and c) *ICT Skills* which captures ICT capability or skills through three indicators such as adult literacy, gross secondary and tertiary scholastic enrolment (ITU, 2010). Based on the countries' IDI performances, ITU has divided economies into four main categories: High, Upper, Medium and Low. Table 4 shows the position of each of the economies of this study in this arrangement.

The above measures are similar to an earlier ICT index called *digital access* introduced by the United Nations' ICT Task Force in 2005. Table1 shows the level of digital access in Asia-Pacific and the Middle East (Shirazi et al., 2010) in comparison with the new IDI index in 2010.

As shown in Table 4, the main changes in the 2005 ranking categories were related to the Middle Eastern countries. In this regard, four Middle Eastern countries (Bahrain, UAE, Saudi Arabia and Syria) improved their ranking positions from a lower category to a higher level. Particularly, countries such as Bahrain and UAE have been advanced to the high ICT developed nations.

Table 4: ICT development in Asia-Pacific and Middles East regions

Digital Access Level (2005)			
High	**Upper**	**Medium**	**Low**
Asia-Pacific			
Hong Kong	Malaysia	China	
Singapore		Indonesia	
		Philippines	
		Thailand	
		Vietnam	
Middle East			
	Bahrain	Iran	Syria
	Kuwait	Jordan	
	Qatar	Oman	
	UAE	Saudi Arabia	

ICT Development Index (2010)		
High	**Upper**	**Medium**
Asia-Pacific		
Hong Kong	Malaysia	China
Singapore		Indonesia
		Philippines
		Thailand
		Vietnam
Middle East		
Bahrain	Kuwait	Iran
UAE	Qatar	Jordan
	Saudi Arabia	Oman
		Syria

Sources: UN ICT Task Force (2005) & ITU (2010)

A Review of Determinants of ICT expansion and Foreign Direct Investment

Many scholars as well as international organizations have argued that ICT expansion has become the core component of today's economic development and growth. In this context, ICT is expected to improve the efficiency of the industrial infrastructure in developing countries enhancing their overall economic performance and strengthening their competitive capabilities in the global market (Indjikian and Siegal, 2005; Meng and Li, 2002; Shirazi et al., 2009, 2010; UNCTAD, 2007, 2008; UNESCO, 2006; WSIS Forum, 2011).

ICT expansion is also expected to facilitate basic social services, the efficiency of governments and enhance the provision of education and health (Braa et al., 2007; Sahay and Walsham, 2006; Silva and Hirschheim, 2007).

A growing number of empirical studies have found that the growth rate of ICT expansion is correlated with the increased level of foreign direct investment flows and the growth rate of Gross Domestic Products (GDP) per capita (Shirazi et al., 2010), the growth of human capital stock as measured by the level of educational attainment (Bontis, 2004), the openness to trade (Baliamoune-Lutz, 2003; Gholami et al., 2006) and the degree of government intervention in business activities (ITU, 1997, 1999; Hargittai, 1999; Salmenkaita and Salo, 2002). As noted at the UNCTAD (2003) conference, "FDI offers recipient economies important potential benefits in the form of capital inflows, technology transfer and improved access to export markets and sources of supply such benefits cannot be taken for granted." (p. vii).

Some scholars argue that the level of FDI flow in host countries is also correlated with the degree of democratic freedoms (Adam and Filippaios, 2007; Busse, 2003; Haggard, 1990; Harms and Ursprung, 2002; Jensen, 2003; Li and Resnick, 2003; Olson, 2000) as measured by the index of civil liberties and political rights, while others are skeptical of the presence of a relationship between FDI and democracy (Huggins, 2007; O'Donnell, 1978; O'Neal, 1994; Tuman and Emert, 2004).

A growing number of empirical studies show that the level of political stability, the absence of violence (e.g., political violence, civil war, interstate war, and transnational terrorism (Li, 2006)) and the level of the rule of law (Kaufmann et al., 2009; Staats and Biglaiser, 2012; UNCTAD, 2003) are the key factors influencing FDI flows in host countries. As argued by Dreher et al. (2007), the role of the legal system and the rule of law play an important role in evaluating the quality of governance and its consequences for development. As such, a strong legal system that protects property rights provides a stable framework for economic activity and plays an important role in controlling corruption (Dreher et al., 2007).

In other words, policies aimed at creating political and macro-economic stability and improving infrastructure and human resources, trade policy, science and technology policies, and labour laws (UNCTAD, 2003) among others, are the key factors in creating an attractive business environment for investors.

Kaufmann et al. (2009) argue that investors make their decisions on the perceived view of the investment climate in the host country and the government's performance. As argued by Aleksynska and Havrylchyk (2013), countries with decent economic institutions that respect property rights and the rule of law, increase incentives to invest and improve the allocation of resources thus leading to a higher growth prospective and making the country more attractive to foreign investors. Institutional resistance, however, in the form of a government's high share in producing goods and services and its spending relative to spending by individuals, households, and businesses (Gwartney et al., 2011), will not only create an unfavourable business environment for private investors, but will also breed corruption. Political and financial corruption are argued by many scholars to be significant contributors to low economic growth (see Dreher et al., 2007). It is also important to note that the institutional legal and economic environment may impact ICT development in a country because national policies can either enhance or hinder the diffusion of a technology, depending on the country's approach to regulating mechanisms, privatization, and free competition outlined in such policies (Shirazi et al., 2009).

The Estimation Framework and Data Collection

The aim of this study is to analyze the bi-directional relationship between ICT expansion and FDI flows (inward and outward), controlling for the effect that other determinants may have on the dependent variables. To assess the above effects empirically, we examine a panel of 17 Middle Eastern and Asia-Pacific countries over the period 1996-2010. The dataset has a pooled time-series cross section (TSCS) structure, allowing us to identify patterns across countries and over time. In the estimates presented in equations 1 and 2, we first capture the link between FDI (inward and outward) and ICT in a model expressed in log-linear form:

$$\ln ICT_{it} = \beta_0 + \beta_1 \ln FDI\_in_{it} + \beta_2 \ln FDI\_out_{it} + X_{it} + d_t + \varepsilon_{it} \quad (1)$$

where the subscript refers to country *i* and year *t*, d_t represents T-1 time dummy variables (for 1996-2010), and ε_{it} is the random error term in the equation. Finally, we assume that the index of ICT depends on a number of control variables (X) which, according to previous literature, may be related to ICT expansion. As expressed in equation 2, variable X represents the following: trade openness (variable *open*) and the annual average growth rate of GDP per capita (*gdpp*) both in log formats, an index of the rule of law *(law)*, an index of socio-political stability *(stab)*, education (*edu*), the political and civil liberties index, as a proxy for democracy *(democ)* and an index of institutional resistance (*resist*).

$$X_{it} = \beta_3 \ln gdpp_{it} + \beta_4 \ln open_{it} + \beta_5 law_{it} + \beta_6 stab_{it} + \beta_7 edu_{it} + \beta_8 democ_{it} + \beta_9 resist_{it} \quad (2)$$

In addition, to investigate the impact of ICTs and other determinants on the growth of FDI flows, equations 3 and 4 were created. In particular, we wish to determine how ICT expansion in these countries attracted FDI flows. While equation 3 assesses the inward FDI flow, equation 4 is evaluates the effects of ICT and other determinants on outward FDI.

Equation (3):

$$\ln FDI\_in_{it} = a_0 + a_1 \ln ICT_{it} + a_2 \ln gdpp + a_3 open_{it} + a_4 law_{it} + a_5 stab_{it} + a_6 edu_{it} + a_7 democ_{it} + a_8 resist_{it} + d_t + \varepsilon_{it}$$

Equation (4):

$$\ln FDI\_out_{it} = \delta_0 + \delta_1 \ln ICT_{it} + \delta_2 \ln gdpp + \delta_3 open_{it} + \delta_4 law_{it} + \delta_5 stab_{it} + \delta_6 edu_{it} + \delta_7 democ_{it} + \delta_8 resist_{it} + d_t + \varepsilon_{it}$$

Data Collection

We use a varied number of data sources to collect the variables of interest for this study. The index of economic freedom (EF) and the index of regulation were obtained from The Heritage Foundation (HF) and the Wall Street Journal (WSJ). The ICT and educational attainment data were mainly collected from ITU, UNDP and the World Bank. The growth rate of GDP per capita was obtained from the United Nation Common Database, while the Political Rights and Civil Liberties indexes were collected from the Freedom House. In the next section we provide a more detailed definition of these indices.

ICT Index

To construct the ICT index, five main ICT components were considered, namely: the number of fixed telephone lines, Internet users, mobile cell phone subscribers and PCs per 100 inhabitants as well as the International Internet bandwidth per Internet user (logarithmic scale). Data was collected from the ITU database for the period 1996 to 2010.

Education Index

To construct the educational index, we applied Orbicom and ITU's (2005) formula which can be applied on primary, secondary, and tertiary gross enrolment ratios: education= (primary + 2* secondary+ 3* tertiary)/6. Data for educational attainment was collected from the UNDP common database.

Traditionally, economists have been optimistic about the contribution of education to economic development; in formal models, the accumulation of human capital is often assigned a central role, particularly in the recent literature on endogenous growth. For instance, in his pioneering contribution to the endogenous growth literature, Lucas (1988) emphasizes human capital accumulation as an alternative source of sustained growth. Lucas distinguishes between two main sources of human capital accumulation; namely, formal education and "learning by doing." Nelson and Phelps (1966) also describe growth as being driven by human capital accumulation, which in turn affects a country's ability to innovate or catch up with more advanced countries. Differences in growth rates across countries are thus primarily due to differences in human capital stocks.

The results of empirical cross country studies on the determinants of educational attainment on economic growth have been largely consistent with the abovementioned view. Landau (1983), Barro (1991) and Mankiw, Romer and Weil (1992), among others, find that a variety of educational indicators show the expected positive effect on output levels.

Regarding the interaction between education and ICT, several studies (Baliamoune-Lutz 2003; Caselli and Coleman 2001; Kiiski and Pohjola 2002) also emphasize the importance of human capital in accessing ICT as well as its role in ICT diffusion. Kiiski and Pohjola (2002) show that tertiary education in developing and OECD countries has a positive and statistically significant influence on ICT diffusion. Using data on computer equipment imports, Caselli and Coleman (2001) find that secondary education also influences technology adoption.

Annual Growth rate of GDP per Capita (GDPP)

Actual GDP per capita data was obtained from the UN common database. While most of the research in this area has found that economic freedom does make a significantly positive contribution to growth (Barro and Sala-i-Martin 1995; Gastil 1978; Gwartney, Lawson, and Block 1996; Islam 1996; Scully 1988), there is also the possibility, as noted by Barro and Sala-i-Martin (1995), of an inverse relationship running from growth to economic freedom. That is, richer countries can afford better institutions (La Porta et al. 1999).

Democracy index

Two main indicators, Political Rights and Civil Liberties, were selected from Freedom House to evaluate the grade of democracy (variable *democ*) for each country. A rating scale developed by Freedom House rates each country's Political Rights (PR) and Civil Liberties (CL) on a scale from one to seven, where one represents the highest degree of democracy, and seven represents the lowest. Those countries that scored an average of less than 3 (combined PR and CL average) are classified as "Free," those with a rating between 3 and 5 are considered "Partly Free," while those countries with a score between 5.5 and 7 are considered "Not Free." While this classification provides a sound metric which presents an overall review of the world's progress towards democracy, it obscures the details of annual performance of civil liberties and political rights within the context of each country. For our estimation purposes, this index was inverted.

The index of political stability and the rule of law (law)

These indices were obtained from the World Bank common database. While the former captures the perception of the likelihood that the government will be destabilized or overthrown by unconstitutional or violent means, including politically-motivated violence and terrorism, the latter captures the quality of the rules of society, particularly the quality of law enforcement and the juridical system in protecting citizens against crime, violence and property rights (Kaufman et al, 2009). As noted by La Porta et al. (2004), the democratic institute emphasizes the separation of the creation of laws and the administration of justice, in which the legislatures make laws, but independent judges enforce them (La Porta et al., 2004). In this context, achieving high levels of economic growth requires a suitable legal and economic environment and requires reform of the rules and regulations that govern the strategic interaction of participants in the political game (Shirazi et al., 2009).

Institutional Resistance Index

The Economic Intervention index introduced by HF and the WSJ was used as a means of measuring the impact of governments' interventions in economic activities through their shares in producing goods and services as well as the magnitude of consuming national resources. Institutional resistance in the form of governments' involvement in economic activities is integral in a noncompetitive market environment. In this study, the variable *resist* takes a value between 0 and 100, where 100 indicates the least institutional resistance and zero the highest resistance.

Empirical Results

Table 5 below shows the impact of FDI flows (inward & outward) on ICT expansion. As shown in column 1, this impact is statistically significant in both regions with a stronger impact on ICTs through the inward FDI variable. A comparison between both regions shows that while FDI inflows in these economies have a positive impact on ICT expansion, the impact on Asia-Pacific economies is much stronger than their Middle Eastern counterpart, signified through a higher variable coefficient as well as a stronger t-statistics at the 99.9% level.

In addition, the growth of GDP per capita and trade openness in general had positive impacts on ICT expansion in both regions. Further, the variable *education* shows a positive impact on ICT expansion; however, this impact for the Middle East countries is stronger as indicated through its statistical significance at 99%.

A thorough investigation of the role of education with regards to FDI flows reveals information regarding key differences between the two regions. While education attainment had a positive impact on inward FDI flow for the Middle East countries, in contrast, as depicted in table 6, when it comes to outward FDI, the results indicate that education has had, in general, an inverse or insignificant effect. Conversely, education has had a positive and significant impact in favor of Asia-Pacific economies.

As depicted in table 5, the variable *instability* has a negative impact on ICT expansion, indicating that any socio-political instability at the country and/or at the regional levels will ultimately impact ICT development negatively (both regions combined) and this impact for Asia-Pacific economies is significant at 99% indicating stronger sensitivity to instability in this region.

The level of rule of law remains as one of the main barriers towards ICT expansion in combination with FDI flows in these regions. As shown in table 5 below, the variable *law* shows a negative sign with regards to ICT indicating its negative impact and this impact is statistically significant.

Table 5: The impact of FDI on ICT Expansion

LnICT	Model (1)	Middle East (2)	Asia-Pacific (3)
lnfdi_in	0.0801***	0.0621**	0.109***
	(5.41)	(3.22)	(4.36)
lnfdi_out	0.0342*	0.0134	0.0657
	(2.38)	(0.83)	(1.97)
lngdpp	0.265***	0.241***	0.241**
	(8.99)	(6.76)	(2.98)
lnopen	0.633***	0.863***	1.078***
	(5.32)	(4.42)	(3.83)
law	-0.00707*	-0.00837	-0.0105
	(-2.01)	(-1.95)	(-1.65)
stability	-0.148***	-0.113	-0.214**
	(-3.40)	(-1.87)	(-2.82)
education	0.00518**	0.00532**	0.00132
	(2.99)	(2.92)	(0.39)
democ	-0.000894	0.00340	-0.00257
	(-0.55)	(1.57)	(-0.99)
resist	-0.000704	-0.00541**	0.00660
	(-0.43)	(-2.99)	(-1.58)
_cons	-2.013***	-2.623***	-2.025***
	(-7.41)	(-6.59)	(-3.55)
N	221	117	104
R2	0.672	0.6444	0.7552
VIF	2.68	2.27	4.39
Time dummy	Yes	Yes	Yes

t-statistics in parentheses; * $p<0.05$, ** $p<0.01$, *** $p<0.001$

This finding is aligned with the UNCTAD's suggestions that the major factors influencing FDI flows into developing countries include a good macroeconomic environment, stability (political, social and economic), an effective legal system and the rule of law (UNCTAD, 2003).

As shown in table 5, institutional resistance (variable *resist*) shows a negative sign in the context of ICT expansion in the Middle East, and this impact is statistically significant. However, its impact on the Asia-Pacific region is reported as insignificant. Also, when it comes to outward FDI flow, the variable *resist* shows a negative sign with variable ICT (for both regions) indicating its negative impacts on ICT expansion. This impact is reported as statistically significant for both regions with stronger negative influences for the Middle East. Moreover, as shown in table 6, institutional resistance is negatively correlated with FDI flows (inward and outward) in both regions.

As discussed earlier, the relationship between FDI flow and democracy has been studied extensively. While some scholars argue that FDI tends to flow more intensively in countries with authoritarian regimes, others claim that FDI flows have been attracted more by countries with higher respect to human rights and democracy. By distinguishing between political rights and civil liberties the empirical study of Adam and Filippaios (2007) shows that multinational firms tend to invest in countries with low civil but high political liberties.

The results of this study shows that despite the negative correlation between the variable *democ* and ICT, when it comes to FDI flows (inward and outward), as shown in table 6, democratic freedoms as measured by political rights and civil liberty does not have significant impacts on FDI flows in these regions. However, among the two indices representing variable democracy, the index of political rights shows a positive and significant impact on ICT development in both regions while its impact on inward and outward FDI flows is reported as insignificant.

The results as depicted in table 5 show that while socio-political and economic instability (variable *stability*) does not have a significant impact on inward FDI flow in Middle East, when it comes to outward FDI, the Middle Eastern investors tend to invest in those countries that are both politically and economically stable. As depicted in table 6, the variable stability shows a negative coefficient with regards to FDI outward flows and this impact is statistically significant at 99%. This finding is aligned with earlier empirical research conducted by Haksoon (2010) indicating that there is a strong correlation between outward FDI and political stability.

Table 6: The impact of ICT on FDI flows (inward and outward)

LnFDI_in	Model	Middle East	Asia-Pacific	Lnfdi_out	Model	Middle East	Asia-Pacific
	(4)	(5)	(6)		(1)	(2)	(3)
lnict	1.699***	1.505***	1.652***	lnict	1.086***	0.747	0.761**
	(6.14)	(3.42)	(4.86)		(3.62)	(1.36)	(2.77)
lngdpp	0.501***	0.223	0.00840	lngdpp	0.391*	0.375	1.485***
	(3.43)	(1.11)	(0.03)		(2.47)	(1.49)	(7.21)
lnopen	0.225	1.102	-4.572***	lnopen	-0.489	-1.485	-3.906***
	(0.40)	(1.09)	(-4.89)		(-0.81)	(-1.18)	(-5.17)
law	0.00737	-0.0191	-0.0135	law	0.00396	0.0324	-0.0364
	(-0.47)	(-0.92)	(-0.57)		(0.23)	(1.25)	(-1.90)
stability	0.787***	-0.148	1.689***	stability	-0.161	0.0739	0.0116
	(4.16)	(-0.50)	(7.04)		(-0.79)	(0.20)	(0.06)
education	-0.0127	0.0184*	0.0149	education	0.0225**	-0.0159	0.0148*
	(-1.66)	(2.07)	(1.17)		(2.71)	(-1.43)	(2.00)

democ	0.00329	0.00906	0.00202	democ	0.00693	0.00383	-0.00851
	(0.46)	(0.87)	(0.21)		(0.89)	(-0.29)	(-1.08)
resist	-0.0217***	0.00381	0.00714	resist	-0.0547***	-0.0530***	-0.0274*
	(-3.49)	(0.47)	(0.46)		(-8.13)	(-5.26)	(-2.19)
_cons	3.330**	1.398	10.08***	_cons	-5.257***	-4.421	3.710*
	(2.62)	(0.62)	(5.02)		(-3.81)	(-1.58)	(2.29)
N	221	117	104	N	221	117	104
R2	0.3354	0.2270	0.5274	R2	0.4036	0.3322	0.6406
VIF	3.06	2.71	4.88	VIF	3.06	2.71	4.88
Time dummy	yes	yes	yes	Time dummy	yes	yes	yes

t- statistics in parentheses; * $p<0.05$, ** $p<0.01$, *** $p<0.001$

As shown in table 6 (*FDI_in*, *FDI_out*), when it comes to inward FDI in the Asia-Pacific region, variable stability plays an important role in attracting FDI flow, while its impact on outward FDI is estimated as insignificant indicating that FDI investors consider economic and political stability in the region as a factor of key importance. Any regional or local instability will ultimately impact the flow of FDI in these countries.

The model's coefficient of determination (R2) for inward FDI for both regions (combined) shows a value of 0.5926. Also, the value of R2 for outward FDI is reported as 0.7623, indicating that the independent variables accounted for 59 percent and 76 percent of variation in FDI inward and outward flows, respectively.

Finally, the results of this study did not confirm the earlier findings that South-South FDI investors are not only discouraged by weak institutions in host countries but are also deterred by an institutional distance between origin and destination countries and the fact that they may be eager and more able to operate in institutionally weak environments (cf. Aleksynska and Havrylchyk, 2013).

Conclusion

For this study, our main research questions were: 1) Can FDI flows (inward and outward) provide insights into the differences in ICT expansion between Asia-Pacific and Middle East countries? And, 2) What are the impacts of other determining factors such as the level of educational attainment, the rule of law, institutional democracy, the growth of GDP per capita, the level of trade openness and socio-political stability on the growth of FDI flow and ICT expansion? To answer these questions, we performed an econometric analysis for a balanced panel of nine Middle Eastern countries and eight Asia-Pacific economies for the period 1996-2010. The results indicate that there is a positive correlation between FDI flows and ICT expansion in the Middle East and Asia-Pacific regions. While inward FDI has generally had a positive impact on ICT development in both regions, the expansion of ICTs in turn imposed positive impacts on attracting more FDI flows in these economies. The results also show that other determining factors such as the growth of GDP per capita, trade openness and the level of educational attainment impose positive impacts on ICT expansion as well as FDI flows, and these impacts are statistically significant. Despite the fact that the index of democracy did not have statistically significant impact on FDI flows in these regions, however, the index of political rights shows a positive and significant impact of ICT development. In addition, the existing level of rule of law and the regional political instability influence both ICT development and flows of FDI in both regions negatively. The existing level of institutional resistance in the Middle East remains one of the main obstacles towards ICT development in the region. The results also indicate that the Asia-Pacific region is more sensitive to any regional conflicts or political instability when it comes to the expansion of ICTs and/or FDI inflow. Moreover, the results indicate that while the expansion of ICT has generally had a positive and significant impact on outward FDI in Asia-Pacific economies, its impact on Middle Eastern economies has been detrimental. The results also indicate that while dissimilarities exist between the economies included in this study in terms of their level of socio-economic and political development, the institutional resistance in economic activities in the form of imposing a noncompetitive market environment is negatively correlated with FDI flows (inward and outward).

Notes

[1] In the context of this research, a 'balanced panel' refers to a data set with an equally long time series for all cross-sectional units.
[2] This study includes non-OECD economies from Asia-Pacific and the Middle East regions.

References

Adam, A. and Filippaios, F. (2007). Foreign Direct Investment and Civil Liberties: A New Perspective, *European Journal of Political Economy*, 23(4), 1038-1052

Aleksynska, M., and Havrylchyk, O. (2013). FDI from the south: The role of institutional distance and natural resources, *European Journal of Political Economy*, 29, 38–53

Austrade (2012). ICT to Hong Kong. Available at: http://www.austrade.gov.au/Export/Export-Markets/Countries/Hong-Kong/Industries/ICT

Baliamoune-Lutz, M. (2003). An analysis of the determinants and effects of ICT diffusion in developing economies. *Information Technology for Development*, 10(3), 151-169

Braa, J. Hanseth, O. Heywood, A. Mohammed, W. and Shaw, V. (2007). Developing Health Information Systems in Developing Countries: The Flexible Standards Strategy, *MIS Quarterly*, 3(12), 381-402

Bontis, N. (2004). National Intellectual Capital Index: A United Nations initiative for Arab Region, *Journal of Intellectual Studies*, 5(1), 13-39

Busse, M. (2003). Democracy and FDI, HWWA Discussion Paper 220, Hamburgisches Welt-Wirtschafts-Archiv (HWWA), Hamburg Institute of International Economics. Available at: http://www.econstor.eu/bitstream/10419/19312/1/220.pdf

Cohen, D., Soto, M. (2007). Growth and human capital: good data, good results, *Journal of Economic Growth*, 12(1), 51-76

Dreher, A., Kotsogiannis, C. and McCorriston, S. (2007). Corruption around the World: Evidence from a Structural Model. *Journal of Comparative Economics*, 35 (3), 443–466

Gholami, R., Lee, S. T. and Heshmati, A. (2006). The Causal Relationship Between Information and Communication Technology and Foreign Direct Investment. *The World Economy*, 29 (1), 43–62

Gwartney, J., Lawson, R., and Hall, J. (2011). *Economic Freedom of the World 2011 Annual Report*, Vancouver: Fraser Institute.

Haggard, S. (1990). *Pathways from the Periphery: The Politics of Growth in the Newly Industrializing Countries*, New York: Cornell University Press

Hargittai, E. (1999). Weaving the Western Web: Explaining differences in Internet Connectivity among OECD Economies, *Telecommunications Policy*, 23, 701–718

Harms, P. and Ursprung, H. (2002). Do Civil and Political Repression Really Boost Foreign Direct Investment? *Economic Inquiry*, 40(4), 651-663

Huggins, C. E. (2007). Macroeconomics, Politics and Policy: The Determinants of Capital Flows to Latin America, Texas Tech University. Available at: http://repositories.tdl.org/ttu-ir/handle/2346/18206

Indjikian, R. and Siegal. D.S. (2005). The impact of investment in IT on economic performance: Implications for developing countries, *World Development*, 33(5), 681-700

ITU (1997). International Telecommunications Union, *World telecommunication development report 1996/97: Trade in telecommunications*. Geneva: ITU

—. (2009). *Measuring the Information Society, The ICT Development Index*, Geneva: ITU Publication

—. (2010). *Measuring the Information Society*, Geneva: ITU Publication

—. (2012). *ICT Adoption and Prospects in the Arab Region*, Geneva: ITU Publication

Jensen, M. (2003). Democratic Governance and Multinational Corporations: Political Regimes and Inflows of Foreign Direct Investment, *International Organization*, 57, 587- 616

Kaufmann, D., Kraay, A. and Mastruzzi, M. (2009). Governance Matters VIII Aggregate and Individual Governance Indicators 1996–2008, Policy Research Working Paper 4978, The World Bank Development Research Group. Available at: https://openknowledge.worldbank.org/bitstream/handle/10986/4170/WPS4978.pdf?sequence=1

La Porta, R., Lo´pez-de-Silanes, F., Pop-Eleches, C., and Shleifer, A. (2004). Judicial Checks and Balances, *Journal of Political Economy*, 112(2), 445-470

Li, Q. and Resnick, A. (2003). Reversal of Fortunes: Democratic Institutions and Foreign Direct Investment Inflows to Developing Countries, *International Organization*, 57, 175-211

Li, Q. (2006). POLITICAL VIOLENCE AND FOREIGN DIRECT INVESTMENT, *Regional Economic Integration Research in Global Strategic Management*, 12, 231–255

—. (2009). Democracy, Autocracy, and Expropriation of Foreign Direct Investment, *Comparative Political Studies*, 42(8), 1098-1127

Meng, Q. and Li, M. (2002). New Economy and ICT development in China, *Information Economics and Policy*, 14(2), 275-295

O'Neal, J. R. (1994).The Affinity of Foreign Investors for Authoritarian Regimes, *Political Research Quarterly*, 47(3), 565-588

O'Donnell, G. (1978). Reflections on the Patterns of Change in the Bureaucratic Authoritarian State, *Latin American Research Review*, 13(1), 3–38

Olson, M. (2000). *Power and Prosperity: Outgrowing Communist and Capitalist Dictatorships*, New York: Basic Books

Orbicom and ITU (2005). From The Digital Divide To Digital Opportunities: Measuring Infostates for Development, Montreal: Claude-Yves Charron

Pohjola, M. (2001). *Information Technology and Economic Growth: A Cross-country Analysis*. In M. Pohjola (ed.), Information Technology, Productivity, and Economic Growth: International Evidence and Implications for Economic Development

Sahay, S., and Walsham, G. (2006). Scaling of Health Information Systems in India: Challenges and Approaches, *Information Technology for Development,* 12(3), 185-200

Salmenkaita J. and Ahti Salo, A. (2002), Rationales for Government Intervention in the Commercialization of New Technologies, *Technology Analysis & Strategic Management*, 14(2), 183 – 200

Silva, L. and Hirschheim, R. (2007). Fighting Against Windmills: Strategic Information Systems and Organizational Deep Structures, *MIS Quarterly*, 31(2), 327-354

Sciadas, G. (2006). Digital Review of Asia-Pacific 2005/2006: Vietnam. Available at: http://www.digital-review.org/

Shirazi, F., Gholami, R., Higon, D. (2009). The Impact of Information and Communication Technology, Education and Regulations on Economic Freedom in Developing Countries, *Journal of Information & Management (I&M),* 46(8), 426-433

Shirazi, F., Higon, D. A.& Gholami, R. (2012). ICT Diffusion and Foreign Direct Investment: A Comparative Study between Asia-Pacific and the Middle Eastern Economies, in Tan, F. B. (ed.) *International Comparisons of Information Communication Technologies: Advancing Applications*, IGI Publications, pp. 294-320

Shirazi, F., Gholami, R. & Higon, D. A. (2010). Do Foreign Direct Investment (FDI) and Trade Openness explain the disparity in ICT diffusion between Asia-Pacific and the Islamic Middle Eastern countries? *Journal of Global Information Management (JGIM)*, 18(3), 59-81

Soper, D.S., H. Demirkan, M. Goul & R. St. Louis. (2006), The impact of ICT expenditures on institutionalized democracy and foreign direct investment in developing economies, Proceedings of the 39th Annual Hawaii International Conference on System Sciences (HICSS'06)

Staats, J. L., and Biglaiser, G. (2012). Foreign Direct Investment in Latin America: The Importance of Judicial Strength and Rule of Law, *International Studies Quarterly*, 56, 193–202

Tuman J. and Emmert, C. F. (2004). The Political Economy of U.S. foreign Direct Investment in Latin America: A Reappraisal, *Latin American Research Review*, 29(3), 9-28

UNCTAD (2003). The Development Dimension of FDI: Policy And Rule-Making Perspectives, Proceedings of the Expert Meeting held in Geneva from 6 to 8 November 2002, Geneva: UN Publication

—. (2008). *World Investment Report: Transnational Corporations and the Infrastructure Challenges*, Geneva: UN Publication

—. (2007). *World Information Society Report 2007 Beyond WSIS*, Geneva: ITU Publication

UNESCO (2006). UNESCO Institute for Statistics ICTs and Education Indicators. Available at:

http://www.itu.int/ITUD/ict/partnership/material/ICT_Education_Paper_Nov_2006.pdf

Wallsten S. (2005). Regulation and Internet Use in Developing Countries, *Economic Development and Cultural Change*, 53(2), 501-23

WSIS Forum (2011). *World Summit on Information Society (WSIS) Outcome Document*, Geneva: International Telecommunication Union (ITU)